GROUP FROM "THE 'BLACK WATCH' (42ND ROYAL HIGHLANDERS) AT BAY AT QUATRE BRAS."
(*From the Painting by W. B. Wollen, R.I.*)

# The Black Watch

## The Record of an Historic Regiment

Archibald Forbes, L.L.D.

HERITAGE BOOKS
2013

# HERITAGE BOOKS
*AN IMPRINT OF HERITAGE BOOKS, INC.*

### Books, CDs, and more—Worldwide

For our listing of thousands of titles see our website
at
www.HeritageBooks.com

A Facsimile Reprint
Published 2013 by
HERITAGE BOOKS, INC.
Publishing Division
100 Railroad Ave. #104
Westminster, Maryland 21157

Originally published 1896

— Publisher's Notice —
In reprints such as this, it is often not possible to remove blemishes from the original. We feel the contents of this book warrant its reissue despite these blemishes and hope you will agree and read it with pleasure.

International Standard Book Numbers
Paperbound: 978-0-7884-2195-2
Clothbound: 978-0-7884-6964-0

# CONTENTS.

### CHAPTER I.
THE GENESIS OF THE REGIMENT—1729-40 . . . 1

### CHAPTER II.
"LOCHABER NO MORE!"—1743 . . . . . . 13

### CHAPTER III.
FONTENOY—THE BAPTISM OF FIRE—1745 . . . 21

### CHAPTER IV.
HOME AND CONTINENTAL SERVICE—1745-56 . . . 34

### CHAPTER V.
SERVICE IN NORTH AMERICA—1756 . . . . . 43

### CHAPTER VI.
TICONDEROGA—1758 . . . . . . . . 49

### CHAPTER VII.
MARTINIQUE AND GUADALOUPE—1759 . . . . 59

### CHAPTER VIII.
NORTH AMERICA—1759 . . . . . . . 67

### CHAPTER IX.
Martinique Once Again—1762 . . . . . 71

### CHAPTER X.
Conquest of the Havannah—1762 . . . . 74

### CHAPTER XI.
Fort Pitt and the Backwoods—1762-67 . . . 86

### CHAPTER XII.
Home Service—1767-76 . . . . . . . 92

### CHAPTER XIII.
The War of Independence—1776-82 . . . . 99

### CHAPTER XIV.
America and Home . . . . . . . . 118

### CHAPTER XV.
Flanders—1794-95 . . . . . . . . 127

### CHAPTER XVI.
West Indies and Minorca—1795-1800 . . . . 142

### CHAPTER XVII.
Alexandria—1801 . . . . . . . . 164

### CHAPTER XVIII.
Home Service—1801-1805 . . . . . . 198

### CHAPTER XIX.
Gibraltar—1805-1808 . . . . . . . 207

## Contents.

### CHAPTER XX.
The Retreat and Battle of Coruña—1809 . . . 211

### CHAPTER XXI.
Home Service and Walcheren . . . . . 228

### CHAPTER XXII.
Wellington's Peninsular Campaigns—1810-1814 . 231

### CHAPTER XXIII.
Quatre Bras and Waterloo . . . . . . 261

### CHAPTER XXIV.
The Crimean War . . . . . . . . 275

### CHAPTER XXV.
The Indian Mutiny . . . . . . . . 286

### CHAPTER XXVI.
The Ashanti Campaign and the Nile Expedition . 300

### CHAPTER XXVII.
Some Pets of the Regiment . . . . . . 307

# A HISTORY

OF

# THE BLACK WATCH

(ROYAL HIGHLANDERS)

*Formerly styled the* 42nd (*the Royal Highland*) *Regiment*
(*The Black Watch*).

---

## CHAPTER I.

### THE GENESIS OF THE REGIMENT. 1729-40.

Duncan Forbes of Culloden the leading Whig within the Highland line. Affair of Glenshiel in 1719. At Forbes's suggestion, the embodiment of certain number of clansmen as a species of local gendarmerie. In 1730 six separate detachments raised, known as "independent companies," engaged in averting depredations on peaceable neighbours outside of Highland line. Plenty of recruits for this service. Incorporated in 1839 into a regiment of the line, under command of Lord Crawford. Names of officers of regiment familiarly known as the "Black Watch." In May, 1740, mustered and embodied under title of the "Highland Regiment with the number of 43rd Foot." Tartan chosen. Lord Crawford succeeded by Lord Sempill. Employed on local service until 1743.

WHAT the first Lord Melville was in Scotland from 1775 until his retirement in 1806, Duncan Forbes of Culloden was in the North-country during the period from 1712 until his death in 1747. He was the leading Whig within the Highland line, and he had the great advantage of enjoying the confidence of Sir Robert Walpole. In the "'15" he distinguished himself by loyal but not

B

cruel exertions against the Jacobite rebels. He and his brother raised forces in support of the Government, and in combination with Lovat, they threatened Inverness, which surrendered just before the battle of Sheriffmuir—that half-humorous, half-tragic conflict, of which, in the words of the old song :—

> "Some say that we wan,
> An' some say that they wan."

Forbes, after the insurrection was quelled, was expected to take part in the prosecution according to law of the rebel prisoners in Carlisle Castle; but he declined that task, and even collected money for the support of the Scottish prisoners immured there. After the absurd expedition from Spain in 1719, which ended so disastrously in the action fought in the valley and on the hillside of Glenshiel, a number of Jacobites of high rank and position found themselves in a very precarious situation; for the Earl Marischal, resolute to burn his bridges, had sent his ships back to Spain, and, as Keith quaintly said, "everybody took the road he liked best." But there was no great choice of roads in a country of which the Whig General Wightman reported that he was "taking a tour through the difficult parts of Seaforth's country to terrify the rebels by burning the houses of the guilty." Duncan Forbes was living at Culloden in 1719, and was furnished by the Provost of Inverness with full details of the affair of Glenshiel. He was a loyal servant of the Whig Government; but blood is thicker than water, and it remained that the leaders of the abortive expedition, after lurking for some time in Knoydart and Glengarry's country, made good their escape, notwithstanding that there was a heavy price on their heads.

It was as the result of a suggestion made to the

authorities by Duncan Forbes of Culloden that in 1729 it was determined on that a certain number of Highland clansmen should be embodied in the character of a species of local gendarmerie. It may be remarked here in passing, that on the approach of the rebellion of 1745 Forbes strongly but vainly advocated the measure, afterwards adopted with great advantage by Chatham, of forming regular regiments consisting wholly of Highlanders. Early in 1730 six separate and distinct detachments of Highlanders were raised, which, because of their being unconnected with each other, came to be known by the term of "independent companies." Of those six companies three consisted each of a captain, two lieutenants, one ensign, and 100 non-commissioned officers and men, and were commanded respectively by Lord Lovat, Sir Duncan Campbell of Lochnell, and Colonel Grant of Ballindalloch. Lord Lovat, formerly a lieutenant of Grenadiers in Lord Tullibardine's Regiment, was particularly proud of his company—the "Fraser" independent company of the Black Watch—and was wont to boast that General Wade, when commander-in-chief in Scotland, had once declared that "he never did see such a company." Lovat, however, was deprived of his independent company, after commanding it nearly fifteen years, was convicted of treason, and was executed on Tower Hill, April 9th, 1747. The three lesser of the independent companies, consisting each of seventy-five men, were commanded respectively by Colonel Alexander Campbell of Finab, John Campbell of Carrick, and George Munro of Culcairn, each holding the commission of captain-lieutenant, with one lieutenant and one ensign to each company. The companies were broken up in small detachments throughout the Highlands, generally in the district wherein each had originally been raised. Thus Fort Augustus and the neighbourhood was occupied by the Frasers under Lord Lovat; the Grants were stationed in Strathspey and Badenoch; the Munros, under Culcairn, in Ross and Sutherland; Lochnell's and Carrick's companies had their quarters in Athole and Breadalbane; and Finab's company in Lochaber, among the disaffected Camerons of Northern Argyle and among the Stewarts of Appin. The officers belonged to the Whig clans of Campbell, Grant, Munro, etc., which had embraced the political principles of the revolution of 1688; but many of the men were of the Athole and other Perthshire clans, which still adhered to the Jacobite interest.

Those six companies were habitually engaged in overawing the disaffected, in preventing reprisals and plunder on the part of rival clans, and in averting the depredations of the mountaineers on their peaceable neighbours outside of the Highland line. Many of the men composing those companies were of a more respectable position than that to which most soldiers of the present day belong; they were cadets of good family, sons and relatives of gentlemen farmers and landholders, either immediately or distantly descended from gentlemen's families; men who held themselves responsible for their conduct to honourable houses, as well as to a country for which they cherished a devoted and single-hearted affection. For the most part they possessed the personal advantage of a bold and striking presence, special care having been taken in selecting men of full height, fine proportions, and handsome appearance. General Stewart mentions as an example a kinsman of his own, one of the gentlemen soldiers in Carrick's company. This person, a man of family and education, was five feet eleven inches in height, remarkable for his personal strength and activity, and one of the best swordsmen of his time in an age when good swordsmanship was almost universal and considered the indispensable accomplishment of a gentleman; yet, with all those qualifications, he was only a centre man of the centre rank of his company.

In a country without commerce and offering no profession for its manhood but that of arms, no difficulty was experienced in finding young fellows eager to engage in a corps stationary within their own vicinity, and the duties of which were for the most part mere pastime. The Highlanders had a special incentive to enter a quasi-military service. At the period under notice the carrying of arms was prohibited by heavy penalties, galling to a high-spirited and warlike race. Hence it became an object of ambition with young Highlanders of spirit to be admitted, even as privates, into a service which gave them the cherished privilege of carrying arms. Thus is explained the great number of men of respectable families who, in the old days, were in the ranks of the Black Watch, a circumstance which has surprised people who were ignorant to what extent the motives referred to operated. When the regiment was first embodied, it is recorded that private soldiers were seen riding to the exercise-ground followed by their servants carrying their weapons and uniforms. Writing of the Black Watch, an English officer of that period remarks: "I cannot forbear to tell you that many of these private gentlemen-soldiers have *gillies*, or servants, to attend them in quarters, and upon a march to carry their provisions, baggage, and firelocks." The sybaritic dhuinnewassal who contemplated a career as a soldier had not yet taken into account the inevitable knapsack.

The "Black Watch," or as is its Gaelic name, "Am Freiceadan Dubh," was the appellation given to the independent companies of which, with reinforcements, the regiment was subsequently formed. From the time that the companies were first embodied until they were regimented the Highlanders continued to wear the dress of their country. Each company wore the clan tartan of its commanding officer, the colours mingling in which being mostly black, blue, and green, with occasionally a stripe of red, yellow, or white; the result afforded the dark and sombre tone whence came the name, and whence also came the contrast with the conspicuous uniform of the regulars, who at this period had scarlet coats, waistcoats, and breeches, and were called in Gaelic "Seidaran Dearag"—the "Red Soldiers"—who must have resembled Mephistopheles, or a detachment of flamingoes.

From 1730 to 1739 the independent companies of the Black Watch performed their allotted duties to the satisfaction of the Government, but in the latter year the constitution of the corps was materially changed. War with Spain—originally caused by the maltreatment of Skipper Jenkins on the high seas at the hands of certain truculent Spaniards, who cut off Jenkins' ear and flung it in his face with "Carry that to your king, and tell him we did it!"—ultimately was enforced by the universal voice of the English nation, and it was declared on 3rd November, 1739. Taking time by the forelock, King George II. resolved to incorporate the Black Watch into a regiment of the line to be augmented to ten companies, in order that the advantage of a Highland corps should be possessed in the impending contest. For this purpose a royal warrant, dated October 25th, 1739, was addressed to

John, twentieth Earl of Crawford, fourth Earl of Lindsay, and thirteenth Lord Lindsay of the Byres. This nobleman was a brilliant and striking personage, a veritable knight-errant of the eighteenth century. Born in 1702, he was elected a Representative Peer of Scotland in 1732. Desirous of acquiring a varied and practical knowledge of his profession, Lord Crawford joined the Imperial army on the Rhine in 1735 as a volunteer, and fought in the battle of Claussen. In 1738 he was serving with the Russians under Marshal Münnich against the Turks. He later joined the Imperialists at the siege of Belgrade, and fought at the battle of Kratza, 22nd July, 1739; when he received a desperate wound, which, after having broken out no fewer than twenty-nine times during the intervals of active service, caused his ending on Christmas Day, 1749, at the age of forty-seven. When in May, 1740, the separate companies of the Black Watch were formed into the historic regiment which now again stands under that title in the Army List, the regimental force had for its commanding officer the Earl of Crawford. "Familiar with the language, fond of the dress, and, although a Lowlander, attached to the manners and customs of the Gael, he was greatly beloved by the Highland soldiers."—so has written General Stewart of Garth—"because of his chivalric and heroic spirit. On his approach to George II. after the victory of Dettingen, he was saluted by that serio-comic monarch with the welcome: 'Here comes my champion!'" During the rebellion of 1745-6 he commanded the forces which held the Lowlands in comparative tranquillity throughout that troubled period, while the Duke of Cumberland was operating with truculent ferocity in the Highlands and islands. Lord Crawford's character has been felicitously described by a distinguished contemporary of his own as "the most generous, the most gallant, the bravest and the finest nobleman of his time."

The commissions of the officers of the new regiment formed in virtue of the royal warrant were dated in November and December, 1739. The following officers received commissions :—

COLONEL : John, Earl of Crawford and Lindsay, died in 1748.

LIEUTENANT-COLONEL : Sir Robert Munro of Foulis, Bart., killed at Falkirk, 1746.

MAJOR : George Grant, brother of the Laird of Grant, removed from the service by sentence of court-martial, for allowing the rebels to get possession of the Castle of Inverness in 1746.

CAPTAINS :

George Munro of Culcairn, brother of Sir Robert Munro, killed in 1746.
Dugald Campbell of Craignish, retired in 1745.
John Campbell of Carrick, killed at Fontenoy.
Colin Campbell, Junr., of Monzie, retired in 1743.
Sir James Colquhoun of Luss, Bart., retired in 1748.
Colin Campbell of Ballimore, retired.
John Munro, promoted to Lieutenant-Colonel in 1743, retired in 1749.

CAPTAIN-LIEUTENANT : Duncan Macfarlane, retired in 1744.

LIEUTENANTS :

Paul Macpherson.
Lewis Grant of Auchterblair.
John Maclean of Kingarloch } Both removed from the regiment in 1744 for
John Mackenzie } having fought a duel.
Alexander Macdonald.

Malcolm Fraser, son of Culduthel, killed at Bergen-op-Zoom in 1747.

George Ramsay.

Francis Grant, son of the Laird of Grant, died Lieutenant-General in 1782.

John Macneil.

ENSIGNS:

Dugald Campbell, killed at Fontenoy.

Dugald Stewart.

John Menzies of Comrie.

Edward Carrick.

Gilbert Stewart of Kincraigie.

Gordon Graham of Drainies.

Archd. Macnab, son of the Laird of Macnab, died Lieutenant-General, 1790.

Colin Campbell.

James Campbell of Glenfalloch, died of wounds at Fontenoy.

CHAPLAIN: Hon. and Rev. Gideon Murray.

SURGEON: James Munro, brother of Sir Robert Munro.

ADJUTANT: Gilbert Stewart.

QUARTERMASTER: John Forbes.

There was not an officer in the regiment—with the exception of the colonel, a Lowlander—who was not a pure Highlander. Most were men of old family, and possessed of landed property for generations back; others were sons or relatives of Highland lairds, cadets of houses of good standing. Family and personal pride was the most salient characteristic of the officerhood of the regiment, as, indeed, was the case for the most part among its non-commissioned officers and the rank and file.

Considerable progress had been made in recruiting, and the several companies were assembled in May, 1740, when the men were mustered and embodied into a regiment under the title of the "Highland Regiment" with the number of the 43rd Foot, but retaining firmly the local name of the Black Watch. It had been generally believed that the muster was in a field midway between Taybridge and Aberfeldy in Perthshire. Sir Robert Menzies, however, has stated that "the detailed companies of the Black Watch met at Weem, and that the whole regiment was first drawn up in the field of Boltachan, between Weem and Taybridge." When the companies were still in a state of independence one from another, each commanding officer naturally wore, and had his company wear, the tartan of his own clan. When the embodiment occurred no clan could arrogate to itself a valid claim to have its tartan made common to the whole regiment, and Lord Crawford, the colonel, as a Lowlander, could have no clan tartan. In this dilemma a pattern of tartan belonging to no clan was selected, and it has ever since been known as the Forty-Second, or Black Watch tartan, distinctive from all other tartans. Lord John Murray gave the Athole tartan for the philibeg; the difference was merely a narrow stripe of scarlet, to distinguish it from the sombre pattern of the belted plaid. The pipers have always worn a tartan chiefly of a brilliant red, of the pattern known as the Stuart tartan. When a band came to be formed, plaids of the pipers' pattern were given to the musicians. General Stewart of Garth, in his interesting and patriotic "Sketches," states that the uniform of the regiment was a scarlet jacket and waistcoat, with buff facings and white lace; tartan plaid of twelve yards, pleated round the middle of the body, the upper part being fastened on the left shoulder, ready to be opened out and wrapped over both shoulders and the firelock in rainy weather. At night the plaid served as a blanket, and was a sufficient covering for the hardy Highlander. It was called a "belted" plaid because kept tight to the waist by a belt; and it was worn on guards, reviews, and all occasions when the men were in full dress. From this belt depended the pistols and dirk when worn. In barracks and when not on duty, the little kilt or philibeg was worn. The head-dress originally was a blue bonnet, with a border of white, red, and green, arranged in small squares to resemble, as has been believed, the "fesse chequy" in the coat of arms of the house of Stuart; and a tuft of feathers, or, perhaps from motives of economy, a small piece of black bearskin. Tartan hose, with buckled shoes, were worn; the sporrans were made of badger-skin. The arms furnished by Government were a musket, a bayonet, and a basket-hilted broadsword. Such of the men as chose to supply themselves with pistols and dirk were allowed to carry those weapons; and some had targets, after the custom of the Highlands. The sword-belt was of black leather, and the cartouch-box was carried in front on a narrow belt round the waist. The officers carried *fusils*, or short muskets, in accordance with the fashion of officers of fusilier and light-infantry corps; the sergeants retained their formidable Lochaber axes.

After its embodiment the Highland Regiment was cantoned on the banks of the Tay and the Lyon for some fifteen months, and was assembled regularly for drill near Taymouth Castle under its Lieutenant-Colonel, Sir Robert Munro of Foulis. On Christmas Day, 1740, the Earl of Crawford was transferred to the 2nd (Scots) Troop of Horse Grenadier Guards, and was succeeded in the colonelcy of the Black Watch by Brigadier-General Lord Sempill on January 14, 1741. Lord Sempill had seen considerable service. He had soldiered in Spain and Flanders under Ormond and Marlborough, also in Ireland and at Gibraltar. He accompanied the Highland Regiment to Flanders in 1743. He is stated to have been transferred from it to the 25th Regiment in "April, 1745," which was somewhat strange since the regiment which he had commanded from the beginning of 1741 was still wholly untried in battle—and battle assuredly was then impending. He is mentioned as having distinguished himself "in 1745" in the defence of Aeth, served under the Duke of Cumberland in Scotland in the following year, and commanded a brigade in the battle of Culloden. He died in November, 1746, when in command of the troops at Aberdeen. In the winter of 1741 the Highland Regiment marched further northwards, and the companies were sent in detachment to different districts of the Highlands to resume the duties which they had formerly performed as the Black Watch, being thus employed until the month of March, 1743, when orders were received for the whole regiment to assemble at Perth.

## CHAPTER II.

### "LOCHABER NO MORE!" 1743.

Regiment in 1743 ordered to march to England. Duncan Forbes's conviction that it was an error to withdraw regiment from the region in which it had been raised. English surprised by warlike aspect of regiment and its orderly deportment. Two chosen privates sent in advance for inspection by King. In April regiment approached London, and on May 14th reviewed by Field-Marshal Wade; appearance and discipline of regiment greatly admired. Mass of regiment marched to Gravesend to embark for Flanders. Part of regiment, about 200 men, refused to take foreign service, and marched in direction of northern homes. The deserters were determined to resist, but after parley, when in Northamptonshire, laid down their arms. Tried by court-martial and condemned to be shot, but sentence executed as regards but three ringleaders, who were shot on Tower Hill. Remainder sent to various destinations abroad.

On arriving at the rendezvous the regiment was informed that it was to march without delay to England. This order was issued in consequence of the Government having selected the Highland Regiment to reinforce the army which, in the previous year, had been despatched to Flanders to support the house of Austria against the Elector of Bavaria and the King of France. The order was unexpected on the part of the men, who expressed no small surprise at the tidings it conveyed. When the intention of employing the regiment on foreign service came to be mooted, many of the warmest supporters in Scotland of the Government strongly disapproved of the measure, among whom was Duncan Forbes, the

Lord President, than whom no one better knew the character of the corps, the nature of the duty on which the men had been employed, and their peculiar aptness for the performance of it.

It has been said in many histories that the order for the Highland Regiment to march into England was contrary to the conditions under which the men had enlisted, that the majority of the Highlanders had joined its ranks on the understanding that they would be required to serve only in their own country, and that consequently to send them abroad would be considered a direct breach of faith. No evidence to this effect has ever come to light. Nothing is forthcoming to indicate that the enlistment of the men of the Black Watch was other than normal, or that it was accompanied by any other than the ordinary conditions expressed in the Regulations. The men of the Black Watch could not well be ignorant that long before the Union numerous Scottish regiments had been serving abroad, and that some were still serving on the Continent. Turenne and the Prince of Condé had lauded the valour and the discipline of Scottish regiments commanded by Hamilton, Douglas, Dumbarton, Kirkpatrick, Collyear, and MacKay. No Government could be expected to maintain and pay a regiment which might think proper to judge for itself whether it should choose obedience or mutiny. It is probable enough that the men of the Black Watch expected—their officers could not have shared the expectation—that they would not be required to quit their own country; and that since their destination had not been officially communicated, they were merely proceeding to London to pass in review under the eyes of the King.

Duncan Forbes wisely discerned that although the

Highland Regiment might be a valuable reinforcement to the army in Flanders, it was a great error in the existing circumstances to withdraw it from the region in which it had been raised. Writing to General Clayton, the commander-in-chief in Scotland, Forbes thus expressed himself: "When I heard that the Highland Regiment was to march southward, I did not concern myself, because I supposed that the intention was merely that it should be seen in England and presently return; but now assured that it is destined for foreign service, I cannot dissemble my uneasiness at a resolution that may, in my apprehension, be attended with very bad consequences. . . . The present system for securing the peace of the Highlands, which is the best I know of, is by regular troops stationed from Inverness to Fort William along the chain of lochs which divides the Highlands, and by a body of disciplined native Highlanders wearing the dress and speaking the language of the country, to execute orders requiring expedition for which neither the dress nor the manner of the regular troops are proper. The Highlanders recently regimented were at first in independent companies; and though their dress, language, and manners qualified them for securing the low country against depredations, yet that was not the sole use of them. Their attributes fitted them for every undertaking that required secrecy and despatch; they served for all purposes of light horse in a country where mountains and bogs render cavalry useless; and if properly disposed throughout the Highlands, nothing that was commonly reported or believed by the Highlanders could be a secret to their commanders, because of their intimacy with the people and the community of language." Forbes's prescience was fully justified two years later, before and when Charles

Edward hoisted his standard in Glenfinnan; and if the Black Watch had been at Aberfeldy in the summer of 1745, instead of being in Flanders, that adventurous youth might never have crossed the summit of Corriarrack. But few statesmen are so wise and far-seeing as was Lord President Forbes.

The Government, acting quite within its rights, adhered to its resolution to send the Highland Regiment abroad. It has been stated, on unauthenticated authority, that in order to prevent an *émeute* their real destination was concealed from the Highlanders, who were told that the object of their march was merely to gratify the curiosity of the King, who was desirous of seeing a Highland regiment. Satisfied, it was alleged, with such an explanation as this, they proceeded on their march. The inhabitants of England, who had regarded the Highlanders as savages, were surprised by the warlike aspect of the regiment and the orderly deportment of the men; and they received most friendly attentions in the country and towns through which they passed.

It was the truth that King George, although not a curious person, had expressed a desire to see a Highland soldier. Two privates, remarkable for their good looks and handsome figures, were despatched in advance to meet the wishes of his Majesty. The Highland soldiers who made obeisance to royalty were Gregor McGregor, commonly called "Gregor the beautiful," and John Campbell, son of Duncan Campbell, of the family of Duneaves in Perthshire. The *Westminster Journal* of the period stated that they "were presented to the King by their Lieutenant-Colonel, Sir Robert Munro; and that they performed the broad-sword exercise and that of the Lochaber axe, or lance, before his Majesty, the

Duke of Cumberland, Field-Marshal Wade, and a number of general officers, in the great gallery of St. James's Palace. They displayed so much dexterity and skill in the management of their weapons as to give perfect satisfaction to the sovereign. Each received a gratuity of a guinea, which they gave to the porter at the palace gate as they passed out." They believed, honest gentlemen, that the King had mistaken their condition in their own country. General Stewart of Garth says in his "Sketches," that "in general the character of the men who originally composed the Black Watch was honourable and lofty." This sentiment of self-respect inspired a high spirit and sense of honour in the regiment, which continued to inform its character and conduct long after the description of men who originally composed it was totally changed. Both Gregor and Campbell rose to rank in the service. Mr. Campbell received an ensigncy for his gallantry at Fontenoy, and he was Captain-Lieutenant of the regiment when he was killed at Ticonderoga. Mr. McGregor was promoted in another regiment, and later purchased the lands of Inverardine in Breadalbane.

At the end of April the regiment, in two divisions, reached the vicinity of London, and on May 14th was reviewed on Finchley Common by Field-Marshal Wade, who well knew the character of the corps, having been for many years commander-in-chief in Scotland. Many thousands of spectators were present at the review, and the appearance and discipline of the regiment were greatly admired; but the King, whom the Highlanders had confidently expected to give himself the trouble of looking at them, had departed for Hanover on the very day they had arrived near the Metropolis. They took his Majesty's non-appearance in great dudgeon, and considering themselves grievously deceived, became exceedingly chagrined and irritated. Then insidious and malicious falsehoods were industriously circulated among the men. The simple yet suspicious Highlanders were told that the Government meant to transport them to the American plantations, there to remain for life. Another report was circulated among the men that they were designed for the West Indies, at that period accounted the grave of Europeans; and again, that the object assigned for bringing them into England was a mere pretext, and that the actual intent of the movement was in order to get out of the country so many disaffected and rebellious Jacobites.

After the review of the 14th the mass of the regiment, in obedience to orders, marched to Gravesend, there to embark for Flanders. But a certain number of misguided men, their minds poisoned by cruel falsehoods and misrepresentations, resolved to shake the dust of London off their feet, and make the best of their way back to their native country. Authorities differ as to the number of the deserters; the "Historical Record" gives it as "upwards of a hundred," whereas, according to General Stewart, two hundred recaptured deserters were sent to different corps abroad; the distribution being fifty to Gibraltar, fifty to Minorca, forty to the Leeward Islands, thirty to Jamaica, and thirty to Georgia. The strength of the regiment, after deductions from desertion, nevertheless amounted after Fontenoy to nearly 900 men fit for service, and its marching-out strength from Perth must have been considerably over 1,000 men, since no mention has been made of a draft having been sent out.

The men of the deserting detachment, in whatever strength, having unsuspectedly obtained some provisions for the journey, and confiding in their capacity to endure privations and fatigue, imagined that they should be able to prevail over any troops that might be sent in pursuit of them. It was on a night soon after the review that they assembled on a common near Highgate, and set out on their wild and romantic march. Keeping as nearly as possible between the two great north roads, they passed from wood to wood so dexterously that it was difficult to follow their track. Their leaders were Corporals Malcolm and Samuel Macpherson, and Private Farquhar Shaw. Warning orders were issued to the commanding officers of forces stationed between the metropolis and Scotland, and the Secretary of War exhorted the civil officers to be vigilant in their endeavours to discover the route of the fugitives. On May 22nd they were overtaken at Oundle in Northamptonshire by a couple of squadrons of cavalry followed by some infantry, whereupon they took up a position in Lady Wood, and expressed their resolution to resist to the last unless they were granted a free pardon. Happily the judicious conduct of Captain Ball of General Blakeney's staff prevented blood being shed, and after a long parley the Highlanders blew the powder out of their pans and laid down their arms before General Blakeney. The deserters were escorted back to London, where they were tried by a general court-martial, found guilty, and condemned to be shot; but the capital part of the sentence was remitted as regarded all but three men—the brothers Macpherson and Farquhar Shaw, who were ordered for execution and shot accordingly on Tower Hill in the early morning of Monday, 12th July. Their more fortunate comrades were drawn out to witness the execution, and joined in their prayers with great earnestness. The doomed men behaved with perfect calmness and propriety. Their bodies were placed into three coffins by three of the prisoners—their clansmen and namesakes—and they were buried in one grave close to the place of execution. Farquhar Shaw, one of the three ringleaders, was no ordinary man. He was the son of an old Celtic warrior from the Braes of Lochaber, who "died sword in hand at the rising in Glenshiel." After his death the old dhuinnewassal's estate was seized by the House of Breadalbane, and Farquhar, his only son, was compelled to enlist in the independent company of the Black Watch commanded by Campbell of Finab. "Farquhar Shaw," wrote the author of the "Legends of the Black Watch," "was a perfect swordsman and a deadly shot alike with the musket and pistol, and his strength was such that he had been known to twist a horseshoe and drive his *skene dhu* to the hilt in a pine log." His activity and power of enduring hunger, thirst, heat, cold, and fatigue became a proverb among the men of the Black Watch. Unhappily he took a prominent part in the mutiny in the Highland Regiment in 1743, and his end has already been told.

## CHAPTER III.

### FONTENOY—THE BAPTISM OF FIRE. 1745.

The regiment, still 900 strong, arrived on the Continent just too late for Dettingen in June, 1743. Exceptionally decent and orderly in quarters. Campaign of 1745. Battle of Fontenoy, May 11th. Marshal Saxe commanding French army of 80,000, Duke of Cumberland commanding British army about 60,000 strong. French position naturally very strong, and fortified with great skill. Advance of British army on the fortified lines. After desperate fighting, Cumberland gave orders to retreat. Conduct of Highland Regiment covering the retreat. Lord Crawford's compliment. Chaplain, afterwards Professor, Ferguson—"Damn my Commission!"

THE unfortunate episode just related did not prevent the embarkation of the regiment from Gravesend. Landing at Ostend it arrived at Brussels on June 1st, 1743; and marching by Tirlemont, Liége, and Maestricht, it joined the allied army commanded by George II. in person, at Hanau, a few days after his Majesty on June 16th had gained the famous victory of Dettingen over the French, the account of which has been amusingly told by Carlyle in his "Frederick the Great." But although the men of the Highland Regiment had not on that occasion an opportunity of evincing themselves good soldiers in the field, all the accounts agree that by their conduct they proved themselves exceptionally decent and orderly in quarters. "That regiment" (Sempill's Highlanders), on the authority of the pious Colonel Gardiner, "was regarded as a trustworthy guard of property. Seldom were any of the men of it seen drunk, and they as seldom swore, notwithstanding that the *locus in quo* was Flanders. The Elector-Palatine conveyed his thanks to King George for the excellent behaviour of the regiment while in his territories in 1743-44; "for whose sake," added that magnate, "I shall always pay a regard to a Scotsman in future." The Highland soldiers had won the good opinion and entire confidence of the inhabitants, whose desire was to have them quartered in their houses, as they were not only quiet and domesticated, but served as a protection against the rudeness of other soldiers.

On April 25th, 1743, Lord Sempill was transferred to the colonelcy of the 25th Regiment, and Lord John Murray, seventh son of the Duke of Athole, succeeded him in the colonelcy of the Highland Regiment. Neither officer, apparently, was at Fontenoy. Lord John, who in 1743 was a comparatively young man and a very keen soldier, took a great interest in everything connected with the Highland Regiment, of which he was colonel for nearly forty-two years. He was the staunch friend of every good officer and soldier in the regiment; and it is stated that when the disabled soldiers from Ticonderoga came home in 1758 to pass the Board, "the morning they were to appear before it, he dressed himself in full Highland uniform, and putting himself at the head of all who were able to walk, he marched his invalids to Chelsea, and advocated their cases so successfully that all received pensions." It is further recorded of this "soldier's friend," that he gave them five guineas wherewith to drink the King's health, and two guineas to each married man; and he obtained for the whole a free passage to Perth, offering as well a house and garden to all of them who chose to settle on his land.

The campaign of 1745 was begun towards the end of April by the siege of Tournay. Marshal Saxe, who was in command of an army of about 80,000 men, opened trenches against that fortified city, the garrison of which consisted of 8,000 Dutch troops under General Baron Dorth. King Louis and the Dauphin hastened from Paris to join the marshal in the camp before Tournay. In March the Duke of Cumberland—Carlyle's "Martial Boy"—was commissioned Captain-General of the British army, the third and last in succession after the Dukes of Marlborough and Ormond who held that high rank. The duke was, moreover, appointed commander-in-chief of an allied army made up of British, Dutch, and Austrian troops. An army of mixed nationalities seldom does great things, especially when its commanders are of little account. Cumberland was brave, but stupid; and so corpulent at the age of twenty-four that he had difficulty in mounting his horse. The Prince of Waldeck, who commanded the Dutch contingent, had neither experience nor skill; and Count Königseck, once a brilliant soldier but now almost in his dotage, commanded a mere handful of Austrian troopers. Thus led, the allied army advanced serenely to measure its strength with the finest army in Europe, commanded by the most brilliant soldier and ablest strategist of the period—Count Saxe, Marshal-General of France, an officer so renowned that the Marshal Duke of Noailles was content to serve under him as his chief-of-staff. Saxe, however, was so feeble from long dissipation that he was unable either to mount a horse or to wear uniform; and since he would not relinquish service in the field, he accompanied the army carried in a litter.

As Cumberland slowly approached on his errand of relieving Tournay, Saxe left to hold the trenches before that place 18,000 men; for the defence of the Scheldt bridges and to keep open his communications he assigned 6,000 more. Then he advanced to the village of Fontenoy, a small village on a rising ground about four miles south-east of Tournay, and on the right bank of the river. A man of great vigilance, forethought, and sagacious precaution, singular in one so dissolute, Saxe had determined to neglect nothing on this occasion. He knew every foot of the ground, having served in his youth in this region. His line of front extended for about seven miles, resting on a chain of villages, of which St. Antoine was on his right, near the river; Fontenoy was on his right centre; and, with a considerable interval, was the village of Barry on his left, on the skirt of the wood of the same name. "In and before each of those villages were posts and defences—in Antoine and Fontenoy elaborate redoubts, batteries, redans connecting; in the wood of Barry an abatis, or defence of felled trees, as well as cannon; and at the point of the wood, well within double range of Fontenoy, was the redoubt of Eu." Saxe was said to have two hundred and sixty pieces of cannon consummately disposed along this front; and his strength in and behind those formidable defences was reckoned to amount to about 60,000 men.

On May 9th the allied army came up and encamped between the villages of Maubray and Beaugnies, at a short distance from the hostile outposts. The allied strength, all told, was about 50,000 men. The Duke of Cumberland, spite of his obesity, was a very keen soldier; and on the evening of his arrival the Highland Regiment was ordered to the front, when his Royal Highness, with Field-Marshal Königseck and the Prince of Waldeck, went out to reconnoitre the French position, covered by the Highlanders, who kept up a brisk fire with the hostile skirmishers lurking in the woods. The veteran Königseck gave it as his opinion that the enterprise was impracticable. He argued that it was impossible to turn either flank of the French position, with the Scheldt on its right and the morasses on its left. Waldeck, however, supported the duke, and the 10th was occupied in placing the artillery, clearing the front, and driving in the hostile outposts. On this duty also was a party of the Highland Regiment, who for the first time stood the fire of a formed enemy. Of their conduct in this their noviciate on the field of battle, the "History of the War" reports—"A detachment of Highlanders acted in support of some Austrian hussars hotly pressed by French light troops, who were promptly repulsed with loss, and the Highlanders were taken great notice of for their spirited conduct."

So early as two o'clock of the morning of the 11th the Duke of Cumberland was busy making his dispositions. The British and Hanoverian infantry were being formed in two lines fronting the space between Fontenoy and the wood of Barry. About four o'clock the Guards and Highlanders began the battle, and attacked a body of French troops near Vezon, where the Dauphin was posted. Although the adversaries were stubborn and were entrenched in the village breast-high, the Guards with their bayonets, and the Highlanders with sword, pistol and dirk, forced them out, killing a considerable number. All the authorities except Colonel Groves mention the Highland Regiment at Fontenoy under the name of "Sempill's Highlanders," which, however, is an error, since Lord John Murray had succeeded Lord Sempill on 25th April. The British and Hanoverians advanced to the attack, and after a bitter contest drove the enemy back on their main entrenchments. The duke from his right had detached Brigadier Ingoldsby with Lord John Murray's Highlanders to silence the Redoubt d'Eu at the front of the wood of Barry, looking towards Fontenoy across the intervening hollow. The redoubt—the taking of which might have given victory to the allies—was not carried. Some thirty Highlanders were killed "in some frantic attempt on it"; and Ingoldsby, who was not energetic, was subsequently tried by court-martial, but vindicated himself after a fashion by denying that he had ever received orders on the occasion—adding, with some discrepancy, that those he did receive were so contradictory that he did not know which to obey. Immediately afterwards his Royal Highness ordered the Highland Regiment to leave the Redoubt d'Eu, and to hasten across the front to assist in the attack on the village of Fontenoy, which still held out against the Dutch, who had failed in every attempt. Notwithstanding these discouragements the duke would by no means accept defeat. Carlyle writes of him: "His Royal Highness blazes into resplendent *Platt-Deutsch* rage, what we may call spiritual white heat—a man *sans peur* at any rate, and pretty much *sans avis*—decides that he must and will be through those lines, please God; that he will not be repulsed at his part of the attack, but will plunge through by what gap there is— 900 yards Voltaire measures it—between Fontenoy and that redoubt, and see what the French interior is like." Cumberland and his officers gathered up and formed the men into columns, which then advanced through bushy hollows, water-courses, and defiles. Gradually they got beyond range of shot from either d'Eu or Fontenoy, till a compact column of some 16,000 men slowly advanced, with frequent halts, and exposed to a torrent of continuous deadly fire. Assailed over and over again, the column still advanced with slow imperturbability, diversified with fierce fire.

Victory for the allies seemed within measurable distance. So thought Saxe, who sent notice to the King to retire further out of danger. He himself quitted his litter; and mounted on horseback supported by a man on either side, he brought up the Household troops of the French monarch. At the suggestion of the Duc de Richelieu, cannon were got ahead of the advancing British column and opened fire on it, to be followed by a final charge. The British guns slackened their fire, and so gave time for the Irish brigade to form—the last resource left to King Louis and Marshal Saxe. It was at the most critical moment of the day that the Irish brigade, consisting of the representatives of 30,000 Irishmen who had followed James into exile, came fully into action against the British—the veteran regiments of Clare, Dillon, O'Lally, Berwick-Rothe, Buckley, and Fitzjames. The encounter between the British and the Irish troops was fierce, the fire constant, the slaughter great; and the loss of the former was such that they were compelled at length to retire. It was about midday that, a second attack made by the Dutch having failed, the Highland Regiment was ordered to support a body of troops which was severely engaged with superior numbers. Sir Robert Munro, the gallant Lieutenant-Colonel of the regiment, brought it into action with a fine ardour tempered with discipline. Doddridge, in his "Life of Colonel Gardiner," records: "Sir Robert had obtained leave of the Duke of Cumberland to allow the Highlanders to fight in their own way. According to the usage of his countrymen, he ordered the whole regiment to clap to the ground on receiving the French fire. Instantly after its discharge the men sprang up, and coming close to the enemy, poured in their shot upon them to the certain destruction of multitudes, and drove them precipitately back through their own lines; then retreating, drew up again, and attacked a second time after the same manner. Those attacks they repeated several times on the same day, to the surprise of the whole army. Sir Robert was everywhere with his regiment, notwithstanding his great corpulency; and when in the trenches he was hauled out by the legs and arms by his own men. But it was to be observed that when he commanded the whole regiment to clap to the ground, he himself alone stood upright, with the colours behind him, ready to receive the fire of the enemy; and this because, as he said, though he could easily lie down, his great bulk would not suffer him to rise so quickly."

The Duke of Cumberland witnessed the gallant conduct of the regiment; and observing a Highlander who had killed nine men making a stroke with his broadsword at the tenth, when his arm was shot off by a cannon-ball, the duke applauded the skilful swordsmanship displayed by the man, and promised him a reward "of a value equal to the arm."

Under cover of the French artillery fire, a combined charge of cavalry and infantry was hurled against the front and flanks of the British column; and this united attack could not be withstood by men who had already experienced long and severe fatigue. The British were forced to give way, and were driven back across the ravine. The Highlanders, who had been ordered up from the attack on the village of Fontenoy, and two other regiments ordered from the reserve to support the line, were borne down by the retreating body, and retired along with the mass. The whole rallied beyond the ravine, and after some delay the duke resolved on a final retreat, ordering that the Highlanders and the 19th Regiment should cover the rear of the retreating army and check the advance of the enemy, who pursued the moment the retreat began. The command of the troops covering the retreat was entrusted to Lord Crawford, who had commanded a brigade of Household Cavalry in the battle, and who conducted the retirement in excellent order until his troops came to the Pass, when he ordered them to file off from the right. He then took off his hat, and, returning them thanks, said that they had acquired as much honour in covering the recent retreat as if they had gained the battle. Such approbation must have naturally been consolatory to soldiers after sustaining a defeat; and to the Highlanders it must have been particularly gratifying, coming from a man who knew them so well as did their first colonel, and whom they so highly honoured for his chivalrous and heroic spirit.

The French author of a pamphlet published in Paris immediately after the battle of Fontenoy writes as follows:—"The British behaved well, and could be exceeded in ardour by none but our officers, who animated the troops by their example, *when the Highland furies rushed in upon us with more violence than ever did a sea driven by a tempest.* . . . In short, we gained the victory—but may I never see such another!"

In the battle of Fontenoy the losses of the Highland Regiment consisted of Captain John Campbell of Carrick, Ensign Lauchlan Campbell of Craignish, and thirty rank and file, killed; Captain Richard Campbell of Finab, Ensigns Ronald Campbell and James Campbell of Glenfalloch, two sergeants and eighty-six rank and file, wounded; one sergeant and twelve rank and file missing. Captain Campbell of Carrick was one of the most accomplished gentlemen of his day. Possessing charming manners and a bravery tempered by gaiety, he was regarded as one of the last of those who had retained the chivalrous spirit of the Highlands of other days. A poet, a soldier, a gentleman, he was the object of general pride and admiration; and the generation of Highlanders to which he belonged took great pleasure in cherishing his memory and in repeating anecdotes regarding him.

The regiment was fortunate in being commanded in its first battle by a man of military capacity, readiness of resource, and a thorough knowledge of his men. Sir Robert Munro of Fowlis, Bart., chief of his name and clan, the first Lieutenant-Colonel of the Black Watch, was promoted to the Colonelcy of the 37th Regiment immediately after Fontenoy. He had served in the latter part of King William's reign, and in Queen Anne's wars under the Duke of Marlborough, who appointed him to a company in the Scots Royals in 1712; in 1714 he was appointed Lieutenant-Colonel. In 1739 he was appointed Lieutenant-Colonel of the newly raised Highland Regiment. In the absence abroad of Lord Crawford the discipline of the regiment was carried on by the lieutenant-colonel, to what purpose may be judged from its conduct at Fontenoy. Sir Robert commanded his new regiment at the battle of Falkirk, January 17th, 1746, but the men of which it was composed were not Highlanders. They ran like sheep before the rebels, and Sir Robert was slain, his manner of death being recounted by his son in the following letter to Lord President Forbes: "My Lord,—I think it my duty to acquaint you of the deplorable situation I am in. The engagement between the King's troops and the

Highlanders on Thursday last, within a mile of Falkirk, proves to be to me a series of woes. There both my dear father and uncle Obsdale were slain. The latter, your Lordship knows, had no particular business to go to the action; but being of a most tender love and concern for his brother, could not be dissuaded from attending him, to give assistance if need required. My father, after being deserted, was attacked by six of Lochiel's regiment, and for some time defended himself with his half-pike. Two of the six, I am informed, he killed; a seventh, coming up, fired a pistol into my father's groin, upon which falling, the Highlander with his sword gave him two strokes in the face, one over the eyes and another on the mouth, which instantly ended a brave man. The same Highlander fired another pistol into my uncle's breast, and with his sword terribly slashed him, whom when killed, he then despatched a servant of my father's. . . . My father's corpse was honourably interred in the churchyard of Falkirk, by direction of the Earl of Cromartie and the Macdonald, and all the chiefs attended his funeral. I am, etc., HARRY MUNRO."

The Duke of Cumberland, after Fontenoy, intimated to the men of the Highland Regiment that he would be pleased to grant them any favour in his power, as a testimony of the high opinion he had formed of them. The reply was on a par with the kindly offer. The men, with respectful acknowledgments, assured the commander-in-chief that no favour he could bestow would gratify them so much as a pardon for one of their comrades, a soldier of the regiment, who had been tried by court-martial for allowing a prisoner to escape, and who was under sentence of a heavy corporal punishment, which, if inflicted, would bring disgrace on the regiment, and on the family and county of every man belonging to it. The favour was instantly granted. The nature of this request, the feeling that suggested it, and, in short, the general qualities of the corps, impressed his Royal Highness with the more force since at the time he had never been in Scotland, and had not had any means of studying the character of the Highland soldier; unless, indeed, he had formed his opinion from the coarse and ignorant ribaldry of the period, when it was the fashion to consider the Highlander "as a fierce and savage depredator, speaking a barbarous language, and inhabiting a barren and gloomy region, which fear and prudence alike forbade all strangers to enter."

The most humorous detail of the battle of Fontenoy, next to the extrication of the commanding officer by the legs and arms of his men from the trenches, whence, because of his corpulence, he was unable to emerge unaided, was the conduct of the worthy chaplain of the regiment, according to an article in *Blackwood's Magazine* of April, 1896: "In his younger days, Adam Fergusson, afterwards Professor of History in the University of Edinburgh, was chaplain of the Black Watch, and was present with it at Fontenoy. When the regiment was advancing into action, Sir Robert Munro, the colonel, noticed his chaplain at the head of the column with a drawn sword in his hand, and ordered him to the rear with the surgeons. Fergusson refused; and when the colonel, in the altercation which ensued, threatened to have the chaplain's commission cancelled, Fergusson bluntly retorted, 'Damn my commission!' Then, charging at the head of his flock, he fought like a valiant Scotsman during the bloody fray. The stout Munro forgave his insubordination for the sake of his valorous example; and no doubt the stern old Presbyterians in the ranks appreciated his subsequent ministrations none the less because they had seen him in time of trial play the brave man in their midst."

The regiment having sustained so moderate a loss in the battle of Fontenoy, and having still nearly 900 men fit for service, was detached on a particular service, which came to nothing. On its return to headquarters it was said that "in the last day's march of thirty-eight miles on, or rather in, a deep sandy road, it was observed that the Dutch grenadiers and cavalry were overpowered by the heat and fatigue, but that not a man of the Highlanders was left behind." At this period there was not a soldier in the regiment born south of the Grampians.

It should be mentioned that John Munro, brother of Sir Robert, and at the date of the embodiment of the regiment its junior captain, was appointed lieutenant-colonel on July 17th, 1745, in succession to his brother Sir Robert, promoted to the colonelcy of the 37th Regiment; and this although a major and three captains were his seniors. Favouritism is not quite obsolete in the present day, but such an exercise of it as that just recorded would send a thrill of amazement through any more modern army. The promotion was said to have been on account of the alleged circumstance that, in effect, he commanded the regiment in its more rapid movements, immediately under Sir Robert, who, from his extreme corpulency and being on foot, could not move with the rapidity sometimes necessary. Lieutenant-Colonel Munro remained in the regiment until his death in 1749.

## CHAPTER IV.

### HOME AND CONTINENTAL SERVICE. 1745-56.

Rumours in Highlands of advent of Prince Charles Edward. Vigilance of Lord President Forbes. Supineness of authorities. The rebellion of 1745. Return of regiment to England, Family feuds in the Highlands —from share in which the regiment mercifully exempted. The three "new companies" true to their salt; one of them all but annihilated at Prestonpans. Quimperlé Bay. L'Orient—attempts unsuccessful. Embarked for Flanders February, 1747. In consequence of reduction of the 42nd, in 1749 number of regiment altered from 43rd to 42nd, which it ever since retained. Service in Ireland. Great cordiality between Highlanders and Irish.

DURING the spring and early summer of 1745 rumours had been rife in the Highlands that Prince Charles Edward was to make his appearance there before the end of the season. The authorities in Edinburgh heard nothing of these reports until after midsummer, and only then by reason of the vigilance of Lord President Forbes. His Lordship came to Sir John Cope, commander-in-chief of the forces in Scotland, and showed him a letter which he had just received from a Highland gentleman, informing him of the rumour. Cope instantly sent notice of what had been communicated to him to the Marquis of Tweeddale, the Secretary of State for Scotland, expressing disbelief in the report, but nevertheless advising that arms should be sent into the forts in the Highlands in anticipation of any attempt which might be made. The marquis replied to Cope, enjoining on him to maintain a vigilant eye on the north, but stating that the Lords of the Regency declined to take so alarming a measure as arming the forts. Cope promptly replied that he would resort to such precautions as seemed called for, avoiding as much as possible the causing of needless alarm. A further correspondence between the marquis and the general shows very conspicuously the zeal and promptitude of the latter, in marked contradistinction to the supineness and false security of the Regency.

The drain of troops for service on the Continent had left Scotland, and especially the Highlands, very inadequately garrisoned. At the outbreak of the rebellion Cope commanded but two regiments of dragoons, both quartered in the Lowlands, three full infantry regiments— one in Aberdeen, another in the Highland forts, and the third in Edinburgh and Leith—and fourteen odd companies dispersed over the low country. But for the warning of the Lord President, Scotland in all probability would have been almost wholly denuded of troops in the course of the summer of 1745; for the greater portion of the forces there, which were newly raised and still raw, were destined for immediate transportation to Flanders. Charles Edward hoisted his standard at Glenfinnan on August 19th, and on the morning of September 21st he and his Highlanders utterly defeated Cope in the battle of Prestonpans. The situation in the north had become extremely serious; and several regiments from the army in Flanders were hurried home in October, on the service of quelling the Highland insurrection. Lord John Murray's Highlanders, as the regiment was now styled, arrived in the Thames on November 4th; and while the other regiments from Flanders were ordered to Scotland under General Hawley, the Black Watch joined a division of the army assembled on the coast of Kent to repel a threatened invasion. The Highlanders were thus mercifully exempted from a cruel duty that would have compelled them to oppose on the field of battle their nearest relatives and friends. Civil war is odious and terrible; how much more awful a fratricidal strife! When it was estimated that more than three hundred soldiers of the Highland Regiment had fathers, brothers, or near kinsfolk taking part in the Jacobite rebellion, the wisdom and humanity of keeping them aloof from such a struggle between duty and natural affection was obvious.

Three new companies had been raised for the regiment early in 1745, with their headquarters at Crieff. The command of those companies, which were raised chiefly in the districts of Athole, Breadalbane, and Braemar, was given respectively to the Laird of Mackintosh, Sir Patrick Murray of Ochtertyre, and Campbell of Inveraw, who had recruited their companies. The lieutenants were James Farquharson, younger of Invercauld, John Campbell, younger of Glenlyon, and Dugald Campbell; the ensigns were Allan Grant, son of Glenmoriston, John Campbell, son of Glenfalloch, and Allan Campbell, son of Balcardine. General Stewart remarks of those new companies that their privates, although of the best character, did not occupy that social position to which so many men of the old independent companies were entitled. Those new companies did not join the regiment immediately on its return from foreign service; two of them were actively employed in Scotland on the Government side during the rebellion in aiding the pacification of the Highlands. The third took part in the battle of Prestonpans, where all its officers, Sir Patrick Murray, Lieutenant Farquharson, and Ensign Allan Campbell, and the whole of its men were either killed, wounded, or taken prisoners. In this instance Highlanders, unfortunately, were opposed to Highlanders. That the company of loyal Highlanders engaged at Prestonpans fought *à outrance* is proved by its casualties; and the rebel Highlanders by whom it was confronted presumably did not refrain from exemplary reprisals. The survivors of the loyal company clung stoutly to their oath in face of entreaties, arguments, offers, and threats employed to prevail upon them to desert their colours and join the cause on which so many of their kindred and countrymen had engaged. All attempts to sap their allegiance proved unavailing; no man forgot his loyalty or abjured his oath.

When the rebellion of 1745 broke out it was a common expedient, in order to save family properties, that father and son, or two brothers of the same house, should take opposite sides. Occasionally, however, family feuds in the highlands of Scotland a century and a half ago were almost as bitter as are the Afghan blood-feuds of to-day. Young Glenlyon, lieutenant of one of the new companies of the Highland Regiment, had a younger brother, who had joined the rebels and fought on the Jacobite side to the bitter end. Old Glenlyon, who had joined the rebellion of 1715, still retained his prejudices and principles so strongly that he never forgave his eldest son for taking service under the hated Hanoverian rule. When the young man went to visit him on his death-bed in 1746 the stubborn old Jacobite refused to see his son. After his father's death in the autumn of that year, the young laird was ordered to garrison his house with a party of men, and to engage in the duty of seizing rebel fugitives, who swarmed in concealment among the woods and caves of the vicinity.

His brother lay hidden in a deep den above Glenlyon House, and was supplied with provisions and necessaries by his sisters and friends. On one occasion the younger brother, having left his retreat before darkness had set in, was observed by his brother the laird, who was walking in the park with some English officers. Pretending to give the alarm, the laird directed the officers to call out their men immediately, while he undertook to keep the "rebel" in sight. Pursuing his brother, he called to him in Gaelic to run for his life and to take to the mountains. When the soldiers came up no rebel was visible, and the outlaw learned a lesson of caution. Ten years afterwards the rebel of 1746 was appointed to Fraser's Highland Regiment, and was shot through the body on the Heights of Abraham.

After the suppression of the insurrection, the three new companies attached to Lord John Murray's Highlanders were employed in a most repulsive service—that of burning the houses and laying waste the lands and property of the unfortunate rebels. It may be easily understood that in a country where rebellion had been so general, frequent occasions must have occurred when loyal officers in the execution of their orders would have been compelled to devastate the estates of their neighbours and friends, and would find their allegiance at cruel variance with their feelings. For example, Campbell of Glenlyon was obliged to burn the houses and harry the lands and property of his neighbours the Laird of Strowan and other gentlemen who had been engaged in the rebellion. The three new companies, already occasionally alluded to, remained in Scotland, sending recruits to the regiment from time to time. They performed various duties in the Highlands; and in March, 1748, the three companies marched to embark for the purpose of joining the regiment in Flanders. But in consequence of the peace the orders were countermanded, and the companies were reduced in the course of the year.

The internal peace of the country having been secured by the decisive victory of Culloden (April 16th, 1746), and the French refraining from the hazard of an invasion in support of a hopeless cause, Lord John Murray's Highlanders became available for general service, and were selected to form part of an expedition against the French possessions in North America. After three failures because of weather, this enterprise was abandoned; but in September-October a descent, in which the Highlanders took part, was made on the coast of France. On September 19th the expedition anchored in Quimperlé Bay, and a landing was effected by the Grenadiers without much opposition. Operations were immediately begun in front of L'Orient, and three heavy batteries were completed against the place. On the 28th the garrison made several sallies. The firing on the town ceased towards evening, and secret preparations were made for a retreat, as the enemy was collecting in great force. The troops re-embarked without interruption, and the expedition sailed for Quiberon. Returning home in the autumn, the regiment was stationed in Ireland until February, 1747, when it proceeded to Flanders to reinforce the army fighting in alliance with the Austrians and Dutch against the French. Excepting, however, at the siege of Hulst, when it incurred some loss, and when covering the embarkation of the allied troops for South Beveland, the Highland Regiment saw but little service during the campaign. The regiment was not engaged either at Lafeldt, where the allies were defeated, nor at Bergen-op-Zoom; and in the winter of 1748-49 it was withdrawn from the Netherlands and returned, first to England, and shortly afterwards to Ireland.

In 1749, in consequence of the reduction of the 42nd, or Oglethorpe's Regiment, which had been raised in 1737 for colonial service in North America, the number of the Highland Regiment was altered from the 43rd to the 42nd. Until this period regiments for the most part were designated by the names of their colonels; but a royal warrant was issued July 1st, 1751, by which the numerical titles were confirmed. By the same warrant the dress of the "42nd," or Highland Regiment, was directed to be scarlet, lined and faced with buff; the national distinctions of bonnet, tartan-plaid, and hose, kilt, or philibeg, were not defined; the Grenadiers to wear bearskin caps with the King's cipher and crown on a red ground in the turn-up or flap. The first, or King's colour, was the great union; the second, or regimental colour, was of buff silk, with the union in the upper canton, and in the centre the number of the regiment in gold Roman characters within a wreath composed of roses and thistles on the same stalk.

Lieutenant-Colonel Munro died in 1749, and was succeeded (May 24th, 1749) by Lieutenant-Colonel John Campbell, afterwards fifth Duke of Argyll. From 1749 until 1756 the regiment remained in Ireland, with frequent changes of quarters. In contrast with the animosities, jealousies, and disputes which were but too rife in Ireland between the military and civil inhabitants, the Highlanders associated familiarly with the Irish people, and great cordiality existed between them and the Highlanders. Probably the similarity of language and the prevailing belief that the Irish and Scotch were of the same origin might have occasioned the mutual good feeling. In the regiment during this long period there were few courts-martial; and for many years no instance occurred in it of corporal punishment. General Stewart states in his "Sketches" that "the punishments most commonly resorted to had not much of a military complexion. The culprit was made to ride astride a wooden horse, with his kilt tied round his neck, or sometimes in a petticoat, as a symbol that his conduct was deemed unworthy of a man. When, rarely, a soldier was brought to the halberts, he was considered, and considered himself, to have become degraded, and little more good was to be expected of him. After being thus publicly disgraced, he could no longer associate with his comrades; and it was a fact that in several instances the privates of a company subscribed from their pay the means to procure the discharge of an obnoxious individual."

Great regularity was observed in the duties of public worship. In the regimental orders, which are still extant, hours are fixed for morning prayers by the chaplain; and on Sundays for divine service morning and evening. The orders state further: "Prayers to-morrow at nine o'clock. Prayers in the barracks on Tuesday at eight o'clock." The greatest respect was maintained towards the ministers of religion. When Dr. Fergusson was the chaplain of the corps, he held an equal, if not in some respects a greater, influence over the minds and conduct of the men than was exercised by the commanding officer. The regiment was equally fortunate in having as its military director so fine a soldier and so judicious a man as Lieutenant-Colonel Campbell, afterwards fifth Duke of Argyll, who commanded as lieutenant-colonel from 1749 until 1755. Later he became aide-de-camp to the King and colonel of the 54th Regiment. After holding the colonelcies of several other regiments, he became general in 1778 and field-marshal in 1796. He had served in Flanders and France; and he died 24th May, 1806. He was Jeanie Deans' Duke of Argyll; and he it was, if we are to believe "The Heart of Midlothian," who, when Queen Caroline threatened to make Scotland a hunting field, replied with a profound bow, "In that case, madam, I will take leave of your Majesty, and go down to my own country to get my hounds ready."

## CHAPTER V.

### SERVICE IN NORTH AMERICA. 1756.

War against French in North America formally declared in May, 1756. Expedition in two divisions sent from home, landed in New York June, 1757; first division commanded by Major-General James Abercromby, of which Lord John Murray's Highlanders formed part. Later came Lord Loudoun, as commander-in-chief in North America. Washington's futile attempts to stir the sluggish Loudoun to active campaign. Montcalm active and successful; Highland Regiment inactive in Albany during 1756. Regiment in 1757, 1,300 strong—all Highlanders. Loudoun recalled, because of delays and inertness. Termination of inglorious campaign of 1757.

FOR years before the Black Watch first crossed the Atlantic in the summer of 1756 there had been intermittent hostilities between the colonists of the British Provinces of North America and the French operating from their base in Canada against the British. On the march towards the Ohio in April, 1754, of a colonial force commanded by Fry and Washington, news was received that a detachment previously sent to build a fort at the junction of the Monongahela with the Ohio had been driven back by a considerable French force, which had completed the work already begun by the colonial detachment, and had named it Fort Duquesne in honour of the Marquis Duquesne, then Governor of Canada. Washington was sent forward with 150 men to retrieve this loss; but being unsupported by the promised reinforcement, was unable to make himself master of the French fort. In the end he was obliged to consent to a capitulation and to surrender his artillery; and he returned in July to Virginia. In the spring of the following year the ill-fated General Braddock arrived in that province with two British regiments, as a nucleus for a formal campaign against the French on the Ohio. The well-known unfortunate issue of this campaign, and the distinguished part borne in it by Colonel Washington in withdrawing the shattered remnants of the army from the field on which Braddock and all his chief officers had fallen (July 9th, 1755), are universally known. That officer's defeat and death, and the massacre by the Indians in the French service of most of the men composing the two regular regiments under his command, stirred the authorities at home to engage in reprisals.

In May, 1756, war against the French was formally declared. An expedition had already been prepared, which was to be despatched to North America in two divisions; and the first division, which was under the command of Major-General James Abercromby, and of which Lord John Murray's Highlanders formed a part, sailed in March and landed at New York in the following June. Before the departure of the regiment on foreign service, several changes and promotions had been made. Major Grant was promoted to be lieutenant-colonel in succession to Lieutenant-Colonel Campbell, promoted colonel of the 54th Regiment. Captain Duncan Campbell of Inveraw became major; Thomas Graeme of Duchray, James Abercromby, son of General Abercromby of Glassaugh, and John Campbell of Strachur became captains; several ensigns were promoted to be lieutenants; and to complete the establishment there were taken from the half-pay list seven lieutenants and nine ensigns.

The second division of the expedition under the Earl of Loudoun, who was appointed commander-in-chief of the army in North America, soon joined General Abercromby's contingent. Washington submitted to Loudoun a detailed account of the recent operations against the French on the Ohio, detailing the reasons of the failure of the operations of the Colonials and of the hapless force which Braddock had led to destruction. Washington urged on Lord Loudoun the prosecution of an active campaign with increased forces, and was grievously disappointed when the British commander informed him of his intention to direct all his efforts against Canada. In point of fact, Loudoun did absolutely nothing. He wasted valuable time in holding abortive councils of war, in making cumbrous preparations, and, in Stewart's sardonic words, "in accustoming the troops to what were called the usages of war. He was so engrossed in schemes for improving the condition of his men that he seemed to have no time for employing them against the enemy; and he allowed a whole season to pass away without having undertaken a single enterprise." Meanwhile the Marquis de Montcalm, who in 1756 had been appointed to the chief command of the French troops in North America, lost no time in getting to business. Within three months of his arrival he captured Fort Ontario, otherwise called Fort Oswego, at the eastern extremity of Lake Ontario. The place held out for two days, but was surrendered on the death of Colonel Mercer, commanding the garrison. The capitulation stipulated that the British soldiers should be conducted to Montreal in safety as prisoners. Those terms were disgracefully violated. The troops were robbed and maltreated by the Indians; several were shot as they stood defenceless; and Montcalm, to his disgrace as a soldier, gave over twenty of the unfortunate prisoners to the Indians, to be sacrificed by them to the *manes* of men of their tribe who had fallen in battle. Montcalm attempted in vain to exonerate himself from the reproach of his inhuman conduct by alleging that the British soldiers had given spirits to the Indians, and that in their intoxication those excesses had been perpetrated. The apology was weak.

During 1756 the Highland Regiment remained inactive in Albany. Throughout the winter and spring of the following year the men were drilled and disciplined for bush-fighting and marksmanship, a species of warfare for which they were well fitted, being for the most part good shots, and expert in the management of their arms. Before the departure of the regiment from Ireland, recruiting parties had been despatched to Scotland which were so successful that at midsummer of 1757 seven hundred excellent recruits were embarked at Greenock for America. A gentleman in New York wrote that "when the Highlanders landed they were petted by all ranks and orders of men, but more particularly by the Indians. On the march to Albany the Indians flocked from all quarters to see the strangers, who, they believed, were of the same extraction as themselves, and whom therefore they received as brothers." By the arrival of this large draft of recruits, a strong regiment in itself, the establishment was now augmented to upwards of 1,300 men—all Highlanders, for at that period none else were admitted into the regiment. To the three new companies of which the draft consisted the following officers were appointed:—James Murray, son of Lord George Murray (Prince Charles Edward's commander-in-chief in the '45), James Stewart of Urrard, and Thomas Stirling, son of Sir Henry Stirling of Ardoch, to be captains; Simon Blair, David Barclay, Archibald Campbell,

Alexander McKay, Alexander Menzies, and David Mills to be lieutenants; and the Rev. James Stewart to be assistant chaplain.

A project having been devised for an attempt against Louisburg, a strongly fortified place on the French island of Cape Breton, an expedition sailed from New York for Halifax in the first instance, where it arrived in June, 1757, with 5,000 troops aboard. The Highland Regiment had been withdrawn from Albany to share in the enterprise. At Halifax Loudoun was raised to a strength of 10,500 men by reinforcements from home, and the expedition sailed from Halifax in August; but it was ascertained that the French were in great force and that their fleet at Louisburg was much stronger than the British naval force with the expedition. The undertaking in consequence was abandoned or deferred. Lord Loudoun returned to New York, taking with him the Highlanders and four other regiments; and towards the end of the year he was recalled home in consequence of his delays and inertness.

During his abortive expedition in the direction of Cape Breton, Montcalm had been active. Collecting all his available forces, he laid siege to Fort William Henry, garrisoned by 3,000 men under the command of Colonel Munro. On the sixth day Munro surrendered, and the garrison were allowed to march out with their arms. When outside the fort they were attacked by the Indians, who committed all sorts of outrages and barbarities, the French troops averring that they were unable to restrain them.

Thus terminated the inglorious campaign of this year. With an inferior force the enemy had been successful at every point, and by the acquisition of Fort William Henry had obtained complete command of Lakes George and Champlain. The destruction of Oswego gave to the French the dominion of the lakes connecting the St. Lawrence with the Mississippi and opened a direct communication from Canada; while by the possession of Fort du Quesne they had obtained an ascendancy which enabled them to maintain their alliance with the Indians.

# CHAPTER VI.

## TICONDEROGA. 1758.

Loudoun succeeded by General Abercromby. Brighter prospects. Expedition against Fort Ticonderoga, commanded by Abercromby with 15,000 men. Fort on tongue of land, surrounded on three sides by water; fortifications very strong. Garrison 5,000 men. On July 5th, 1758, Abercromby disembarked at head of Lake George, and marched in four columns towards forts. In skirmish on march was killed Brigadier-General Viscount Hood. On morning of 8th, believing assault practicable, Abercromby engaged, although guns not up. Place found very strong, with regularly constructed breastworks, abatis, and other defences. First attack failed; then Highlanders rushed forward from reserve, and assailed with great fury. Desperate struggle lasting four hours. Highlanders reluctantly withdrew, after loss of more than half of strength and of twenty-five officers. Retired in good order unmolested, 647 officers and men of Black Watch *hors de combat*. Intrepidity of Highlanders admired greatly. Remains of regiment covered retreat and brought off wounded. Arrival of reinforcements to fill depleted ranks. General Stewart's comments on impetuosity of Highlanders. Highland characteristics.

THE command of the army devolved on General Abercromby on the departure of Lord Loudoun, and the campaign of 1758 opened with brighter prospects. The Cabinet had determined to efface the discredit of former campaigns, and the stimulus of popular favour imparted energy and alacrity to the projects of the new ministers. The commands were transferred to officers in whom confidence could be reposed, and who undertook with energy the enterprises proposed to them. A great naval armament and a military force of 32,000 men afforded good hopes of a vigorous and successful campaign, and the people of England gladly forgot the delays, vacillations, and disasters which they had impatiently borne during the three previous years. Of three expeditions proposed for this year, the one against the Fort of Ticonderoga was commanded by Major-General Abercromby, with a force of 15,390 men, of whom 6,337 were regulars and 9,000 provincials with a train of artillery. Among the regular troops were Lord John Murray's Highlanders.

Fort Ticonderoga stood, and its ruins still stand, on a tongue of land projecting into the tortuous river connecting Lake George with Lake Champlain. It was surrounded by water on three sides; part of the fourth side was protected by an impassable morass, and the remaining part was covered by a line of fortifications eight to ten feet high, defended and flanked by three batteries. The advance was rendered extremely difficult by abatis and other obstacles. The garrison numbered about 5,000 men, of whom half were regulars. On July 5th General Abercromby embarked his troops on Lake George in 100 batteaux and other craft, with provisions, ammunition, and artillery; several pieces of cannon being mounted on rafts to cover the landing, which, however, was effected on the following day without opposition.

The troops landed near the northern extremity of the lake, whence they marched in four columns through a wild, thickly wooded region, great confusion being caused owing to the guides mistaking the direction through the trackless woods. One of the columns came by accident on an advanced post of the enemy consisting of one battalion, covered by a breastwork of logs. The French abandoned this position without a shot, after burning their tents and implements and setting on fire their breastwork. Another column met by haphazard with a body of French troops in the wood, when a sharp action ensued, in which the enemy was routed with the loss of three hundred killed and a hundred and fifty taken prisoners. In this affair was killed Brigadier-General Viscount Howe, of the 55th Regiment, who, as was his brother the admiral and his successor in the title, was greatly beloved in the army, and his death was deeply regretted. "He had distinguished himself in a peculiar manner by his courage, activity, and rigid observance of military discipline; and he had acquired the esteem and affection of the soldiery by his frank generosity, his sweetness of manner, and his engaging address."

General Abercromby, perceiving that the soldiers were much fatigued, ordered them to return to the landing-place, where supplies were awaiting them on the shore. On the 7th, the army advanced to within easy distance of the outlying defences of the fort, and the night was spent in and about an abandoned saw-mill. On the morning of the 8th the British commander, having received information from prisoners that General Levis, with a force of 3,000 men, was marching to aid in the defence of Ticonderoga, resolved to anticipate such an attempt by striking a decisive blow, if possible, before the hostile column should come up. He sent his engineer-officer, Mr. Clerk, across the river opposite to the fort to reconnoitre the defences of the enemy; and when his report was that the works were still unfinished, and that the place might be attempted with a prospect of success, the General decided to hazard an immediate assault without waiting for his guns to be brought up. The attack was begun by the picquets, supported by the grenadier companies of battalions, and the 27th, 44th,

46th, and 60th Regiments; the 42nd and 55th constituting the reserve. When the troops approached the defences, they were surprised to find a regularly constructed breastwork, which, with its formidable *chevaux de frise* defended by a strong force in its rear, could not be reached without the greatest exertions, especially in the absence of the guns. Unexpected as those formidable obstructions were, the troops fought gallantly, although exposed to a very heavy fire from enemies well covered and in position to take deliberate aim with but little danger to themselves. The assaulting columns could not press through the abatis, and so suffered severely. Then the Highland soldiers of the 42nd could endure no longer. Impatient of their position in the rear, they rushed forward, hewed their way through the obstacles with their broadswords, and since no ladders had been provided, made strenuous efforts to carry the breastworks, partly by mounting on each others' shoulders, and partly by fixing their feet in holes which they had excavated with their swords and bayonets in the face of the work. The defenders were so well prepared that the instant an assailant reached the top, that instant he was thrown or shot down. At length, after great exertions, Captain John Campbell, one of the two soldiers presented to George II. at Whitehall, in 1743, and a handful of valiant followers, forced their way over the breastworks, but were instantly despatched by the bayonet. Much time had been expended in the preliminary operations, and many men had fallen from the fire of the defenders who manned the trenches in rear of the breastworks, and who retreated within the fort when the assailants had all but penetrated the exterior defences. This destructive fire from the fort was continued with great effect. After a desperate struggle, which lasted four hours, under conditions so disadvantageous, the general, seeing no possible chance of success, ordered a withdrawal; but the soldiers had become so exasperated by the opposition which they had encountered, and by the loss of so many of their comrades, that they could with difficulty be recalled. The Highlanders in particular were so obstinate that it was not until the third peremptory order from the general that Lieutenant-Colonel Grant, the commanding officer of the regiment, was able at length to prevail on them to withdraw, after more than one half of the men and twenty-five of the officers had been either killed or desperately wounded.

Abercromby's retreat from before Ticonderoga was not molested by the garrison, and his force retired in good order, carrying with it all the wounded, amounting to sixty-five officers and 1,178 non-commissioned officers and men. Twenty-three officers and 567 rank and file were killed. The 42nd suffered terrible losses. Eight of its officers, nine sergeants, and 297 men lay dead on or before the breastworks of Ticonderoga; there were wounded seventeen officers, ten sergeants, and 306 men. With 647 officers and men of its strength *hors de combat*, the regiment was reduced almost to a skeleton. The officers killed were Major Duncan Campbell of Inveraw, Captain John Campbell, Lieutenants George Farquharson, Hugh McPherson, William Baillie, and John Sutherland, Ensigns Patrick Stewart of Bonskied, and George Rattray; the wounded were Captains Gordon Graham, Thomas Graham of Duchray, John Campbell of Strachur, James Stewart of Urrard, James Murray (afterwards General); Lieutenants James Grant, Robert Gray, John Campbell of Melford, William Grant, John Graham (brother of Duchray), Alexander Campbell, Alexander

Mackintosh, Archibald Campbell, David Miller, Patrick Balneaves; Ensigns John Smith and Peter Grant.

Severe as were its loss and disappointment on this occasion, the resolute intrepidity of the Highland Regiment had the greatest gratification that soldiers could receive in the approbation of their country and the warm appreciation of their companions in arms. The periodical publications of the time were full of anecdotes and panegyrics of the corps. "With a mixture of esteem, grief, and envy," wrote an officer of the 55th, present at Ticonderoga, "I am penetrated by the great loss and immortal glory acquired by the Highlanders engaged in the late bloody affair. Impatient for the fray, they rushed forward to the entrenchments, which many of them actually mounted. Their intrepidity was rather animated than damped by witnessing their comrades fall on every side. They seemed more anxious to avenge the fate of their deceased friends than careful to avoid a like death. With their co-operation we trust soon to give a good account of the enemy and of ourselves. There is much harmony and friendship between the two regiments." The following extract from a letter written by Lieutenant William Grant, an officer of the regiment, gives an interesting *résumé* of the conflict. "The attack," wrote Grant, "began a little past one in the afternoon, and about two the fire became general on both sides. It was exceedingly heavy and without any intercession, insomuch that the oldest soldiers never saw so furious and incessant a fire. The affair at Fontenoy was nothing to it—I saw both. We laboured under insurmountable difficulties. The enemy's breastworks were about nine or ten feet high, on the top of which they had plenty of wall-pieces fixed, and which (the breastworks) were well lined inside with small arms. But the difficult access to the enemy's lines was what gave them a fatal advantage over us. They had taken care to cut down monstrous large trees, which covered all the ground from the foot of their breastworks about a cannon-shot in every direction in their front. This not only broke our ranks but put it entirely out of our power to advance until we had cut our way through. I had seen men behave with courage and resolution before that day, but so much determined bravery can scarcely be paralleled. Even those who lay mortally wounded cried aloud to their companions not to mind or waste a thought upon them, but to follow their officers and remember the honour of their country. Nay, their ardour was such that it was difficult to bring them off. They paid dearly for their intrepidity. The remains of the regiment had the honour to cover the retreat of the army, and brought off the wounded, as we did at Fontenoy. When shall we have so fine a regiment again? I hope we shall be allowed to recruit." Lieutenant Grant's hope had been anticipated, as letters of service for raising a second battalion had been issued before the disaster of Ticonderoga had become known in England. Moreover, previous to the arrival of the tidings of that glorious though unfortunate affair, a royal warrant had been promulgated conferring on the regiment the title of "'Royal,' as a testimony of his Majesty's satisfaction and approbation of the extraordinary courage, loyalty, and exemplary conduct of the Highland Regiment." This mark of approbation was naturally the more gratifying that it should have been conferred before the conduct of the corps at Ticonderoga was known at home, and it no doubt proved an additional inducement for young men to join its ranks.

Writing on the subject of the Highlanders at Ticonderoga, General Stewart, who thoroughly knew the character of the Highland soldier of the last century, makes some interesting observations which deserve to be read. "The impetuosity of Highland soldiers," he remarks, "and the difficulty of controlling them in the most important part of a soldier's duty, have frequently been noticed and reprobated. To forget discretion and break loose from command is an unmilitary characteristic; but as it proceeds from a fine principle, it deserves serious consideration how far any attempt to allay this ardour may be advisable. It has been observed that the more modern Highland regiments display less of that chivalrous spirit which marked the earlier corps from the mountains. If there be any good ground for this observation, it may probably be attributed," says General Stewart, "to the fact that these corps do not consist wholly of native Highlanders."

Were the general alive in these latter days he would alter his impressions. There is not a Highland regiment of to-day that consists "wholly of native soldiers"; in every one there is a large mixture of Lowland Scotch, Englishmen, Irishmen, and even foreigners. Yet, as in the days of Ticonderoga, so at Quatre Bras, so in the days of the Crimea, so in the fierce onslaught at Tamai, many of the traditional characteristics of the Highland soldier of the last century have inured in the kilted man of to-day, Cockney, Paddy, or yokel though he may be. The men who, standing in the "thin red line" at the head of the Balaclava gorge, were objurgated by Colin Campbell in the rough warning words, "Ninety-third!— Ninety-third! damn all that eagerness!" were simply the military descendants of the Highlanders who could scarcely be dragged away from the breastworks of Ticonderoga. An older and a more staid regiment than the 93rd, the Black Watch controls its lurid internal fires in the hour of combat under the mask of traditional discipline and a steadfast regimental pride; but no grander cry was ever heard on a battlefield than the unanimous shout of the 42nd—"Rally roun' the cornel!"—which rose above the turmoil of the desperate *melée* at Tamai.

Other days, other manners. General Stewart loved and was proud of the old Highland soldier, whom, perhaps, he to some extent idealised. "In the earlier part of the service of the 42nd," he wrote, "and when the ancient habits of the Highlanders remained unchanged, the soldiers retained much of their habits in their camps and quarters. They had their bards for reciting ancient poems and tales, and for composing laments, elegies, and panegyrics on departed friends. Those were useful and appropriate when none save Highlanders were present, who understood them, and whom they could warm and inspire.

"Another cause has contributed to change the character of the Highland soldier—the reserved manners and more distant etiquette of military discipline. While many of the officers were natives of the mountains, they spoke in their own language to the men, who in their turn addressed the officers with that easy but respectful familiarity and confidence which subsisted between the Highland people and their superiors. Another privilege of the Highlander of the old school was that of remonstrating with and counselling an officer when the case seemed to him to require it." General Stewart relates that when he joined the regiment as a very young soldier, his colonel gave him a steady old soldier, named Fraser, as his servant—perhaps as his adviser and director. The colonel himself could not have been more frequent and attentive in his remonstrances and cautions with regard to the youngster's conduct and duty than was his old soldier-servant when he thought he had cause to disapprove. Those admonitions he always administered in Gaelic, calling young Stewart by his Christian name, with an allusion to the colour of his hair, which was fair, or in the Gaelic, *bane*, and never prefixing " Mr." or " Ensign " except when he spoke in English. General Stewart, when a callow subaltern, must have been a much-enduring youth; and his servant Fraser, when communing with himself, must have sometimes found himself surprised that he should be allowed to escape death at the hands of a maddened subaltern.

## CHAPTER VII.

### MARTINIQUE AND GUADALOUPE. 1759.

Recruitment; "O's" and "Macs." Second battalion sent to West Indies with expedition destined for Martinique and Guadaloupe under General Hopson, January, 1759. Citadel of Port Royal. Fort Negro captured. Army landed January 16th. Venue changed to Guadaloupe. Fierce attack on Basse-Terre, capital of island. Town in blaze. Madame Ducharmey, the Amazon. Lieutenant Maclean, of the 42nd. Storm of Fort Louis. General Hopson's death; his successor General Barrington. Surrender of island by French troops and inhabitants, May 1st. Severe loss from climate.

THE second battalion of the Royal Highlanders was formed of the three additional companies raised in 1757, and of seven other companies of a hundred and twenty men each, embodied in the summer of 1758. The three companies embarked for North America to reinforce the first battalion, as soon as its severe losses at Ticonderoga were known at home. It was not until August that the recruiting officers received their instructions in regard to the seven new companies, and in October 840 men were embodied at Perth. Eighteen Irishmen were enlisted at Glasgow by two gentlemen anxious to obtain commissions. The orders of Lord John Murray, the colonel of the regiment, were peremptory that none but Highlanders should be accepted. Several of the aspirants were O'Donnels, O'Lachlans, O'Briens, &c. The "O'" was changed to "Mac," and they passed muster for the Highland regiment as genuine Macdonnels, Maclachlans, and Macbriars without being questioned. The second battalion was brought into a state of discipline and efficiency so speedily that in four months from the date of the order for its being raised it was reported fit for active service and ordered to proceed abroad. An attack on the French West Indies having been resolved upon an expedition was fitted out for that service under Major-General Hopson, and it sailed in the autumn. The second battalion of the Royal Highlanders was selected to take part in this enterprise, and two hundred men belonging to it embarked at Greenock for the West Indies. This detachment joined the expedition in Carlisle Bay, Barbadoes, in the beginning of the following year. From Barbadoes the expedition sailed under convoy of the squadron commanded by Commodore Moore, and was off Martinique on January 14th (1759). Next day the squadron entered the great bay of Port Royal, where some of the ships were exposed to the fire of a battery erected on the little Isle de Ranières, half-way up the inlet. At the first appearance of the British squadron in the bay, the *Florissant*, a French seventy-four, with two frigates withdrew under shelter of the fortifications; but one of the latter, *La Vestale*, made her escape in the night and sailed for European waters. The chief stronghold of the island was the citadel of Fort Royal, a regular structure once of some importance, then garrisoned but by a few companies of infantry and some gunners. The cisterns of the garrison were empty, the ammunition was very short, and the walls were ruinous.

On the 16th, three ships of the line from the squadron attacked Fort Negro, the guns of which were soon silenced, and it was presently occupied by a body of sailors and marines, who, having landed, had scrambled up the rocks and masses of mangroves till they entered the fort through the embrasures, when the garrison promptly fled. The Union Jack was hoisted with loud cheers, the enemy's guns were spiked, the carriages were broken, and the powder was destroyed; the detachment remained in possession of the fort. The battery at Cas de Navire was next silenced. The French troops had marched from the citadel to oppose a landing; but on seeing the British squadron with the transports full of soldiers and Fort Negro already in possession of marines, they retired to Port Royal, leaving the beach open; and next day the whole army landed. The Grenadiers, the King's Regiment, and the two companies of Royal Highlanders moved forward, and soon fell in with some parties of the enemy, with whom they maintained an irregular fire, until within a short distance of Morne Tortueson, an eminence that overlooked the town and citadel of Port Royal, and the strongest post in the island. There they maintained a sharp skirmish, during which it was said of the Highlanders, "that although debarred the use of arms in their own country, they now showed themselves good marksmen, and had not forgotten how to handle their weapons."

In the skirmish of Morne Tortueson, sixty-three officers and men were killed or wounded; among the casualties was Lieutenant Leslie of the Royal Highlanders. General Hopson intimated to the commodore that he could neither maintain his ground nor attack the citadel unless the squadron would furnish him with heavy guns, which seemed impracticable; he therefore gave orders to re-embark without delay. A council of war having suggested that it might be for the public service to attack St. Pierre, the fleet proceeded to that part of the island, and entered the bay on the 19th. The commodore told General Hopson that as the town was open it could be reduced with ease; but as the ships might be so disabled as to become unfit for more important efforts, it was proposed that further attempts on Martinique should be abandoned; and the conquest of Guadaloupe was suggested. Accordingly the British squadron took position in line before Basse-Terre, the capital of that island; and on the morning of the 23rd opened a fierce attack on the town, the batteries, and the citadel, which was armed with forty-two guns and two mortars. The firing was promptly returned, and it was kept up on both sides with great spirit for several hours. Towards the end of the afternoon the fire of the citadel slackened, and in the tropical darkness four bomb-ketches anchored near the shore hurled their flaming missiles into the town, which was soon in a blaze. On the following morning the troops landed without opposition, and took possession of the town and citadel, the governor having retired into the interior of the island, which he was resolved to defend to the last extremity. The main body of the second battalion of the Royal Highlanders, which had been detained for want of transport, arrived from Scotland and joined the expedition here in Guadaloupe. For several days nothing occurred but the establishment of some small posts on the hills nearest the town. On one of these eminences an officer of the 38th took up a position over against some entrenchments formed by Madame Ducharmey, a lady of high spirit, who, despising the French governor, the Chevalier Nadau d'Estriel, had armed her negroes and servants for a strong resistance. Madame Ducharmey, at the head of her armed slaves, having made many furious attacks upon the post of Major Melville, that officer at length considered himself under the necessity of attacking this Amazon sword in hand, and of carrying her works by storm. She made her escape, but her houses and plantations were destroyed. Some of her people were killed and a number taken. Of the major's party twelve were killed and thirty wounded, including three officers, one of whom lost an arm. This officer was Lieutenant Maclean, of the 42nd. "It would appear," says General Stewart, "that this very noisy and unpolite intrusion on a lady's quarters did not injure Lieutenant Maclean in the esteem of the ladies of Guadaloupe; for we find that although he got leave from General Barrington to return home for the cure of his arm, he refused to leave the regiment, and remained at his duty. He was particularly noticed by the French ladies for his gallantry and spirit, and the manner in which he wore his plaid and Scottish regimental garb."

The total reduction of Guadaloupe involving unexpected obstacles, it was resolved to transfer the area of operations to the eastern or Grande Terre part of the island, and to attack Fort Louis, a place of arms with a strong battery in that quarter. The work was bombarded and cannonaded by the squadron; and during the contest a column of Highlanders and marines landed in boats. Their progress towards the shore being impeded by long, trailing water-plants and mangrove roots, they leaped into the water, which rose breast-high on them, drove the French from their works with fixed bayonets, captured the fort, tore down the French ensign, and hoisted in its place the Union Jack. "No troops could behave with more courage than the Highlanders and Marines did on this occasion."* By this time, however, 1,800

---

* Beatson's "Naval and Military Memoirs."

officers and men were dead or in hospital from the effects of the climate. General Hopson died of fever in the end of February, and the command devolved upon General Barrington, who resolved to prosecute the reduction of the island with vigour. All the batteries in and about Basse Terre were destroyed except the citadel, in which was left a battalion under Colonel Debrissay, an officer of great experience; and the army re-embarked for Grande Terre, on the other side of the island. When the enemy perceived the squadron under weigh they assailed the citadel with a heavy fire and attempted a regular attack, but were repulsed with loss; but the gallant Colonel Debrissay, several officers, and a number of soldiers were blown up and destroyed by the explosion of a powder magazine. General Barrington, on learning of this disaster, sent Colonel Melville to assume the command at Basse Terre, and to repair the fortifications. Having established himself in Grande Terre, General Barrington despatched a force of 600 bayonets, consisting of detachments of the 4th and 42nd Regiments, under Colonel Crump, to attack the towns of St. Anne and St. Francis, both of which places were promptly captured under a heavy fire. The losses were trivial, and only one officer, Ensign Campbell of the Highlanders, fell in the assault.

On the following day Colonel Crump drove the enemy from another position, and stormed a battery of twenty-four-pounders. The detachments of the 4th and Highlanders were subsequently sent, under Brigadier-Generals Clavering and Crump, to land in the vicinity of the town of Arnonville, when the enemy retreated to a fortified position behind the river Lecorn. The position was accessible only by two narrow passes through a mangrove swamp, and they were defended by a redoubt, entrenchments mounted with cannon, and a numerous force of local militia. Despite those disadvantages, the brigadiers resolved on an assault. A heavy fire on the entrenchments was opened from the field guns and howitzers, under cover of which the Royal Highlanders and the regiment of Duroure (38th) pushed forward, when the enemy began to waver. " Then," we are told in " Letters from Guadaloupe," " slinging their muskets, the Highlanders drew their swords and, supported by part of the other regiment, rushed forward with their characteristic impetuosity, and followed the enemy into the redoubt, of which they took possession." In the storm of this position sixty-five officers and men were killed or wounded. After this gallant exploit the little force advanced on Petit Burg, where were encountered fortified lines and a redoubt garnished with cannon; but when the British troops advanced to turn the hostile position the enemy fled. The Royal Highlanders furnished a detachment against Bay Mahaut, which took part in the capture of the town and its defences. The regiment was also engaged in driving the French from the strong port of Stes. Maries, where many guns were captured; and it subsequently penetrated the rich and beautiful district of Capestarre.

After a gallant defence, lasting from the end of January to the beginning of May, the French troops and the inhabitants of the island found themselves compelled to surrender, and on May 1st a capitulation was signed. The British loss in this expedition was severe, but more from the climate than by the enemy. The service was a trying experience for Highland soldiers, who a few months earlier were herding cattle and sheep on their native hills at a very different temperature; but the Highlanders conquered the climate as well as the enemy, and proved themselves stout soldiers on the march and gallant men in action. The losses of the regiment were—Ensign Maclean, killed; Lieutenants Maclean, Leslie, St. Clair, and Robertson, wounded; Major Anstruther and Captain Arbuthnot died of fever; and 106 soldiers killed, wounded, and died of disease.

## CHAPTER VIII.

### NORTH AMERICA. 1759.

In May, 1759, first battalion joined force under General Amherst, designed to take part in renewed attempt on Ticonderoga. Second battalion joined from West Indies. Total strength of force 14,500. Preparations begun for attack on Ticonderoga. Siege actually begun when French commander abandoned fort and withdrew. Further operations prevented by want of shipping; two vessels built; but winter set in, and army spent winter at Crown Point and Ticonderoga. Result of campaign of 1760 was cession of Canada to Great Britain, following on combined movement punctually accomplished on Montreal. French Governor-General surrendered; ten French battalions became prisoners of war. General Amherst made peer. Submission of inhabitants.

FROM its winter quarters on Long Island the first battalion of the Royal Highlanders joined, in May, 1759, the force, then at Fort Edward, which was designed under General Amherst, now commander-in-chief, to take part in a renewed attempt on Fort Ticonderoga; while General Wolfe was to attack Quebec from Lower Canada; and General Prideaux was to proceed against Niagara to prevent the enemy from interrupting General Amherst's operations on that side, and endeavour to gain the strong and important post below the great falls. This well-planned and comprehensive combination, should it be successful, it was hoped would drive the enemy out of all their territories in North America.

The force which was under the immediate command of the commander-in-chief was assembled at Fort Edward, the point of rendezvous, on June 19th. It consisted of four line regiments, one of which was the Royal Highlanders, Montgomery's Highlanders, nine battalions of provincials, some other details, and a detachment of artillery. When joined subsequently by the second battalion of the Royal Highlanders from the West Indies, this army had a strength of about 14,500 men. On the 20th, Colonel Grant, of the Royal Highlanders, moved forward with the first battalion of his regiment and the light infantry of the army. The main body followed next day, and encamped at General Abercromby's landing-place of the previous year. Some time passed in preparations for the attack on Ticonderoga, which formidable position the enemy seemed determined to defend. The British force advanced towards the fort, driving the French outpost from the saw-mills, and the siege was actually begun when M. Bourlemaque, the French commander, finally despairing of being able to defend the place, set fire to the magazines and buildings, abandoned the fort, and withdrew, first to Crown Point Fort, and afterwards down the lake to Isle aux Noix. The endeavour of the French in this campaign appears to have been to embarrass and retard the opposing army, but not to hazard any considerable engagement, or to allow themselves to be so completely invested as to fail to make good a retreat; and to effect such a concentration as might arrest General Amherst in his progress down the St. Lawrence to Montreal. When the French abandoned the fortified position of Isle aux Noix, Amherst moved forward and took possession of that place, where he landed and encamped on August 4th. He then ordered up from Oswego the second battalion of the Royal Highlanders, Captain James Stewart being left to hold that port with 150 men, and the general was preparing to embark on Lake Champlain. But the enemy possessed a naval force on that lake, and operations were suspended until a brigantine mounting eighteen guns and a sloop mounting sixteen had been completed, when the army again embarked and continued its progress along the lake on October 11th. On the following morning the boats containing part of the Royal Highlanders fell in with a division of the French naval force; and one boat, containing an officer and twenty men, was captured by the enemy. The progress of the expedition was arrested by severe frosts, and the season being too late for military operations the army returned to Crown Point and Ticonderoga for the winter.

The crowning campaign of 1760, which gave Canada to Great Britain, was conducted on new and bold lines. In May General Amherst recommenced operations, and made arrangements for a combination of his army at Montreal with the force commanded by General Murray; that position being now the only place of strength possessed by the enemy. Both battalions of the Royal Highlanders marched in General Amherst's army across country from Crown Point to Fort Oswego, at which latter place the army was assembled in the beginning of August. On the 7th the Grenadiers, first battalion of the Highland Regiment, and two companies of Rangers, embarked on Lake Ontario as the advance guard of the army under the command of Colonel Haldimand, and navigating the lower portion of that great expanse of water, took post at the head of the river St. Lawrence for the assistance of the armed vessels in passing to La Galette. On the 10th the main body followed, and the whole army proceeded down the great river, capturing Fort Levi after a short siege. After this was accomplished the army continued its progress down the river, experiencing much difficulty in the dangerous navigation of the rapids; on one day a corporal and three men of the 42nd were drowned, and three days later sixty-four boats were wrecked and eighty-four men of various corps lost their lives. The progress of the army was continued; the French opposition was ineffective; and a landing was accomplished on the island of Montreal on September 6th. On the evening of the same day General Murray appeared below the town with his force; and so admirably were all the dispositions executed that Colonel Haviland, from his base at Isle aux Noix on the northern extremity of Lake Champlain, appeared on the following day with his troops, coming out on the south bank of the St. Lawrence. Thus, after traversing vast tracts of unknown and intricate country, the three bodies of troops coalesced with admirable punctuality and promptly set about the investment of Montreal. The French Governor-General of Canada, the Marquis de Vaudreuil, finding himself surrounded by greatly superior forces and with no prospect of relief, surrendered Montreal, and with it all Canada, to the British arms—ten French battalions becoming prisoners of war. Thus was accomplished a conquest the most important that Great Britain had achieved in the New World; and the vast, loyal, and fertile territory thus acquired has continued to form part of the possessions of the British Crown. Lord Rollo was immediately sent with a body of troops to take possession of the outposts and to receive the submission of the inhabitants, who came in from all quarters. General Amherst, in recognition of his high military capacity as Commander-in-Chief of the British army in North America from 1755 to 1764, was worthily elevated to the peerage in 1776 as Baron Amherst of Holmesdale in Kent, and he received the bâton of a field-marshal twenty years later.

## CHAPTER IX.

### MARTINIQUE ONCE AGAIN. 1762.

Troops ordered from North America to West Indies in summer of 1761. Encomia on Royal Highlanders, both battalions of which regiment were included in expeditionary force. Arrival at Barbadoes. Rodney's fleet in St. Ann's Bay; partial landing of troops. Capture of Morne Tortueson after stubborn contest. Folly of garrison of the Garnier. Brilliant and successful assault by Highland soldiers.

AFTER the annexation of the great province of Canada to the British Crown the regiment remained for some time in that country, until the inhabitants had taken the required oaths and the government of the colony should have been established. In the summer of 1761 orders arrived from England for a body of troops to be despatched from North America to the West Indies. The Royal Highlanders were particularly named as one of the corps for this service; "as their sobriety and abstemious habits, great activity, and capability for bearing the vicissitudes of heat and cold, rendered them well qualified for that climate, and for a broken and difficult country." In October both battalions of Lord John Murray's Highlanders, along with ten other regiments, among which were Montgomery's Highlanders, sailed from North America and arrived at Barbadoes in December, there to join an expedition against Martinique and the Havannah, two of the most important possessions of the French and Spaniards. The land force consisted altogether of eighteen regiments, under the command of Major-General Monckton.

On January 8th the fleet, consisting of eighteen ships of the line commanded by Rear-Admiral Rodney, anchored in St. Ann's Bay, Martinique. A partial landing was immediately effected without loss. Brigadiers Grant and Haviland encountered no opposition in the vicinity of the Bay of Ance Darlet. Several days later the whole army landed near Cas de Naviers, under Morne Tortueson and Morne Garnier, two considerable eminences commanding the town and citadel of Fort Royal. Till those points were carried, the town could not be attacked with reasonable prospect of success. Morne Tortueson was first attacked. The position was to be turned on both flanks, and the central attack was to be made by the Grenadiers and the Highlanders, supported by the main body of the army. After a stubborn contest the enemy were driven from the Morne Tortueson, but no decisive result could be obtained without gaining possession of the sister eminence of Garnier, which, from its loftier elevation, enabled the enemy holding it to annoy and oppose the British forces. But the enemy on the Morne Garnier ruined themselves by their precipitation. While preparations were going forward for carrying the hostile posts, the garrison of the Garnier rushed down from their summit and assailed the advanced posts of the British troops. They came on gallantly, but were instantly repulsed. A passage from the *Westminster Journal* states that "when they began to retire the Highlanders, drawing their swords, rushed forward like furies, and being supported by the Grenadiers under Colonel Grant and by a party of Lord Rollo's brigade, the hills were stormed, the batteries were seized, and numbers of the enemy, unable to escape from the rapidity of the attack, were taken." The French regulars retired into the town, but the militia fled all over the country. The action proved decisive, for the town, commanded as it was from the heights, surrendered on February 7th. This point gained, the general was preparing to move against St. Pierre, which was the capital of the island, when his operations were arrested by the arrival of commissioners who had come to arrange terms for the whole island, together with the islands of Grenada, St. Vincent, and Ste. Lucia. This capitulation gave to Great Britain the possession of all the Windward Islands.

The losses in this expedition amounted to 500 officers and men killed and wounded. Of this loss the proportion falling on the Royal Highlanders consisted of Captain William Cockburn, Lieutenant David Barclay, one sergeant and twelve rank and file, killed; Major John Reid, Captains James Murray and Thomas Stirling, Lieutenants Alexander Mackintosh, David Milne, Patrick Balneavy, Alexander Turnbull, John Robertson, William Brown, and George Leslie, three sergeants, one drummer, and seventy-two rank and file, wounded.

## CHAPTER X.

### CONQUEST OF THE HAVANNAH. 1762.

Formidable expedition to the Havannah. Admiral Knowles's survey of vicinity. Earl of Albemarle commander-in-chief of land forces Admiral Pocock commanding fleet. The Keppel brothers—William, the soldier, Augustus, the sailor; fortress of "Moro" very strong and commanded crowded harbour. Spanish militia successfully attacked by Albemarle. Difficulties encountered in making approaches. Repulse of sortie. The sailors' batteries. Failure of Captain Hervey's project. Burning of besiegers' principal battery. Abortive sortie of Spaniards. Successful storm of Moro. Gallantry of Highlanders. Devotion of Spanish chiefs. The guns of the Punta silenced. Capitulation of the Havannah. Distribution of prize-money.

In the month of January, 1762, war was proclaimed against the Spaniards, and at the same time there was set on foot a grand secret expedition, which proved to be destined for the conquest of the Havannah, the capital of Cuba, then the greatest emporium of the Western hemisphere, and the depôt of the precious metals of Mexico and Peru before their final despatch to Old Spain. The undertaking was first suggested by Admiral Knowles, after having made a careful survey of the island, and the plan was submitted by the Duke of Cumberland to the Government, which, in his capacity as the first military authority of the time, gave him the nomination of the officer by whom the operations of the enterprise were to be conducted. His choice fell upon George, third Earl of Albemarle, who had served as aide-de-camp to the duke at the battle of Fontenoy, who was his friend and pupil, and who for nineteen years had been his inseparable companion and comrade. The commander-in-chief of the expedition, who received the local rank of full general, was assisted by Lieutenant-General Elliot as second in command, by Major-General La Fausillé, and by his brother William Keppel. To the latter was assigned the conduct of the siege operations against the Moro Castle, the fortress which commanded the Havannah and defended the entrance of the harbour.

Admiral Sir George Pocock commanded the fleet, which consisted of nineteen ships of the line and eighteen frigates, carrying in all 2,042 guns; and there were no fewer than 150 transports having on board 10,000 land forces, which were to be joined from North America by 4,000 more. Sir George Pocock had been in the service for four-and-forty years, and had distinguished himself in various parts of the world, particularly in India. In 1757 he led the attack on Chandernagore, and though he was wounded in seven places he would not quit his deck till the end of the action, which lasted for three hours. He was the conqueror of the brave but ill-fated Lally, who, when brought a prisoner to England desired to be introduced to Sir George. "As the first man in your profession," said the gallant Frenchman, "I must respect and esteem you, although you have been the greatest enemy I ever had. But for you I should have triumphed in India instead of having been made a captive." Lord Albemarle's brother, Captain the Hon. Augustus Keppel, was second in command of the naval forces with the distinguishing pennant of commodore. Upon him devolved the conduct of the active operations of the fleet during the siege. He was an experienced and distinguished sailor; and he so loved blue water that his visits on shore had been almost limited to the brief intervals between hauling down his pennant from one ship and hoisting it on another.

Under his command Lord Albemarle had nineteen regiments of the line, inclusive of both battalions of the Royal Highlanders, two corps of American provincials, and a detachment of marines—in all upwards of 11,000 muskets, without counting the seven or eight regiments which were expected from New York. The fleet assembled at its assigned rendezvous off the north-west point of Hispaniola; and from thence, sailing in seven divisions, it was conducted with skilful seamanship through the Old Channel of Bahama and on June 6th arrived in sight of the far-famed Havannah. The same evening the admiral gave Commodore Keppel orders to take six ships of the line and some frigates under his command, to protect the transports and the siege material; and he himself, with the rest of the ships of the line, the greater part of the frigates, and all the tenders, bore away to the westward to make a feint of disembarking. The object of the long and perilous voyage and of so many ardent hopes was at length before the eyes of the adventurers. Nor did the spectacle disappoint their expectations. The view of the city from the approach to the port is one of the most beautiful and picturesque within the Tropics, and the island of Cuba has well been termed the "Pearl of the Antilles." The strong fortifications which crown the rocks on the eastern side; the noble inner basin where more than a thousand ships might anchor, sheltered from every wind; the majesty of the groves of palm-trees, which there grow to a great height; the city itself, with its white houses of Saracenic and Gothic styles, their quaint galleries and deep red roofs, their pillars and pinnacles, towers and domes—half seen and half hidden amid the forest of masts and sails—all unite to present a brilliant and imposing whole.

The landing was made on the morning of June 7th, between the forts Bocanao and Coximar, without the loss of a man, the squadron commanded by Commodore Keppel having previously silenced a small battery on the beach. It was on this side that the main body of the troops was meant to act. The army was divided into two corps, one of which under Lieutenant-General Elliot was to cover the siege and protect the detachment employed in procuring water and provisions. The other corps, commanded by General the Hon. William Keppel, was intended to effect the reduction of the Moro; and a detachment, commanded by Colonel Howe, was encamped near the western end of the city to cut off its communications with the country and divide the attention of the enemy. The Spaniards had a considerable body of militia in arms which was very active in driving in the cattle and picking up the stragglers of the recently landed force. On June 8th, Lord Albemarle marched to attack a body of them about 8,000 strong; and their cavalry, in a strength of about 1,600, came down threateningly on the right of the British line; but their hearts failed them, and the commander-in-chief took possession of the village of Guanamacoa, making it his headquarters.

The Spaniards made strenuous efforts to prevent the British ships from effecting an entrance into the harbour. On the 8th and 9th they sank across its mouth three of their ships of the line. Albemarle was struck by the importance of the famous Cavannos or Quarry hills, and they were promptly seized by Colonel Carleton with the light infantry and a battalion of Grenadiers, driving about 1000 Spaniards from a recently made redoubt, which, however, he could not hold, as it was within range of grape-shot from the Moro. The wood of the Cavannos and that between the Moro and the Coximar were cut down, and preparations were being made for the erection of batteries against the Moro, situated as it was on a high rock commanding every approach, and with the advantage of the town, Punta, and shipping in the harbour to prevent it from being enfiladed. Great hardships were endured during those operations. The earth was so thin that it was almost impossible to make the approaches under cover, and the scarcity of water, combined with the heat, was overpowering.

Many soldiers and sailors, worn with toil, drenched with perspiration, and parched with thirst, fell dead on the drag-ropes, in the trenches, and at their posts, slain by sheer heat and over-labour. But there was no respite.

Colonel Howe was detached with four battalions and six guns to secure the pass of St. Lazare, to watch the operations of the enemy, and to protect the troops while watering at the mouth of the River Chorera. On 30th June a sortie was made from the Havannah of about a thousand troops and a great host of negroes and mulattoes. They were repulsed, leaving on the ground about 200, the British loss being trivial. At length the batteries were ready, the guns of which were to be concentrated on the Moro. The two sailors' batteries were named the "Namur" and the "Valiant," the names of the ships respectively of the admiral and commodore. The "Valiant" battery, manned by Keppel's squadron, mounted eighty thirty-two pounders, and it fired oftener than any other work in the ratio of three to two. The scarcity of earth and the slowness of the engineers brought it to the morning of the 1st of July before the batteries were ready for being opened. Captain Hervey, of the *Dragon*, prevailed on the admiral against the opinion of Lord Albemarle that he should send three ships of the line to be stationed as near to the Moro as the depth of water permitted, with the object of dismounting the guns of the fort and if possible of breaching the wall. The *Cambridge*, *Dragon*, and *Marlborough* anchored under the Moro with great skill and daring; and on the morning of July 1st the bombardment of the Moro was opened. A furious cannonade lasted for several hours, when the *Cambridge*, whose captain had been early killed, had to come out of action owing to the damages she had received from the Spanish shot. The *Dragon*, commanded by Captain Hervey, soon followed, his ship severely injured; and not long after the *Marlborough* retired, the losses in the three ships amounting to over 150 men. The damage done by the ships to the fort was inconsiderable, since it commanded them so as to sweep them with grape, while the ships' guns could not obtain the requisite elevation. The only service done by the ships was to draw some of the fire of the fort from the British land batteries. They continued to maintain a steady fire with great success until the following day, when the principal battery of the besieging force, constructed as it was mainly of timber and fascines, caught fire and was consumed down to the ground. But for this misfortune, Lord Albemarle was persuaded that the fort would have fallen in a few days. As it was, the labour of 600 men for seventeen days was destroyed in an hour, and the works had to be reconstructed at a time when the hardships of the soldiers were all but intolerable. Albemarle, writing to his patron the Duke of Cumberland, stated: "I am sorry to say that almost everyone who relied on the success of this battery upon the loss of it began to despair and despond. Your Royal Highness may be assured I did not, and we have been hard at work ever since to get more guns up. The enemy in the mean time, who are very active, seem determined to defend this fort and have repaired their almost destroyed works. I have mounted as many guns as we had lost, and every one of our new batteries opened yesterday with great success. I shall open another of six guns to-morrow, and another of four next day. I have no doubt myself, if my soldiers last—they grow very sickly—that I shall take both fort and town." Albemarle was a determined and a sanguine man; he was almost alone in his optimism. It seemed, nevertheless, as if ill-fortune would thwart him. Another battery took fire before the first had been entirely repaired. Many eyes were turned seaward, looking for the long-expected arrival of the strong contingent from North America. Part of the North American force on its way to Cuba was taken by the French squadron of M. Blenac; another portion was delayed by the wreck of many of the transports in the Straits of Bahama. General Stewart states that part of the North American force ultimately did reach Cuba; but on the other hand Lord Albemarle wrote on July 13th that he had heard nothing of the North American force, adding in momentary despondency, "If any accident happens to it, I shall be undone." He made no further allusion to any subsequent arrival of that body or any part of it, and he certainly was not "undone." Fortunately the Jamaica fleet on its passage home under the convoy of Admiral Sir James Douglas, touched at Havannah. It was able to afford supplies for the troops, and necessaries for siege purposes, particularly bales of cotton, which were of the utmost service to the engineers who could not otherwise have pushed on their saps, the soil being so scanty above the stratum of rock as not to afford adequate cover.

The troops thus were inspired with fresh vigour. The batteries were reconstructed, their fire became more formidable, and it soon proved superior to that of the fort. The obstinate Moro still held out, but its guns were silenced and its upper works were dismantled and partially destroyed; and on July 20th the assailants succeeded in making a lodgment in the covered way. As the British troops approached the Moro they began to hope that they were now soon to reach the completion of their labours; but a formidable and unexpected obstacle suddenly presented itself. This was an immense ditch, cut for the most part in the solid rock, eighty feet deep and forty wide. It seemed at first sight impossible to fill up such a chasm in any expeditious way. Fortunately a thin ridge of rock facing the sea had been left to protect the ditch from the action of the waves. Along this ridge, which would only allow men to move in single file, the miners made their way unclothed and soon burrowed into the wall. By July 22nd they had penetrated eighteen feet under the face of the bastion opposite to the British right. It now became evident to the valiant and resolute Governor of the Havannah that a desperate effort must be made to arrest the advance of the besiegers. At daybreak of the 22nd 2,500 Spanish soldiers climbed the hills and made three separate assaults upon the British posts. All three sorties were unsuccessful, and the posts attacked were promptly reinforced by General Keppel, who ordered his left brigades to the Spanish redoubts and marched himself with the Royal Highlanders to the right of the

British batteries. The enemy fell into terror and confusion, and were driven down the hill with great slaughter. Some gained their boats, but many were drowned. A fire was kept up in their favour from every point of the defence—the Punta, the west bastion, the lines, and the ships in the harbour. But the Spaniards were hurled back with the loss of 400 men, while the loss of the assailants was only fifty.

This was the last attempt made to relieve the Moro, the garrison of which, abandoned as it was by the city and with an enemy undermining its walls, sullenly and sternly held out; but at noon of the 30th two mines were sprung, part of the wall fell into the ditch, and when the smoke and dust drifted away there was seen in the massive face of the Moro a breach which Lord Albemarle described as scarcely wide enough to admit a file of men. General Keppel, relying on the bravery of his troops, lost not a moment in making the assault. On arriving at the summit of the breach the assailants, led by Lieutenant-Colonel James Grant of the Highlanders, formed with extraordinary celerity and precision. The Spaniards fled on every side and an indiscriminate slaughter ensued. The loss of the enemy in killed, wounded, and prisoners reached in all 706 men. "The attack," wrote Lord Albemarle, "was so vigorous and impetuous that the enemy were instantly driven from the breach, and his Majesty's standard was promptly planted upon the bastion." The garrison was taken by surprise. The Marquis de Gonzales, the second in command, was killed while making an ineffectual effort to rally his men. The Governor, Don Louis de Velasco, collected a hundred men in an entrenchment he had made round his colours, but seeing that all his men had either fled or were slaughtered before him, disdaining to accept quarter he received a mortal wound and fell offering his sword to his conquerors. The King of Spain to commemorate the fate of this hero created his son Viscount de Moro, and decreed that ever after there should be a ship in his navy bearing the name of Velasco. The fall of those two officers augmented the confusion in the ranks of the enemy; 150 Spaniards were shot or bayoneted, 400 threw down their arms and were made prisoners, and the rest were either killed in the boats or were drowned while attempting to escape to the Havannah. Thus was the Moro won after a vigorous struggle of forty days from the time of its investment. The cost to the assailants was comparatively small. Only two officers and thirty men fell of those engaged in the assault, who numbered thirty-nine officers, twenty-nine sergeants, and 421 rank and file. The reduction of the Moro, however, was not immediately followed by the surrender of the Havannah. No sooner did the Spaniards in the city and in Fort Punta see the British flag flying on the Moro than they directed all their fire upon it. Meanwhile the victors, encouraged by their success, set about restoring the Moro and remounting its guns. They also wrought energetically in erecting batteries on an eminence commanding the city, and soon sixty heavy pieces of cannon were ready to open upon it.

On August 10th the commander-in-chief, being prepared to break ground, sent an aide-de-camp with a letter to the new governor, Don Juan de Prado, summoning him to surrender, " thereby to prevent the fatal calamities which always attend a siege "; and pointing out to his Excellency that "however much his disposition might incline him to humanity, it might not be possible to extend its influence to the preservation of the Spanish troops in a manner so recently experienced at the reduction of the Moro." To this curiously involved and somewhat sarcastic sentence the governor's answer was civil but resolute—he would defend the town to the last extremity; and he forthwith reopened fire. At daybreak next morning on the signal of a rocket, the British batteries, which consisted of forty-five cannon and eight mortars, fired on the enemy so energetically that by ten o'clock the Punta, the fort commanding the harbour opposite the Moro, was completely silenced, and the north bastion very nearly so. At three o'clock in the afternoon of the 11th flags of truce were hung out all round the town and on the Spanish admiral's ship; and one of them soon arrived at the English headquarters with the town mayor and an interpreter. A suspension of hostilities was agreed on until the 12th; and as soon as the terms of capitulation were adjusted the city of Havannah and the Spanish ships in the harbour were surrendered to his Britannic Majesty. The garrison, reduced to less than 800 men, in testimony of esteem for their heroic defence were allowed all the honours of war, and were to be conveyed to Spain with their private baggage. The value of the conquest altogether was estimated at three millions sterling; and the prize-money divided between the fleet and the army in equal shares was £736,185 2s. 4½d. Writing to his patron Cumberland, the Earl of Albemarle intimated his expectation of receiving "from first to last £100,000 for my share." He did better; he took £122,697. Elliot, the second in command, had £24,539; the two Keppel brothers had each £6,816; and the pittance allotted to the Tommy Atkins of the period—the man who did the work—was £4 1s. 8½d. As the Havannah was restored to Spain a few months after its conquest, the wags said with some reason, in reference to the share of the three brothers' prize-money, that the expedition was undertaken solely to put money into the Keppels' pockets. Three years after the reduction of the Havannah the Earl of Albemarle received the order of the Garter. Burke has recorded a high estimate of the Havannah expedition. "It was without question," says he, "the most decisive conquest we have made since the beginning of the war, and in no operation were the courage, steadiness, and perseverance of the British troops and the conduct of their leaders more conspicuous. The acquisition of this place united in itself all the advantages which can be acquired in war. It was a military advantage of the highest class. It was equal to the greatest naval victory by its effect on the enemy's marine, and in the plunder it equalled the produce of a national subsidy." The news of the victory caused great rejoicings in England and the bearer of the intelligence came in for his share of the honours. In the broad-sheets of the day appeared the following greeting to Captain Hervey:—

> "Welcome, brave hero, to thy native shore;
> Blessed with thy news, Britannia asks no more.
> The King hereafter to young George shall tell
> How Hervey fought when proud Havannah fell."

The British loss in the siege of Havannah amounted to 1,657 officers and men; there were killed 345; wounded 640; and 672 died by sickness. The loss of the two battalions of the Royal Highlanders was but twelve men killed and wounded; there died of sickness Major Macneil; Captains Robert Menzies and A. Macdonald; Lieutenants Farquharson, Grant, Lapsley, Cunninson, Hill, and Blair; two drummers, and seventy-one rank and file.

## CHAPTER XI.

### FORT PITT AND THE BACKWOODS. 1762–67.

From Cuba to North America. Regiment landed in New York, October, 1762. Following winter in Albany. Relief of Fort Pitt. Considerable losses. Wintering at Fort Pitt. Summer of 1764 in constant patrolling against Indians. Skeleton of regiment, after decade of service in North America, ordered home. Departure regretted in colony because of good conduct. Officers of Black Watch a band of brothers.

IMMEDIATE preparations were made for removing from Cuba the main body of the army. The first battalion of the Royal Highlanders was ordered to embark for New York, where it landed in October, 1762. The men fit for service of the second battalion had been drafted into the first; the rest, with the officers, remained till reduced. During the following winter the Royal Highlanders were quartered in Albany, and in the summer of 1763 they, with two detachments of other regiments, the total strength being 950 men, under Colonel Bouquet, were ordered to the relief of Fort Pitt. The Indian warriors of various tribes had united, and attacked in succession all the small British forts between Lake Erie and Pittsburg. In those enterprises they displayed considerable sagacity and a great improvement in their discipline and manner of fighting. While on the march in the end of April, towards evening Bouquet's advanced guard was suddenly attacked by Indians. After several days of sharp intermittent fighting, preparations were ostentatiously made for a feigned retreat, and then at last the Indians exposed themselves within reach and rushed forward with impetuosity. Charged in front and in flank they were thrown into great confusion, and they were pursued so far that they did not attempt to rally. Colonel Bouquet resumed his march and reached Fort Pitt without further molestation. The losses of the Royal Highlanders in this bushwhacking affair were: Lieutenants John Graham and James Mackintosh, one sergeant, and twenty-six rank and file killed; Captain John Graham of Duchray, Lieutenant Duncan Campbell, two sergeants, two drummers, and thirty rank and file wounded.

The regiment wintered at Fort Pitt, and in the early summer of 1764 was employed under Brigadier-General Bouquet in service against the Indians. His force consisted of eight companies of the Royal Highlanders, part of the 60th, and 400 colonial marksmen having their faces painted and their clothes made in the Indian fashion. In this service the troops patrolled many hundred miles, cutting their way through dense forests and frequently attacked by or attacking scouting parties of Indians, who were at length so harassed that they sued for a peace which was not interrupted for many years. In the six months from July, 1764 to January, 1765 —during three of which they were exposed to extreme heat and three to equally severe cold, with very little shelter from either extreme and frequently disturbed by an active and cunning enemy—the Highlanders did not leave a man behind from fatigue or exhaustion. Three men died of sickness, and when the force returned to Fort Pitt there were but nineteen men in charge of the surgeon.

The regiment was now in better quarters than for

several years past. It was, however, greatly reduced in numbers from the extent, nature, and variety of service in which, during the tropical heat of the West Indies and the rigorous winters of North America, it had been for years engaged. At length, after more than a decade of faithful and arduous service the gallant 42nd, now reduced to a mere skeleton, was ordered home. Such of the men as preferred to remain in America were permitted to volunteer into other regiments. The second battalion was reduced and several officers were placed on half-pay. The volunteers for remaining in America were so numerous that, along with those who had earlier been discharged and sent home as disabled, and others who had been discharged in America where they settled, the strength of the regiment was reduced to a very small proportion of that which had left Scotland in 1756. It embarked at Philadelphia in June, 1767, to the great regret of the colonists, who esteemed the Highlanders for "their unswerving loyalty, fidelity and orderly behaviour"; and it arrived at Cork in the following October. During the seven years the 42nd was employed in North America and the West Indies, it had thirteen officers, twelve sergeants, and 382 men killed; thirty-three officers twenty-two sergeants, and 508 men wounded—in all 970 officers and men killed and wounded, a number equal to a full regiment.

By their courage in the field and their integrity and orderly conduct in quarters, the men of the 42nd Regiment seem to have made a most favourable impression on their brethren of North America. A proof of this appreciation is furnished in the following extract from an article published in the *Virginia Gazette* of July 30th, 1767:—"Last Sunday evening the Royal Highland Regiment embarked for Ireland. Since its arrival in America it has been distinguished for having undergone amazing fatigues, made long and frequent marches through an unhospitable country, bearing excessive heat and severe cold with alacrity and cheerfulness, frequently encamping in deep snow, such as those who inhabit the interior parts of this province do not know, and which only those who dwell in the most northern parts of Europe can have any idea of, continually exposed in camp and on their marches to the alarms of a savage enemy, who in all their attempts were forced to flee. It has ensured to us peace and security; and along with our blessings for those benefits it has our thanks for that decorum in behaviour which it maintained during its stay in this city, giving an example that the most amiable conduct in civil life is in no way inconsistent with the character of the good soldier; and it has every wish of the people for health, honour, and a pleasant voyage."

General Stewart writes:—"Comparing the loss sustained by this regiment in the field with that of other corps, it has generally been less than theirs, except in the unfortunate affair at Ticonderoga. I have conversed with several officers who served in the regiment during that period (1756-67), and they uniformly accounted for the moderate loss from the celerity of its attack and the use of the broadsword, which the enemy never could withstand. This, likewise, was the opinion of one of the original soldiers of the Black Watch, in the ranks of which, although a gentleman by birth and education, he served until the peace of 1748. He informed me that although it was believed at home that the regiment had been almost destroyed at Fontenoy, the truth was quite the reverse, and that it was the subject of general observation in the army that its loss should have been so small, considering how actively it was engaged in different parts of the field. On one occasion," continued the veteran, "a brigade of Dutch were ordered to attack a rising ground on which were posted the troops called the King of France's Household Guards. The Dutch were to be supported by the Highlanders. The former conducted their march and attack as if they did not know the road—halting and firing and halting every twenty paces. The Highlanders, losing all patience with this kind of fighting, which gave the enemy time and opportunity to fire at their leisure, dashed forward, passed the Dutch; and the front ranks, handing back their firelocks to the rear rank, drew their swords and quickly drove the Frenchmen from their ground. When the attack was over it was found that of the Highlanders not above a dozen men were killed or wounded, while the Dutch, who had not come up at all, lost more than five times that number."

During the first American war the regiment was specially fortunate in possessing a corps of officers—men of respectable character, education, and family, several of whom were distinguished for superior professional acquirements, and for their accomplishments as cultured gentlemen. The number of officers in 1759, for instance, including the chaplains and medical staff of both battalions, was eighty-three. Of this number seven only became general officers—Francis Grant of Grant, John Reid of Straloch, Allan Campbell of Glenure, James Murray (son of Lord George Murray), John Campbell of Strachur, Thomas Stirling of Ardoch, and John Small. Many more could have attained general rank had they desired to do so. But this was not the case; probably no regiment in the service has produced fewer general officers than the Royal Highlanders. And this simply because the officers of this regiment have for the most part chosen to remain in it and perform regimental duty in it during their military service, in preference to being detached as aides-de-camp, staff officers, men aspiring for "billets," and other votaries of non-regimental service. The pride of the officerhood of the Black Watch has been to regard it as a family which lives in itself and for itself; and when a member departs from out this military family, it is not for promotion, but to go into civil life, always retaining while life endures pride and affection for the "old corps." The field officers of this period were men of high character, a considerable proportion of whom were landed proprietors. While Colonel Graham was unremitting in his exertions to procure the appointment of good officers, and the men had a respect for their own character and that of the regiment, the corps of Royal Highlanders could not fail to maintain the attributes for which it was justly distinguished.

# CHAPTER XII.

## HOME SERVICE. 1767–76.

Landed at Cork October, 1767. Recruiting in the Highlands. Royal Warrant concerning colours. Changes in clothing and arms. Eagerness to enlist. Quartered in Glasgow after absence from Scotland of thirty-two years. Peculiar regimental administration. Lord John Murray's devotion to regiment. Pride in grand old corps. Embarked for North America at beginning of War of Independence. Embarking strength of rank and file, 1,013. Sailed May 1st, 1776.

As has already been stated, the Royal Highland Regiment landed at Cork in October, 1767, after an absence from home of eleven years, General Lord John Murray, the colonel of the regiment, had been in Cork for some weeks awaiting the arrival of his regiment, and on its landing he marched into the town at its head, himself and the officers attired in full Highland garb, with broadsword, pistol and dirk. Recruiting parties were promptly despatched to the Highlands, and on May 28th of the following year, when reviewed in Galway by General Armiger, the regiment was complete to the establishment, and every man in it, with two exceptions, born north of the Tay.

By the Royal Warrant of 19th December, 1768, the 42nd, or Royal Highlanders, were authorised to bear—

"In the centre of the Colours, the King's cypher within the garter, and crown over it. Under it *St Andrew*, with the motto *Nemo me impune lacessit*. In the three corners of the second colour, the King's cypher and crown. On the Grenadier caps the King's crest; also *St. Andrew*, as in the colours. On the drums and bells of arms the same device, with the rank of the regiment underneath."

It is recorded that at this period the uniform of the regiment had a very dingy appearance. The jackets were of a brickdust-like red; for economy was strictly observed in the matter of clothing. The old jacket, after having been worn for a year, was made into a waistcoat, and the plaid, at the end of two years, was taken into service as the philibeg. The hose supplied by Government were of so shoddy a character that the men paid an additional price in order to furnish themselves with a better material. Instead of feathers for the bonnets they were allowed only a shabby piece of black bearskin; but the men supplied themselves with ostrich-feathers and spared no expense in fitting up their bonnets handsomely. In its sombre black and green tartan—the same in hue as the tartan of to-day, and with the dark blue facings of a Royal regiment—it had a far less brilliant appearance at a distance than English regiments, with their white breeches and belts; but on a closer view the Highland line presented a more imposing and warlike aspect. The men possessed what an ingenious writer has called "the attractive beauties of the soldier—sunburnt complexion, a hardy, weather-beaten visage, with a penetrating eye, and firm, expressive countenance, sinewy and elastic limbs, muscles strongly developed; indicating capacity of action and marking experience of service." In 1769, when the regiment removed to Dublin, the men received white cloth waistcoats, which were regarded as an improvement on the vests of red cloth, and the colonel supplied them with white goatskin sporrans in lieu of the purses made of badger-skin. During the war the officers had worn only a narrow edging of gold lace round the edges of the facings, and very often no lace at all—epaulets and all glittering ornaments having been laid aside to render them less conspicuous to the Indians, who always aimed particularly at the officers. During the stay of the regiment in Ireland the officers wore their coats edged with gold lace. On ordinary occasions they wore light hangers, using the basket-hilted claymore only in full dress. They also carried fusils. The sergeants were furnished with carbines instead of the Lochaber axe, or halbert, which they formerly carried. In 1775 the soldiers were provided with new firearms, three and a half inches shorter in the barrel than the long old musket. The sergeants wore silver lace on their coats, which, however, they furnished at their own expense.

At this period the regiment was held in so high respect in the Highlands, and young men so eagerly enlisted into it, that recruiting parties of other regiments frequently assumed the dress of the Old Highland Regiment, for which they pretended to be recruiting. While the regiment was quartered in Dublin a large party of recruits arrived from the Highlands to join the 38th Regiment, then in Cork. When the recruits saw their countrymen they refused to go any further, asserting that they had engaged to serve in the Black Watch. The officer in charge of the draft reported the situation to the officer commanding in Dublin. The Lord Lieutenant ordered a court of inquiry, and after full investigation it was found that the 38th officer and party had gone to the north of Scotland in Highland dress, and that it was the general belief that the recruiting was for the Black Watch, and that although the attestations bore to be for the 38th, no explanation was made to the recruits, who, ignorant of the English language, understood that their engagement was to serve in the familiar regiment of their own country, and not along with men whose language they did not understand and whose dress they so much disliked. As the result of the investigation the Highland recruits were all discharged in Dublin, whereupon, to a man, they enlisted in the 42nd.

The regiment remained in Ireland until the year 1775, when it landed at Portpatrick and thence marched to Glasgow, after an absence from Scotland of thirty-two years since the march into England in 1743. Many of the old soldiers, as Scotland was approached, leaped on shore with tears of joy, kissed their native earth with enthusiasm, and grasped it in handfuls.

An interesting account of the conduct of the regiment and of its internal administration and discipline during its eight years' service in Ireland, from 1767 to 1775, has been preserved by one who served in it throughout the period stated. The regiment is described as still possessing the character which it had originally acquired in Flanders and America, although there were not more than eighty of the men who had served in America, and only a few of those who had served abroad previously to 1748. The attachment of the soldiers of the Royal Highlanders to their native dress, and their peculiarity of language, habits, and manners, contributed to preserve them as a race of men separate from others of the same profession, and to give to their system of regimental discipline a distinctive and peculiar character. Their messes were managed by the non-commissioned officers, or old soldiers who had charge of the barrack-rooms; and those messes were so arranged that in each room the men were in friendship or intimacy with each other, belonged to the same glen or district, or were connected by similar kindred tie. Thus each barrack-room was a large family circle. After the weekly allowances for food and small necessaries had been provided, the surplus pay was deposited in a stock-purse, each member of the mess drawing for it in his turn. The accumulation thus acquired soon mounted up, and instead of it being hoarded it was lent out by those military economists to the inhabitants, who were surprised that soldiers should be saving money. At each tri-monthly settlement of accounts with their officers they enjoyed themselves very heartily, but with a strict observance of propriety and good humour; and as the members of each mess considered themselves in a manner answerable for each other's conduct, they took measures with such severity regarding any impropriety as to render the interference of superior authority quite unnecessary.

The standard height was five feet seven inches for mature men, and five feet six for growing lads. When companies were complete on parade, none under five feet eight inches were allowed to be in the front rank. The grenadiers were always a body of tall men. Although the standard was nominally retained at the above height, there were men of five feet five inches in the centre rank, and those undersized men were frequently able to undergo greater fatigues than the biggest men in the corps. With the exception of two men who had been recruited at Glasgow, no desertions occurred during the stay of the regiment in Ireland. Lord John Murray, the colonel of the regiment, exerted himself to procure for it Scotch and Highland officers, well aware how greatly their influence would avail to procure men from

## HOME SERVICE. 97

the hill-country, and sensible also of its possessing officers who understood the dispositions and character of the men. Soon after the regiment arrived in Glasgow, the establishment was increased to 105 rank and file each company, thus forming when complete a battalion of 1,155 rank and file, exclusive of officers, sergeants, and drummers. The establishment was completed in a few weeks; for young men were proud to enter the grand old corps, and the old mountaineers honoured it as a memorial of the achievements of the race of Highlanders. The bounty offered was at first one guinea and a crown; but in the North-country the increase had no influence on the success of the recruitment. The sentiments of the people were moved by the anticipation of meeting their fellow-countrymen in the regiment, and the bounty was left or sent to their parents or families.

At the instance of the Lord-Lieutenant of Ireland, notwithstanding the strenuous remonstrances of Lord John Murray, three English officers received commissions in the Royal Highland Regiment. A number of Highland officers were brought in from half pay. On April 10th the regiment was reviewed by General Sir Adolphus Oughton. It was pronounced complete to establishment, and so unexceptionable that none were rejected. The War of Independence had broken out in North America, and the Royal Highlanders were now destined to serve against a people in great part of their own race—a people for the safety and protection of whom they had been fighting only a few years previously, and who had been indebted to them for a peaceful and unchequered existence. But obedience is the first duty of the soldier; and so, hostilities having been begun in America, every exertion was made to teach the recruits the manual of

H

the musket exercise, for which purpose they were drilled even by candlelight. New accoutrements were supplied to the men; and broadswords and iron-stocked pistols were furnished at the cost of the colonel. The embarking strength of rank and file was 1,012; of whom 931 were Highlanders, seventy-four Lowland Scotch, five English (bandsmen), one Welshman, and one Irishman.

# CHAPTER XIII.

### THE WAR OF INDEPENDENCE. 1776-82.

May 1st, 1776, regiment, along with Fraser's Highlanders, embarked for America. A transport captured by American privateer. The Highland Company rose against American crew, and navigated the transport to Jamestown. Republican Government made prisoners of Highland Company, men of which rejected all inducements to forfeit allegiance. Battle of Brooklyn gained by Howe—American loss 3,300 men. Washington's activity. Storm of Fort Washington. Fort Lee reduced, Winter quarters. Defeat by Washington of Hessian garrison of Trenton. Combat of Princetown. Surprise of Highlanders by American force— enemy beaten off. Movement of British Army to Chesapeake. Battle of Brandywine—defeat of Washington. Entry into Philadelphia of British troops. General Howe succeeded by General Clinton. Destruction of American privateers by General Grey. Destruction by Highlanders of American stores at Portsmouth, in Virginia. Highland Regiment deteriorated by draft of blackguards.

THE regiment embarked at Greenock under the command of Colonel Stirling, and, along with Fraser's Highlanders, consisting of two battalions, sailed on May 1st, 1776. Four days later the transports separated in a gale of wind. The *Oxford* transport, carrying a company of the 42nd, was captured on the passage by an American privateer. The officers and ship's crew were conveyed on board the privateer, and a prize crew and guard sent to the transport with directions to make the first friendly port. A few days later the soldiers overpowered the American crew, navigated their transport into the James river, and anchored at Jamestown. Virginia had, however, been evacuated by Lord Dunmore and his British adherents, and the colony was now under a Republican Government. The transport was seized, and the Highland soldiers were marched prisoners to Williamsburg, the chief town of the province. There every effort was made to induce them to abandon their allegiance and join the American cause. When offers of military promotion were rejected, the Scottish soldiers were told that they would receive grants of fertile land on which to settle in freedom and happiness, and that they would all be lairds themselves with no rents to pay. Those inducements also failed. Those trustworthy and honourable men declared that they would neither receive nor possess any land but such as they should have deserved by service under their King, whose health they could not be restrained from drinking, although in the midst of enemies; and when they were found resolute, they were sent in small detached parties to the back settlements. They were, however, exchanged two years later, and rejoined the regiment. The other transports crossed the Atlantic safely, and joined the armament under General Sir William Howe which landed on Staten Island on August 3rd.

As soon as the three Highland battalions landed, their grenadier companies were formed into a grenadier battalion commanded by Major Sir Charles Stewart. The three light companies of the 42nd and Fraser's were also formed into a battalion in the brigade commanded by Lieutenant-Colonel Abercromby. The eight battalion companies of the 42nd were formed into two temporary battalions, the command of one being given to Major William Murray of Lintrose, and the other to Major William Grant of Rothiemurchus, both officers of that regiment; the whole being under its commanding officer, Lieutenant-Colonel Thomas Stirling. Those small battalions were brigaded under Sir William Erskine, and were placed in the reserve with the grenadiers and light infantry of the army under the command of Earl Cornwallis, whose own regiment, the 33rd, was also with the reserve.

About this time the broadswords and pistols, which the men had received in Glasgow, were ordered to be discontinued. The pistols being considered unnecessary except in the field, were not intended, like the swords, to be worn in quarters. The reason given for discontinuing the broadswords was that they retarded the men by getting entangled in thick woods. "Admitting," wrote General Stewart, "that the objection was well founded as regarded the swords, it certainly could not apply to the pistols. In a closely wooded country, where troops were liable to sudden attacks and surprises by a hidden enemy, the pistol was peculiarly of service. It was therefore difficult to find a good reason for laying that weapon aside. I have been told by old officers and soldiers who bore a part in those attacks that an enemy who had stood for hours the fire of musketry invariably gave way when an advance was made sword in hand. But those weapons were never restored, and the regiment had neither swords nor pistols since."

From the day of the landing of his regiment Colonel Stirling was indefatigable in training his men to the manner of fighting practised in the former war with the Indians and French bushmen, which experience had shown to be so well suited for a closely wooded country. Well versed himself in this mode of warfare, Colonel Stirling imparted it to his troops by first training the non-commissioned officers himself, and then superintending their instructions given to the soldiers. The Highlanders made rapid progress in this discipline, being already excellent marksmen, and requiring only to have their natural impetuosity restrained, which too often had caused them to disdain the idea of fighting in ambush.

The British force commanded by General Sir William Howe, including 13,000 Hessians, amounted to about 30,000 men. The campaign was opened by a landing on Long Island on August 22nd. The whole army encamped in front of the villages of Gravesend and Utrecht. The American General Putnam was encamped at Brooklyn, a few miles westward from the British position. The two armies were separated by a range of wooded elevations intersecting the country from east to west. The direct road to the enemy lay through a pass beyond the village of Flatbush, and Clinton held it with a battalion. At nightfall of the 26th the main body of the army advanced to the heights in front, crossed them without opposition, and then descended into the lower ground between the hills and General Putnam's lines. Meanwhile Major-General Grant with his brigade, supported by the Royal Highlanders, marched from the left along the coast towards the Narrows with intent to strike the enemy's right. On the morning of the 27th the British right attacked the American left, and the enemy after a short resistance retired to their lines in great confusion, pursued by the British troops, Major Stewart leading with his battalion of Highland Grenadiers. The Hessians advanced from Flatbush at the sound of the firing and charged the American centre, drove it through the woods, and captured three guns. General Grant had earlier assailed the right of the enemy, and after a sharp cannonade had routed his opponents. The hostile position had been considerably strengthened; but it could offer no effectual resistance to troops so eager to close with their antagonists. But the cautious Howe would not permit his troops to attack the enemy's position, although he must have seen both the spirit animating his own people and the despondency of the Americans. Unfortunately the same lack of enterprise and want of confidence which characterised Sir William Howe also on this occasion influenced General Grant; and instead of moving rapidly forward in pursuit he halted, and sacrificed not only the opportunity of capturing many fugitives but also of intercepting the enemy's retreat from Flatbush.

Nevertheless, the Americans lost some 3,300 men killed, taken prisoners, or drowned in the morass. Among the prisoners were Generals Sullivan, Uddell, and the "Earl of Stirling," a gentleman named Alexander, who, born in America, claimed and assumed that ancient but extinct title. The British lost five officers and fifty-six non-commissioned officers and privates killed and twelve officers and 245 non-commissioned officers and men wounded. The loss of the Royal Highlanders was Lieutenant Cramond and nine men wounded. There were left on the field by the enemy twenty-six brass and iron guns, and a vast quantity of pikes and other arms. Among the killed were one officer and twenty marines, who mistook the enemy for Hessians, and fell among the ranks of the former.

The British army encamped in face of the American lines, and next day broke ground opposite the left redoubt of the hostile position. Washington, however, had crossed over from New York during the action at Brooklyn, and had resolved on a retreat. In the course of a single night he transported 9,000 men with guns, ammunition, and stores across the East River to New York, and so secretly was the movement effected that the British were not aware of it until the following morning.

Active operations on the part of the British were resumed on September 15th, when the reserve, which the Royal Highlanders had rejoined after the action at Brooklyn, crossed the East River to New York, and after some opposition took possession of the heights above the town. A corps of New England men and Virginians retiring from New York was intercepted by the Highlanders and Hessians advancing towards Bloomingdale. Next day the light infantry were despatched to dislodge a hostile force which had possessed itself of a wood facing the British left. A smart action ensued, and the Highlanders were sent in support of the light infantry. The Americans were forced back within their entrenchments; they renewed the action with strong reinforcements, but were again repulsed with a loss of 300 men. The British loss was fourteen men killed, five officers and seventy men wounded. The 42nd had a sergeant and five privates killed; Captains Duncan Macpherson and John Macintosh, and Ensign Alexander Mackenzie (who died of his wounds), and one piper, two drummers and forty-seven privates wounded.

No further operations occurred for some days, and the enemy were gradually regaining their spirits. Washington had established his army on commanding ground in rear of the White Plains, and with the object of inducing the enemy to quit its strong position, on October 12th Sir William Howe embarked his army in flat-bottomed boats, and passing through the intricate channel called Hell's Gate, disembarked his army the same evening at Frog's Neck near West Chester. The bridge connecting this place with the mainland had been destroyed by the enemy, and on the 14th the army reached White Plains, where the Americans had concentrated their whole force. Both armies being in position, the British took the offensive by seizing a rising ground held by 4,000 of the enemy ; but General Washington refrained from bringing on an action, and General Howe proceeded against Fort Washington, the possession of which was necessary to keep open the communication between New York and the mainland. The garrison of the fort numbered nearly 3,000 men, and the strong ground round it was covered with lines and works. The Hessians under General Knyphausen, supported by the whole of the reserve—with the exception of the 42nd, which was to make a feint on the eastern face of the fort—were to make the chief attack. Before daybreak of the 16th the 42nd embarked in boats and landed in a small creek at the foot of the rock in the face of a smart fire. The Highlanders then formed hastily and scrambled up the precipice, assisted by each other and by the shrubs which grew out of the crevices of the rocks. Gaining the summit they rushed forward and attacked the enemy so suddenly that upwards of 200 threw down their arms. The Highlanders pursued their advantage, penetrated beyond the intervening eminence, and met Lord Percy's brigade coming up on the further side. Thus the Highlanders, with their characteristic impetuosity, turned a feigned into a real attack, and so contributed greatly to the success of the day. When the Hessians approached from another direction the enemy surrendered at discretion, of whom about 2,700 men were made prisoners. The British loss was but 120 men ; that of the Royal Highlanders eleven men killed, and Lieutenants Patrick Graeme, Norman Macleod, four sergeants, and sixty-six men wounded.

In order to command the North River and gain a communication with New Jersey, Fort Lee was next reduced, in which service the Royal Highlanders were employed. The enemy, pursued by the British, retreated successively to Elizabeth, Newark, and Brunswick, where Lord Cornwallis halted for a week while the main body moved forward and reached Princetown on the 17th, an hour after it had been evacuated by Washington. The winter having set in, General Howe put his army into winter quarters. For a time the Royal Highlanders were quartered in Brunswick, but later were ordered to the advanced posts, being the only British regiment in the front.

The enemy were greatly dispirited by their reverses, and if General Howe had been an energetic commander the Americans might have been reduced to the last extremity. But Washington availed himself of the inactivity of his adversary by making frequent partial attacks on the hostile advanced posts, whereby he at once improved the discipline of his inexperienced troops and revived their drooping spirits. On January 22nd, 1777, by a successful stratagem he surprised and completely defeated the Hessian garrison of Trenton. Because of this reverse the situation of the Highlanders, who formed the left of the line at Mount Holly, became seriously compromised, and they were therefore ordered to fall back on the light infantry at Princetown. Lord Cornwallis, who had been on the eve of embarking for England, returned to the army on learning of the reverse of the Hessians, and he promptly advanced on Trenton with a considerable force in which was included the two Highland regiments. He found Washington in position on high ground beyond Trenton, and a long cannonade ensued. But the Americans decamped during the night and effected their retreat in good order. Declining a general engagement, the active and resourceful Washington marched to surprise the British troops left by Lord

Cornwallis at Princetown. As Colonel Mawhood was preparing to follow his lordship to Trenton in accordance with the orders of the latter, the Americans suddenly struck his flank and rear, a sharp musketry fire being the first notice of their approach. Colonel Mawhood resolved to hazard an action, and when the enemy advanced he poured in a heavy discharge of artillery which did great execution. But the American attack was so sudden and unexpected that the British force fought with no concerted plan, and while one regiment made good its retreat to Maidenhead, the other corps retired on Brunswick with a great loss in killed and wounded, most of the latter being taken prisoners.

Lord Cornwallis established his headquarters at Brunswick, where he passed the winter. On January 6th, 1777, the Royal Highlanders were detached to the village of Pisquatua, on the line of communication between New York and Brunswick by way of Amboy. The duty there was severe and the season extremely rigorous. The Americans annoyed the Highlanders with nightly alarms, but never made any regular attack on this post, as they frequently did on that of the Hessians, who, when first landed, were held in great dread by the people. To remove this impression Washington had the Hessian prisoners taken at Trenton led through several towns, to accustom the inhabitants to the sight of those formidable-looking soldiers, whose whiskers, beards, and rough caps originally inspired much awe.

After a considerable pause in the operations, on the afternoon of May 10th the American generals Maxwell and Stephens attacked the Royal Highlanders in Pisquatua with 2,000 men. Advancing with secrecy and favoured by the ground, their approach was unperceived till they suddenly rushed on to a level space in front of the Highland picquets. The attack was so unexpected that the men had scarcely time to seize their arms, but they kept the enemy in check till the reserve picquet came up. Pushing on in strength the enemy mixed with the picquets, who retired disputing every step to gain time for the regiment to turn out. Thus time to assemble was obtained, and the enemy were driven back with great precipitation, leaving upwards of 200 men killed and wounded. The Highlanders, pursuing ardently, were only prevented by nightfall from pushing on to attack the hostile camp. The loss of the Highlanders was but three sergeants and nine privates killed; Captain Duncan Macpherson, Lieutenant William Stewart, three sergeants, and thirty privates wounded. When the picquet was overpowered Sergeant Macgregor was severely wounded and left insensible on the ground. The sergeant had that day put on a new jacket with silver lace, and large silver buckles on his shoes; and he attracted the notice of an American soldier, who reckoned him a good prize. The retreat of the sergeant's comrades not allowing the American time to strip the Scotsman on the spot, he took him on his back to a more convenient distance. By this time Macgregor began to recover; and perceiving whither the American was carrying him, he drew his dirk, grasped the other by the throat, and swore he would run him through if he did not turn back and carry him to the camp. The American, finding this argument irresistible, complied with the demand, and meeting Lord Cornwallis and Colonel Stirling, was thanked for his care of the sergeant; but he honestly told them that he was only carrying the Scottish sergeant to camp because he wished to save his own life. Lord Cornwallis gave the American his liberty, and procured for Sergeant

Macgregor a billet under Government. The fighting in this skirmish was very bitter, most of it being at close quarters. Lieutenant Stewart and three sergeants were disabled for life, as well as many of the men. The loss of six sergeants, all men of the best conduct and character, was counted a serious one to the regiment.

Summer being now well advanced, preparations were made for taking the field. Much time had already been lost in waiting for supplies of camp-equipage and stores from England. The Royal Highlanders, along with the 13th, 17th, and 44th Regiments, were in this campaign under the command of Major-General Charles Grey. Sir William Howe, having assumed the command in mid June, attempted to entice Washington from his position at Middle Brook; but the American commander knew too well its advantage to be induced to abandon it, and the prudent Howe considered it a place too strong to attack. Seeing no prospect of making any effectual impression on the enemy in the Jerseys, he determined to change the seat of war. He embarked for the Chesapeake with thirty-six battalions of British and Hessian troops, including the flank battalions of grenadiers and light infantry. Before the embarkation the Royal Highlanders were joined by a detachment of 170 recruits from Scotland, who, as they were all of the best description, more than supplied the loss which the regiment had sustained from various casualties. After a tedious voyage the army landed at Elk Ferry; but it was not until September 3rd that the march towards Philadelphia was begun. This delay enabled Washington to march across the country and to take up an advantageous position at Red Clay Creek, whence he pushed forward detachments with the intent of annoying the British troops by partial skirmishes while on the march. General Howe did not reach the Brandywine River until the middle of September, in consequence of the difficulties experienced in traversing a country, wooded, and full of defiles. On reaching that river he found that the enemy had taken up a strong position behind it, with the intention, apparently, of opposing the further advance of the British army. The Americans had secured all the fords; and at Chad's Ford, where it was expected that the British would attempt to cross, batteries had been erected and entrenchments thrown up to command and defend the passage. While the attention of the enemy was occupied here, Cornwallis with a division of the army, made a circuit of some miles, crossed Jeffery's Ford without opposition, and turning down the river, fell in with the American general Sullivan, whom Washington had detached with a strong force to oppose Lord Cornwallis's division. An action took place in which the British troops rushed on the enemy and drove them through the woods from all their posts towards their main army. Meantime General Knyphausen with his division made a demonstration of passing the river at Chad's Ford, and as soon as he was aware from the cannon-sound that Lord Cornwallis' movement had succeeded, he crossed the river and carried the batteries and entrenchments of the enemy, and following up his advantage, a general rout ensued. Washington, with such force as he was able to keep together, fled with his cannon and baggage to Chester, whence next day he proceeded to Philadelphia, where he collected his scattered army.

Such was the issue of the battle of Brandywine. The loss of the British was less than might have been expected in a battle fought against an enemy on strong ground of its own choice. The British had fifty officers killed and wounded, and 438 men. The battalion companies of the Royal Highlanders were not brought into action, but of the light company six men were killed and sixteen wounded. The Marquis de la Fayette and several other French officers who had joined the American cause distinguished themselves conspicuously in the battle.

In this disastrous war it was the ill-fortune of the British army that its successes led to no important consequences. For example, instead of pursuing a broken and defeated army, preventing its re-assemblage, and capturing its stores and magazines, General Howe remained passive and permitted the indefatigable Washington to recruit his army and replenish his stores at his leisure.

It was ascertained that the American general Wayne with some 1,500 men was concealed in the woods, watching for an opportunity to harass the British rear on its march towards Philadelphia. Major-General Charles Grey was despatched on the 20th with the 2nd Light Infantry and the 42nd and 44th Regiments to cut off this body. General Grey directed his men to use the bayonet only. The enemy were surprised at dead of night when asleep, and before the Americans could seize their arms more than 300 were bayoneted and 100 prisoners made; the rest owed their escape to the darkness. The British loss was one officer, one sergeant, and one private killed; a few men were wounded. On the 25th the British army moved forward to German Town, and on the following morning the Grenadiers entered Philadelphia, of which they took peaceable possession, the enemy having previously retired.

General Washington, having received considerable

reinforcements and his army having recovered the defeat at Brandywine, determined on an enterprise bold in itself and unexpected on the part of the British. Marching from his camping ground at nightfall, he reached German Town in the middle of the night and surprised the British with a sudden attack. A vigorous resistance was made by the two battalions in German Town, but they were forced to give way before superior numbers. With six companies of the 40th, however, Lieutenant-Colonel Musgrave threw himself into a large stone house, from which he annoyed the assailants with such effect as to arrest their progress till General Grey arrived with his brigade and supports and forced the Americans to retreat. In this short but sharp affair the losses on both sides were greater than in the action of Brandywine.

In May, 1778, Sir William Howe was re-called, and was succeeded as commander-in-chief by General Clinton. The new commander opened the summer campaign with the evacuation of Philadelphia. He then crossed the Delaware and reached Monmouth on June 28th, in the vicinity of which place the American general was in considerable force. He made several attacks on the rear of the British column which were uniformly repulsed; but as they occasioned delays, General Clinton determined to attack the enemy's main body, which was drawn up behind Monmouth Court House. The ground being favourable, the cavalry made several successful charges, and the Guards and Grenadiers advanced rapidly on the hostile front, which, after a vigorous resistance, at length gave way. The enemy, however, re-formed, but in order so good and on ground so strong that General Clinton did not push the attack and withdrew the troops. Marching during the night, the column next morning reached New York. The loss incurred in this by no means satisfactory affair was three officers and fifty-six soldiers killed, and sixteen officers, seven sergeants, and 137 rank and file wounded.

In the beginning of September an enterprise was prepared under the direction of General Grey, who embarked with the Grenadiers, Light Infantry Brigade, and the Royal Highlanders, for the purpose of proceeding to the Acushnet river to destroy a great assemblage of privateers, which with their prizes lay at New Plymouth. This expedition was completely successful. The troops landed on the banks of the Acushnet river on September 5th, and by noon the following day the whole force was re-embarked, after having destroyed seventy vessels, and all the stores, cargoes, wharves, etc., along the whole extent of the river.

The winter of 1778 was mainly a season of rest; but in February, 1779, Colonel Stirling with a detachment of the Guards and the Royal Highlanders attacked and took a post at Elizabeth Town. In April the Highland regiment was employed in an expedition to the Chesapeake, to destroy the stores and merchandise at Portsmouth in Virginia. In the summer of 1779 Colonel Stirling became an aide-de-camp to the King and a brigadier-general; and the command of the Royal Highland Regiment devolved on Lieutenant-Colonel Charles Graham. This officer had served in the regiment during the whole of his military life, having joined as an ensign in September, 1760. With his own regiment and a detachment of Fraser's Highlanders, under Major Ferguson, he was entrusted with the commands of Stony Point and Verplanks. In October both of those posts were withdrawn, and the regiment fell back on Greenwich, in the vicinity of New York.

In the autumn of this year there befell the Royal Highland Regiment a misfortune from which it did not recover for several years. A draft of 150 men, for the most part the sweepings of London and Dublin, was despatched for the regiment by order of the Inspector-General at Chatham. They were of the most depraved character, and of habits so dissolute that one-half of them were unfit for service. Fifteen died on the voyage and seventy-five went straight from the transports to the hospital. As a contrast it is on record that only three years earlier the three battalions of the 42nd and of Fraser's Highlanders embarked for America 3,248 strong; during a passage of more than three months not a man died; there were only a few sick, and those not dangerously. The infusion of ingredients so degraded could scarcely fail to impair the characters and sink the habits of men who held their self-respect as a cherished possession; and in consequence of strong representations made by Colonel Stirling to the commander-in-chief, those men were drafted into the 26th Regiment in exchange for an equal number of Scotsmen. Their introduction into the regiment would have destroyed the influence which for nearly forty years had protected the Highlanders from contamination. During that long period there were few courts-martial, and for many years no instance of corporal punishment had occurred. So high was their sentiment of honour that, as we have already said, "if a soldier was brought to the halberts, he was regarded as degraded, and little more good was to be expected of him. After being publicly disgraced he could no longer associate with his comrades; and in several instances the privates of a company had subscribed from their pay to procure the discharge of an obnoxious person." But when punishments were found indispensable for men newly introduced, and the men of the regiment became more habituated to the sight, the sense of honour was necessarily blunted.

The HISTORICAL RECORD of the regiment states :—An illustration of the strong national feeling with which the corps was regarded by the Highlanders occurred in April, 1779, when two detachments of recruits belonging to the 42nd and 71st regiments arrived at Leith for the purpose of embarking to join their respective regiments in North America. Being told that they were to be turned over to the 80th and 82nd, the Edinburgh and Hamilton regiments, the men remonstrated and declared firmly that they were determined to serve only in the corps for which they had enlisted. After some negotiation troops were sent to Leith to convey the refractory Highlanders as prisoners to Edinburgh Castle, should they persist in their determination. As they were resolute, attempts were made to enforce the orders; but the Highlanders rushed to arms, and a desperate conflict ensued in which a captain of a Fencible regiment and nine men were killed and thirty-one soldiers wounded. Being at last overpowered, the mutineers were carried to the castle. In the following May three of those prisoners, Charles Williamson and Archibald Macivor, soldiers of the 42nd, and Robert Budge, soldier of the 71st, were brought before a court-martial, "charged with having been guilty of a mutiny at Leith, and of having instigated others to be guilty of the same, in which mutiny several of his Majesty's subjects were killed and many wounded."

Their reasons for resisting the orders to embark were thus stated in their defence :—" The prisoners Archibald Macivor and Charles Williamson had enlisted as soldiers in the 42nd, an old Highland regiment wearing the Highland dress. Their native language was Gaelic—the one being a native of the northern parts of Argyllshire and the other of the western parts of Inverness-shire, where the language of the country is Gaelic only. They have never used any other language, and are so ignorant of the English tongue that they cannot avail themselves of it for any purpose of life. They have always been accustomed to the Highland dress, so far as never to have worn breeches, a thing so inconvenient and even so impossible for a Highlander to do, that when the Highland dress was prohibited by Act of Parliament, though the philibeg was one of the forbidden parts of the dress, yet it was necessary to connive at it, provided only that it was made of a stuff of one colour and not of tartan, as is well known to all acquainted with the Highlands, particularly with the more mountainous parts of the country. Those circumstances made it more necessary for them to serve in a Highland regiment only, as they neither could have understood the language nor have used their arms or marched in the dress of any Lowland regiment."

The other prisoner, Budge, stated that he was a native of the upper parts of Caithness, and being ignorant of the English language and accustomed to wear the Highland garb, he enlisted to serve in Fraser's Highlanders, and in no other regiment. In continuation, the three prisoners stated that " when they arrived at Leith they were informed by the officer who had conducted them that they were now to consider the officers of the 82nd Regiment, wearing the Lowland dress and speaking that tongue, as their officers. They were told that they must immediately join the Hamilton and Edinburgh regiments. A great number of the detachment represented, without any disorder or mutinous behaviour, that they were altogether unfit for service in any other corps than Highland ones, particularly that they were incapable of wearing breeches as a part of their dress. At the same time they declared their willingness to be transferred to any Highland regiment, or to continue to serve in the regiments into which they had been regularly enlisted. But no regard was paid to those remonstrances, which, if they had had an opportunity, they would have laid before the commander-in-chief. The idea naturally suggested itself to them that they should insist on serving in the regiment in which they had been enlisted. They accordingly drew up under arms on the shore of Leith, each detachment by itself. Had the orders to carry them prisoners to the castle been explained to them, they would have submitted, and with proper humility have laid their case before those who could have given them redress. But, unfortunately, the sergeant who undertook to explain to them in Gaelic represented that they were immediately to embark as part of the Hamilton regiment, but which they with diffidence maintain that they did not conceive they could lawfully do." After the defence was read, " Captain Innes of the 71st Regiment showed an attestation to the court, which he said was in the uniform style of the attestations for that regiment; and it expressly bore that the persons thereby attested were to serve in the 71st Regiment, commanded by General Simon Fraser of Lovat, and that they were to serve for three years only, or during the continuance of the present war."

The prisoners were sentenced to be shot, having been guilty of mutiny; but the King gave them a free pardon, "in full confidence that they would endeavour, by prompt and loyal behaviour, to atone for this atrocious offence." The prisoners, along with the rest of the detachment, joined the second battalion of the 42nd, and justified the confidence of his Majesty by steadiness and good conduct in the regiment.

## CHAPTER XIV.

### AMERICA AND HOME.

Fortune of war adverse to Great Britain. Siege and surrender of Charlestown. Lieutenant Grant's remarkable wound. Regiment's re-embarkation for New York. Loyalty of Highland Regiment; no deserter in five years. Reduction to eight companies. Casualties during War of Independence. Six years' stay in Halifax. Presentation of new colours there. Return to England, October, 1789, after fourteen years' foreign service. Service in England and Scotland. Troubles in Ross-shire and Lowlands.

IN the end of 1779, after five long years of bitter struggle between the mother country and her revolted children, the fortune of war was becoming more and more adverse to Great Britain. Sir Henry Clinton was not the man to reverse the situation, but he was anxious to be doing something, and he resolved on making an attack on Charlestown, the chief town of the province of South Carolina. Leaving General Knyphausen in the New York command, he embarked the troops destined for the Charlestown enterprise, and sailed from New York on December 26th. Such was the severity of the weather that it was not until February 11th, 1780, when the troops disembarked on John's Island, thirty miles from Charlestown. Several of the transports had been driven from their course, others were captured, and a great proportion of the horses died on the voyage, which never should have been undertaken at a season so tempestuous. So difficult were the approaches and so cautious the movements of the general, that it was the 29th of March before the force crossed the Ashley river. On the following day it encamped in face of the American lines, and on April 1st broke ground before Charlestown. The American general Lincoln had so strengthened the place that the siege proved a tedious and difficult operation. Clinton realised that his enterprise was more serious than he had anticipated, and ordered down from New York the Royal Highlanders and the Queen's Rangers who joined him in the middle of April. The siege plodded on until May 12th, when the garrison surrendered prisoners of war. The British loss was seventy-six killed and 189 wounded; that of the Royal Highlanders Lieutenant Macleod and nine privates killed, and Lieutenant Charles Grant and fourteen privates wounded. The wound of Lieutenant Grant was remarkable for its severity. A six-pound ball struck him in the back in a slanting direction near the right shoulder, carrying away the entire scapula with several other bones, and leaving the whole surrounding parts in such a condition that he was allowed to remain on the ground, the only care of the surgeons being to alleviate his state for the short time they believed he could survive. To their surprise he was found alive the following morning, free of fever and all bad symptoms. In a short time he completely recovered, and served in the army for many years in perfect health.

The Royal Highlanders re-embarked for New York on June 4th, and after being stationed in different parts of the province went into winter quarters, where was received a draft of 100 recruits, all young men in full vigour and ready for immediate service. The regiment was not again employed on active service during the remainder of the war, which came to an end in November, 1782. On April 28th of that year Major Graham became lieutenant-colonel of the Royal Highland Regiment, in succession to Colonel Stirling who was promoted to the colonelcy of the Fraser Highlanders. During the five years of active service in which the regiment was engaged in North America, the men preserved so completely their original habits of temperance and moderation that, while rum and other spirituous liquors were served out daily to the other troops, the Highlanders received their allowance every third or fourth day in the same manner as the officers. Desertions from other corps were frequent, but in this regiment it was otherwise : not a man deserted, and of more than a thousand men of whom the corps consisted there was but one man punished during the whole of those five years. One man who had been refused leave of absence went away, settled his business, and returned to the regiment. For this defiance of orders he was tried and punished. But the unfortunate man endured a double punishment. The soldiers considered the honour of the corps tarnished by one of their number being thus publicly brought to shame; and such was the horror of the castigation and of the disgrace attached to it that not a soldier in the regiment would mess with him. But in the interval between the end of the active service of the regiment and its removal from the United States in 1783, while the regiment was quartered at Paulus Hook a marked deterioration was unfortunately evinced, and some occurrences took place which were equally unexampled and disgraceful. The prevailing idea was that the men from the 26th Regiment, who had been prisoners at Saratoga, had been seduced while in the hands of the Americans by promises of grants of land, and several men deserted to the enemy. One of these deserters, Anderson by name, was taken, tried, and shot—the first instance of an execution in the regiment since the mutiny in 1743.

At the close of the long war the establishment of the regiment was reduced to eight companies of fifty men each. The officers of the ninth and tenth companies were not put on half pay, but were retained as supernumeraries in the regiment to fill up vacancies as they occurred. Many of the men were discharged at their own request, and their places were supplied by those who desired to remain in America in preference to returning home. During the War of Independence the losses of the regiment were eighty-three killed and 286 wounded.

In October, 1783, the regiment was sent to Halifax where it remained until 1786, when six companies were removed to the island of Cape Breton, the remaining two companies being despatched to the island of St. John. In this year the second battalion was formed into a separate regiment and numbered the 73rd, with its facings green instead of the Royal blue. The 73rd has always upheld the character which it had honourably acquired as foster-brother to the old Highland Regiment, and when the system of linked battalions was put in force in 1872 the 73rd rejoiced greatly to be reinstated as the second battalion of the grand old corps which now stands in the Army List as "The Black Watch (Royal Highlanders)."

In consequence of preparations for war with Holland two companies were added to the regiment, to the command of which Captains William Johnstone and Robert Christie respectively succeeded, having purchased the commissions declined by the Lieutenants

Stewart. Lieutenant Robert Macdonald, brother of Macdonald of Sanda, from half-pay of Fraser's Highlanders, and Ensign James Rose, were appointed lieutenants, and Ensigns David Stewart (afterwards Major-General, and author of the "Sketches") and James Stewart, nephew of the Earl of Moray, ensigns on the augmentation. In May, 1787, Lord John Murray died in his seventy-seventh year, and in the forty-second year of his command of the regiment. At the time of his death he was the senior officer of the army. Till he was disabled by old age, he was the friend and supporter of every deserving officer and soldier. He had served in the Netherlands in 1747 at the relief of Hulst, the defence of Fort Sandberg, and the retreat to Welshorden, and subsequently as a volunteer in the defence of the lines of Bergen-op-Zoom. He was succeeded in the command of the Royal Highlanders by Major-General Sir Hector Munro on June 1st, 1787. Sir Hector was the descendant of the ancient Ross-shire family of Novar. He was a very distinguished officer. In 1777 he became commander-in-chief in the Madras Presidency, and two years later his services in India were rewarded with the Knighthood of the Bath.

On January 1st, 1784, new colours were presented at Halifax to the regiment by Major-General John Campbell, who made an eloquent address in which in glowing language he spoke of the numerous engagements in which the regiment had won honour and renown, and he concluded by urging upon the Highland soldiers ever to study to sustain the high character of their regiment, and never to forget that they were the citizens and defenders of a great country, and Christians as well as soldiers.

In August, 1789, the regiment embarked for England

and landed at Portsmouth in October after an absence from home of fourteen years. Marching northward it passed over Finchley Common of chequered memory. Numbers flocked to see the historic regiment, no Highland corps having been in that vicinity since 1745, when this identical regiment, then the 43rd, or Sempill's Highlanders, was stationed there for a few weeks on its return from Flanders. The regiment passed the winter in Tynemouth Barracks, where it was reinforced by 245 young recruits, raised by the officers who had remained at home for that purpose. About this time the black leather belts for the bayonet were laid aside and white buff belts were supplied instead. Officers' epaulets, which were formerly very small, were enlarged considerably.

In May, 1790, the regiment marched to Scotland by way of Berwick and Edinburgh. In Scotland, as in England, its reception was cordial, but not so enthusiastic as on later occasions when the regiment, as in 1802 and 1816, came home direct from fighting the battles of the country. The service in America had been far away and not very stirring; and the period of eight years' peace abroad before the arrival of the regiment at home weakened the memories of earlier service in the field. Fortunately its stay in Glasgow was short, since ill-judged hospitality on the part of the citizens of that good city tempted the soldiers to forget themselves in the matter of ardent spirits, with the result that the discipline of the regiment became somewhat relaxed. General Stewart observes that a removal in November to Edinburgh Castle cured the evil. There may have been some sarcasm in this remark, since in the matter of strong drink, according to general acceptation, from Glasgow to Edinburgh is simply " out of the frying-pan into the fire."

In consequence of the expectation of a rupture with Spain, the establishment of the regiment was ordered to be augmented in 1790; but owing to troubles in the Highlands recruiting was not successful. It was therefore fortunate for the Royal Highland Regiment that in this year its strength was increased by an independent company, consisting of a fine body of young Highlanders recruited by the Marquis of Huntly, which joined the regiment with his lordship, who had exchanged with Captain Alexander Grant. After being reviewed in June, 1791, by Lord Adam Gordon, the regiment marched to the north in the following October. It was considerably broken up during the winter. Headquarters were at Fort George; one company was stationed at Dundee, another at Montrose, two at Aberdeen, and one at Banff. The regiment was re-assembled at Fort George in the spring of 1792, whence it marched in the summer to Stirling, where it was reviewed by Lieutenant-General Leslie and then returned to its former stations along the north-eastern coast. The regiment, however, had scarcely returned to quarters when it was ordered to proceed by forced marches into Ross-shire, where disturbances had occurred among the farmers and peasantry, of whom great numbers had been evicted from their farms and crofts in consequence of the system of converting vast tracts of country into pasturage for sheep. It appeared that after those wholesale ejectments such of the people as had been permitted to remain as cottagers and crofters had risen in a body, gathered together all the sheep which had been placed by the great stock farmers on the tenements and farms which they themselves had formerly held, and drove the flocks before them beyond the precincts of the county; imagining in their simplicity and despair that if the sheep would thus be got quit of they would be reinstated in their original holdings. Yet few acts of violence or outrage were committed; though pressed with hunger the peasants were guilty of no depredations. When the Royal Highlanders marched into Ross the people had already separated and disappeared of their own accord. Happy was it that the affair ended thus, as the task of turning their arms against their own kith and kin must have been to the last degree painful to the best feelings of the soldiers, as well as laying a great strain on their discipline. As to the cruel evictions, one may recall the biting words which the patriot Galgacus addressed to Agrippa: "Solitudinem faciunt, pacem appellant." Eighteen of the so-called rioters were sent to Inverness for trial. They were eloquently defended by an advocate of their own race; but as their conduct was illegal and their offence clearly proved, they were found guilty and condemned to be transported to Botany Bay. It would appear, however, that though the legality of the verdict and sentence could not be questioned, this circumstance did not carry along with it public opinion; which, probably, was the cause that the escape of the prisoners was in a manner connived at, for they disappeared from prison, no one knew how, and were never inquired after or molested.

The summer and autumn passed with the Royal Highland Regiment in marching and countermarching through Ross-shire; and in the course of the following winter it was not less actively employed against the disaffected Lowlanders, who were rioting turbulently, and hanging, drowning, and burning the effigies of those whom they regarded as their political oppressors. This distasteful work ended when, hostilities having been declared against France, the regiment was assembled at

Montrose, in April, 1793, preparatory to marching southward. The establishment had been ordered to be augmented to 750 men, but the recruiting was very unsuccessful. It was now no longer, as in 1756 and 1776, that the regiment could be completed to its strength of 1,100 in a few weeks—as quickly, indeed, as they could be gathered in from the outlying districts. Nor was it as in 1755, when the Laird of Mackintosh raised a complete company in a single morning. The self-same regiment in 1793 must have gone on foreign service with scarcely 400 men, had not orders been issued for raising independent companies. Two of those raised by Captain David Hunter of Burnside, and Alexander Campbell of Ardchattan, were ordered to join the Black Watch. On the whole those were good men, but they were not of the same description as those who in former times were so eager to join the standard of the old regiment.

## CHAPTER XV.

### FLANDERS. 1794-95.

June, 1794, regiment embarked for Flanders. Stupendous preparations on the part of France. March from Ostend to junction at Malines with Duke of York's army. Hon. Arthur Wellesley, afterwards Duke of Wellington, in command of brigade. His first commission and subsequent connection, through 73rd, with 42nd. Sharp fighting at Nymeguen, Thuyl, and adjacent places. The history of the "Red Heckle," related by eye-witnesses. State of English hospitals. Disastrous retreat from Holland to Bremen. Endurance of Highlanders. Return to England, and encamped at Danbury.

In May the regiment marched from Montrose to Musselburgh, and embarked from that port on the 8th for Hull, in which town the Highlanders occasioned great interest, as no plaids or bonnets had hitherto been seen in that region. The worthy "Tykes" showed them great hospitality; and so well had the regiment behaved, that after it had embarked for Flanders the town of Hull sent for each man a pair of shoes, a flannel shirt and worsted socks—a very seasonable kindness in a November encampment. From Gosport the regiment sailed for Ostend, landing there on October 1st; and two days later it joined his Royal Highness the Duke of York, then encamped in the vicinity of Menin. The 42nd, however, with three other regiments, were presently ordered to return to England, to join there an expedition then being prepared under their old commander in America, General Sir Charles Grey, against the French colonies in the West Indies. While the regiments lay in Ostend harbour the enemy pressed the town of Nieuwport so vigorously that immediate relief was demanded, since the place was garrisoned only by the 53rd Regiment and a small battalion of Hessians. Sir Charles Grey and General Thomas Dundas hurried to Ostend, and the 42nd, with the light companies of the other regiments, was disembarked and marched on to Nieuwport. The enemy had kept up a fire so heavy that upwards of 400 houses were destroyed or damaged; but on the appearance of the British reinforcement, after having maintained a brisk fire throughout the night they departed at daylight in great haste, leaving several cannon and mortars with their ammunition. This sudden withdrawal gave great disappointment to many young soldiers of the light infantry, and the Highlanders were not less disappointed because of the loss of their opportunity of facing the enemy under such commanders as Generals Sir Charles Grey and Thomas Dundas. The losses were insignificant. After the retreat of the enemy the regiment was re-embarked for England to join the expedition in preparation against the West Indies; but on arriving at Portsmouth its destination was altered, and it was ordered to take part in an expedition which was being fitted out against the French coast, under the command of the Earl of Moira, afterwards Marquis of Hastings. Colonel Graham, who had commanded the regiment since 1781, was at this time promoted to a brigade command, and the command of the regiment devolved upon Major Dalrymple.

Although the expedition duly sailed on November 30th, no landing took place, and after remaining some time in Guernsey, it returned to Portsmouth in the beginning of January, 1794. The troops remained in

England until June 18th, when they were re-embarked for Flanders under the command of the Earl of Moira, and landed at Ostend on the 26th. During the preceding winter and spring, France had been making stupendous preparations. She had mustered a force more than 200,000 strong, and provided it with a vast accumulation of stores and artillery in anticipation of imminent war in Flanders. The partial defection of Prussia after having accepted the British subsidies augmented the difficulties of the situation; and the allied armies found themselves in a very precarious position, more especially the comparatively small section which belonged to the command of the Duke of York at Malines. The French Convention sent into Flanders its ablest commanders; such men as Pichegru, Jourdan, and Moreau, who, exasperated by their defeats at Cambray, Landrecy, Cateau-Cambresis, and Tournay, were determined to bring into the field the utmost strength which they could command. To meet those hostile advances, the original destination of the force under Lord Moira was changed to the arena of Flanders, which has aptly been termed "the cock-pit of Europe," and, sailing for Ostend, it landed there on June 26th. This re-inforcement consisted of ten regiments, aggregating 7,000 men, and including the Royal Highlanders.

The alternatives before Lord Moira were either to hold Ostend, and stand a siege against an enemy which had already reduced Ypres and Thourout and was preparing to advance upon him, or to fight his way through the enemy and join hands with the Duke of York. He resolved to quit Ostend, and to resort to the active offensive. The stores and garrison of Ostend were embarked just as the advanced guard of the enemy entered the place. The troops were stationed under arms, in light marching order, on the dunes in the vicinity; the officers left all their baggage behind, except what they carried on their backs. The force moved off on the evening of the 28th, and after a halt ten miles from Ostend, resumed its march at midnight towards Ostaker, and reached Alost on July 3rd. While halted in the streets of Alost a regiment of hostile cavalry dashed into the town *ventre à terre*, and being mistaken for Hessians, was allowed to push forward to the marketplace, but was soon driven back by the 8th Light Dragoons and the picquets. On the 9th the force joined the Duke of York's army at Malines. The march from Ostend had been fatiguing; but so well had it been conducted that a very superior enemy commanded by Vandamme, attempted nothing except the dash into Alost. A series of petty skirmishes were carried on until Lord Moira resigned his command on July 20th, and was succeeded by Lieutenant-General Ralph Abercromby, to whom the command of the third brigade, in which were the Highlanders and Guards, was assigned with the reserve.

That able officer, on the tidings that the enemy were in possession of Boxtel, marched on September 14th with the reserve to compel them to evacuate that position. The third brigade, now under command of Lieutenant-Colonel the Hon. Arthur Wellesley of the 33rd Regiment, marched on the early morning of the 15th to join the brigade of Guards. When the three bodies concentrated as Boxtel was approached, it was clear that the enemy were in too great force in the place to justify an attack with any prospect of success.

It was on this occasion that the Royal Highlanders first saw him under whom in later years they were to fight so often and so bravely in campaign after campaign of the memorable Peninsular war. Almost by a hair's-breadth the old Highland Regiment missed the honour of being able to rank Arthur Wellesley among the officers of the gallant old "Forty-Twa." Wellington's first commission in the British army, as an ensign in the 73rd Regiment, bears date March 7th, 1787. The 73rd was originally the second battalion of the 42nd. It became a separate corps with green facings instead of the Royal blue, under the denomination of the 73rd Regiment, and its first commanding officer was Sir George Osborn. It achieved its independent existence in Dinapore in Bengal, on April 18th, 1786. Wellington received his ensign's commission in the 73rd Regiment while the regiment was still in Dinapore. It was in the home dépôt of the 73rd that Wellington, then the Hon. Arthur Wellesley, was initiated into the mysteries of the goose-step at the age of eighteen, on his return from the celebrated military school of Angers in France. On December 2nd of the same year he was promoted to a lieutenancy in the 76th Regiment, and after numerous changes to a lieutenancy in the 13th Light Dragoons (now Hussars). The interest of his brother Lord Mornington (afterwards Marquis Wellesley, Governor-General of India) was exerted to advance his progress in the army, and in 1793 he obtained his majority, and a few months later the lieutenant-colonelcy of the 33rd Regiment, now the Duke of Wellington's (West Riding) Regiment. In the spring of 1796 the 33rd went to India. Delayed by severe illness, the colonel did not accompany it; but on his recovery he took passage on a fast sailing-ship, overtook his regiment at the Cape, and landed with it at Calcutta in July, 1797. He first saw his original regiment, the 73rd, when before Seringapatam. The 42nd first came under

Wellington's command after the battle of Vimiero, for which the regiment, coming from Gibraltar, was too late. Although Wellington was Irish by birth, his favourite staff officers and companions in the Peninsular war were such men as Sir George Murray, Sir John Macdonald, Sir Colin Campbell (his favourite aide-de-camp), and Colquhoun Grant, his famous scout. When the system of linked battalions came into force in 1872, the 73rd Regiment became again the second battalion of the regiment whose present title is the Black Watch (Royal Highlanders); and thus that corps may claim a special connection with the Great Duke in the earliest period of his military career.

Various unimportant movements took place up to November 6th, when the army crossed the Waal at Nymeguen; and in this position there were several smart engagements until the morning of the 20th, when the enemy made a general attack on the advanced posts of the British army. They were repulsed, and the enemy were driven back with great gallantry; but the 37th Regiment, mistaking a detachment of the enemy for Rohan's hussars, allowed them to approach too closely. In consequence of this error, that gallant regiment sustained a severe loss in officers and men. On the 27th and 28th the enemy renewed their assaults on the outposts; and in a hostile attempt on Fort St. André General Abercromby was wounded. By incessant attacks in superior force the British outposts were finally driven in, and the enemy established themselves in front of Nymeguen and began to erect batteries preparatory to a siege. It was determined to attempt the destruction of those works; and on November 4th Lieutenant-General de Burgh, with a force of six line regiments supported by two battalions of Swiss in the Dutch service and some dragoon regiments, undertook this duty. The works were partially destroyed after a brave resistance on the part of the enemy. They quickly repaired their batteries; and as they continued their approaches with unabated determination, it was found necessary to evacuate the town. The British loss was not severe—one sergeant and thirty-one rank and file were killed; and eleven officers, ten sergeants, and 149 rank and file were wounded.

After this evacuation, which occurred on November 7th, the army was cantoned along the banks of the Waal. The troops suffered greatly from the severity of the weather and the lack of necessaries, as the clothing for the year had not been received. So intense was the frost that the enemy crossed the river on the ice, and availing themselves of their superior strength began active operations. As they threatened the towns of Culenborg and Gorcum, it was resolved to force them to re-pass the Waal; and about 8,000 British troops, among them the 3rd Brigade, moved against them on December 13th. The French were in possession of Thuyl, the access to which was flanked by batteries in position on the island of Bommel; and the place itself was surrounded by entrenchments. Those obstacles were surmounted, and the French were compelled to recross the Waal with the loss of a considerable number of men and several guns. The British loss was comparatively slight. The enemy, however, were not content. They again crossed the river on January 4th, 1795, and retook Thuyl. General Walmoden sent instructions to Generals David Dundas and Dulwich to drive them back, but they proved to be too strong. They attacked General Dundas at Gildermalsen, but were received with great firmness, and were repulsed with the loss of 200 men. The British lost three privates killed, and one general officer (Sir Robert Lawrie), two captains, one subaltern, and fifty-four privates wounded; the loss of the 42nd being one private killed and Lieutenant-Colonel Lamont and seven privates wounded.

An incident occurred in the course of this combat which is one of the most cherished traditions of the Royal Highland Regiment. For a century every officer and man serving in that regiment has worn in his feather bonnet the historical "red heckle," or, as it used to be termed in the early years of the century, the "red feather." Much has been said, and more has been conjectured, regarding the exploit on account of which the "red heckle" was awarded as a distinctive mark to be worn in the feather bonnets of the regiment, but comparatively few are aware of the origin of the distinction. The bare narrative of the affair is as follows:—On January 4th, 1795, the British retired upon the village of Gildermalsen, where the 42nd and several other regiments halted and formed up to cover the retreat through the village. The French cavalry, however, cut through the retreating picquets, and attacking the regiments holding Gildermalsen, met with a severe repulse. As the French horsemen retired they seized two guns which had been posted in front of the village and abandoned by the picquets, and were dragging them off, when the 42nd, under Major Dalrymple, charged with great impetuosity, re-took the guns, and brought them safely into the village. For their gallantry on this occasion the Royal Highlanders were rewarded with a distinctive badge—the "red heckle," or vulture plume.

On dingy paper and faded ink there now lies before the writer the quaint and honest narrative by a long since dead and gone soldier of the "Forty-Twa," of the affair which won for his regiment the "red heckle," or, as he styles it, the "red feather." The chronicler has not dated his story, but he has appended his name, "Rowland Cameron, pensioner, 42nd Regiment." And the following is his narrative, told in his own words:—

"A movement of the army having taken place on the last days of December, 1794, the 42nd Regiment, quartered at Thiel [Thuyl], received orders to march late on the night of 31st December, towards Bomell [Bommel], distant about twenty miles on the opposite [south] side of the river Waal, and arrived about four o'clock, 1st January, 1795, near the bank of the river, having taken a circuitous route, as also a number more regiments, and rested till daybreak, when an attack was made, and drove the French across the river on the ice, and held a position on the bank of the river till the evening of the 3rd, when a partial retreat took place, leaving strong picquets. The picquets were overpowered by the French and obliged to retreat [northward] towards the village of Guildermansen [Gildermalsen], where the 42nd and other Corps were stationed. The cavalry of the French pushed their way on the retreating picquets to the very Ranks, some of which fell into our hands, a Trumpeter of which remained with the regiment for some time after our arrival in England, and which was given over to the York Rangers for a Trumpeter at the formation of that corps.

"The 11th Light Dragoons [now Hussars] were stationed in front of the village to cover the retreat of the picquets with their two field-pieces, and instead of resisting the charge of the French cavalry, they immediately retreated at a furious Rate to the rear of the village, leaving the guns in possession of the French cavalry, who commenced dragging them off. An aide-de-camp [Major Rose] came and ordered the Commanding Officer [Major Dalrymple] of the 42nd Regiment to advance and re-take the guns of the 11th Dragoons, which was immediately complied with, with the loss of one man killed and three wounded.

"The Guns were dragged in by the Corps as the harness had been cut and the Horses disabled; there was no notice taken of this affair at the time, as all was bustle and confusion. A further retreat took place on the 5th to Bueherun [Buren], where the Prince of Orange had a palace, which the 27th, 28th, and 42nd Regiments occupied for the 6th and 7th, and on the 8th January, 1795, commenced a retreat across the Rhine, and continued it until early in April, when the British army embarked at Bremalie [Bremen or Bremerhafen] in Hanover, for England, and landed at Harwich. Much had been said and conjectured about the conduct of the 11th Dragoons on the 4th January, 1795; and although it was rumoured that some distinctive mark was to be awarded to the 42nd Regiment, it never was thought that the transfer of the Red Feather from the 11th Dragoons to the Corps was to be the distinctive mark conferred. The 11th Dragoons were substituted with a White Feather and yellow Top. On the 4th June, 1795, when quartered at Royston, near Cambridge, after fireing three Rounds in Honour of H.M. George 3rd's birthday, a box containing the Feathers arrived on the Common, which were distributed to the Officers and Men; the Commanding Officer giving a Speech on the Subject of which the Honour of Wearing the Red Feather was conferred on the 42nd Regiment for their gallant conduct on the 4th January, 1795.

"The Officers and Men placed the Feathers in their

Bonnets and marched into Royston, and on the evening of the 4th June were paid the Arrears due for Eighteen Months, with a caution to keep close to their own Billets and be regular."

Pensioner Cameron adds: "I have seen some time ago in a newspaper that the Red Feather was awarded for their exploits in Egypt. How could that be? The Red Feather floated over the heads of the 42nd men in the West Indies and taking Minorca long before the exploits that took place in Egypt. It will not be long," he remarks with feeling, "till there will be but few who can give any account of How, Where or When the transfere took place, but I daresay there are individuals still at Royston who remembers shareing in the Washing of the Red Feather, 4th June, 1795."

Another description of the winning of the "red feather" by the gallantry of the 42nd has been preserved, the recorder being a man in the ranks, participating in the honour achieved by the regiment. Private Andrew Dowie is more succinct than his comrade, Rowland Cameron, but he describes the incident more vividly. "On January 1st, 1795," so writes Andrew while a pensioned veteran, "our army consisting of the 42nd, 78th, 80th, and 19th," probably a brigade, "drove the French again across the Waal; the 42nd retired to Guildermaslen, about three miles to the rear. The French crossed a second time, and attacked the 78th in our [42nd] front; the 11th Light Dragoons covering the 78th with two pieces of cannon. The French being very superior in numbers pressed the 78th so hard that they were obliged to give way; the cavalry also giving way, leaving their guns, which the enemy turned upon us. In the affair General Sir Robert Lowrie [Lawrie] received a severe rub on the right cheek, and was along with Sir David Dundas when he

[Sir David] called out 'Forty-Second! for God's sake and for the honour of your country retake those guns!' Two companies were sent out which were repulsed; other two companies were then sent out and succeeded in recapturing them with great loss [to the French]. Lieutenant James Jonathan Fraser commanded our company in the absence of Captain Anstruther; on the guns being brought in, General Sir David Dundas called out, 'Forty-Second, the 11th Dragoons shall never wear the red plume on their helmets any more, and I hope the 42nd will carry it so long as they are the Black Watch!' I heard Sir David pronounce those words; when we arrived in Essex we got the red heckle." Andrew was a few miles out in his geography—Royston is in Cambridgeshire.

In 1822, because of an erroneous direction in a book of dress for the guidance of the army, some of the other Highland regiments considered that they too had a right to wear "a red vulture feather." The 42nd, however, remonstrated, and its representations to headquarters resulted in the following memorandum:—

"*For officers commanding Highland Regiments.*

"HORSE GUARDS, 20*th August*, 1822.

"The Red Vulture feather prescribed by the recent regulations for Highland regiments is intended to be worn exclusively by the Forty-Second Regiment; other Highland Corps will be allowed to continue to wear the same description of feather that may have been hitherto in use.

"H. TORRENS, *Adjutant-General.*"

The severity of the weather, and the heavy and prolonged duties which pressed on the British troops in consequence of the superior numbers and successive reinforcements of the enemy, were such as few constitutions could endure for any length of time. It was therefore determined to fall back and take up a more defensive position behind the Leck. During the preliminary movements in execution of this operation the enemy assailed the troops under Lord Cathcart. Each force alternately attacked and was repulsed four times in succession, till at length the enemy abandoned the contest and retreated with considerable loss. But the French were not to be denied; on the 10th they crossed the Waal in great force and pressed strenuously on the British troops, now reduced by disease and accumulated hardships, of which the most distressing was the state of the hospitals, for it was regarded as a certainty that whoever entered hospital never came out except as a corpse. On the 14th Pichegru made a general attack along the whole line from Arnheim to Amerongen, and the British, after a stubborn resistance which lasted until nightfall, were at length forced to retire at all points. The sufferings of our soldiers during this cruel winter campaign were exceptionally severe because of the severity of the weather. The misery of the retreat to Deventer and thence across the province of Overyssel and through Western Hanover and Oldenburg, was such as had not then been experienced by any modern army, and has since been exceeded only by the French in their disastrous retreat from Moscow. There have been few situations where the courage, constancy, and temper of British soldiers have been more severely tried than in the concluding period of this unfortunate campaign, pursued by an enemy of more than thrice their numbers, and through regions so hostile that every house contained inveterate adversaries eager to refuse the meanest shelter to the harassed soldiers. Exhausted by an accumulation of obstacles and hardships, the army at length in the beginning of April reached Bremen in two divisions. There the hospitality of the inhabitants exhibited a noble contrast to the conduct of the peoples through whose country they had marched as they suffered, and whose malignant hatred little merited the forbearance with which they had been treated by the British. In the middle of April the regiment embarked for England. Its total loss from its landing at Ostend in the end of the preceding June was only twenty-five men killed and dead of disease; but several regiments had lost above 200 men from disease alone. The comparative immunity of the 42nd proved the superior capability of Highlanders to endure the vicissitudes of war and climate. Yet of the soldiers belonging to the 42nd, 300 had been recently recruited. It was true that those young men had a great advantage in forming themselves on the habits and example of the more experienced soldiers, of whom many still remained in the regiment who had served in America. The Highlanders on landing at Harwich marched to Chelmsford, and in June were encamped in the vicinity of Danbury under the command of General Sir William Medows.

In September the regiment was increased to a strength of 1,000 men, from several Highland regiments which had been raised in the preceding year, and which were now to be broken up and the men of them drafted into several regiments. General Stewart has remarked that although those drafts furnished many good and serviceable men, they were in many respects very inferior to former recruits. This difference of character was more particularly marked in their habits and manners in quarters than in their conduct in the field, which was always unexceptionable. Having been subject to a greater mixture of character than was usual in older

Highland battalions, those corps had lost much of their original manners and of that strict attention to their religious and moral duties which were wont to distinguish the Highland youths on quitting their native glens, and which, when in corps unmixed with men of different characters, they always retained. The intermixture from the disbanded corps, General Stewart lamented, produced a sensible change in the moral conduct and character of the regiment.

# CHAPTER XVI.

### WEST INDIES AND MINORCA. 1795-1800.

Regiment joined Abercromby's expedition against French West Indies, October, 1795. Disasters at starting—dispersal of fleet. Half of regiment driven to Gibraltar, where it remained; other half reached Barbadoes. Abercromby's care for troops. Surrender of Demerara and Berbice. Landing on St. Lucia in four divisions, Highlanders in Moore's division. Successful attacks on Morne Fortunée and Morne Chabot, and later on Morne Duchassaux. Prolonged struggle for the Vizie, with ultimate surrender of garrison. Insalubrity of St. Lucia. Awful mortality among troops. Moore's narrow escape. Abolition of drafting. Attack on St. Vincent. Surrender of French garrison. Major Graham's wound and the soldier's wife. Mortality of troops from May, 1796, to June, 1797, amounting to 264 officers and 12,387 soldiers. Attack and capture of Trinidad and St. Kitts. Regiment arrived home July, 1797, without a sick man. Sent first to Gibraltar and later to Minorca, where a large army was being accumulated.

In October, 1795, the Royal Highland Regiment joined the expedition under Lieutenant-General Sir Ralph Abercromby designed to accomplish the deliverance of the French West India Islands from the possession of the Republican Government. In fitting out this armament, an exemplary attention was paid to the comfort of the troops and to the preservation of their health. The medical staff, so essential an efficient accompaniment in all military enterprises, consisted of officers of talent, zeal, and experience. Ships of war were appropriated as transports; and several East Indiamen and a number of excellent and well-appointed West India ships were chartered for the same purpose. The troops were protected by flannel from the damps and chills of the tropical nights, more destructive to soldiers than is heat in a West India campaign. Abundant supplies of potatoes and other vegetables were procured for the use of the troops; the water was plentiful and sweet; and, in fine, nothing was wanting to contribute to their comfort when on board ship. The yellow fever having been very destructive in the West Indies during the two preceding years, many precautions were taken to guard the soldiers against its effects by a change of clothing and other measures. Among the alterations was the temporary doing away by the Highlanders of their plaids, kilts, and bonnets, the place of which was supplied by Russia duck pantaloons and round hats. On the subject of this change there was no little controversy. Some people argued that no species of dress was worse calculated for a tropical climate than the Highland garb; others, again, reprobated the pantaloons, which, it was held, when wetted by the frequent torrents of rain to which the men would necessarily be exposed, would cling to their legs and thighs, and before they were dried after one shower would be wet again by the next; and that thus by keeping the lower part of the body constantly damp, agues, rheumatism, and other kindred diseases would be generated. And as to the hat instead of the feather bonnet, since it was of coarse felt and cheap and trashy, the first rainfall would destroy its shape; it would then stick close to the men's heads, and would afford no protection against the sun; whereas the bonnet, being of thick woollen stuff and covered with feathers, formed a complete protection against the effects of a tropical sun, and made a warm and convenient nightcap without at all injuring its form. When the kilt and hose became wet, if they were taken off and wrung they might be immediately worn again with perfect safety. The mosquitoes were the most troublesome annoyance to be guarded against by men wearing the kilt, but as they seldom attack in daylight and only in certain places at night, that objection was not serious. Experience proved that neither the duck pantaloons nor the round felt hats were suited to a campaign in the West Indies.

The lieutenant-general commanding-in-chief was well supported by his principal subordinates. Major-General Charles Graham was the second in command; the other major-generals were Campbell of Monzie and Morshead; the brigadier-generals were Perryn, John Moore, Colin Mackenzie, the Hon. John Hope, afterwards Earl of Hopetoun (adjutant-general), and the Hon. John Knox (quartermaster-general). Lieutenant-Colonel Donald Macdonald of the 55th Regiment commanded the reserve, which consisted of eighteen companies of Grenadiers and the Royal Highland Regiment. All the officers named, including the commander-in-chief, were Scotsmen with the exception of Generals Morshead and Perryn; and three of them were Highlanders. The cavalry regiment was the 26th Light Dragoons, and apart from the reserve there were twenty infantry regiments, reckoning 16,479 bayonets. While this formidable expedition was being prepared at Portsmouth, another, intended also for the West Indies, was fitting out at Cork, the general officers belonging to which were Brigadier-Generals Keppel, Wilford, Churchill, Howe, and Whitelocke. It consisted of six light cavalry regiments mustering 2,600 men, and of seven infantry regiments amounting to 5,680 rank and file. The total force of the combined expeditions destined for the West Indies was 3,060 cavalry and 22,159 infantry. No part of the Highlands of Scotland is more broken and rugged than was the proposed theatre of war in Guadaloupe, St. Vincent, and Grenada. The cavalry were therefore totally useless; and the horses died so fast that in a few months the 26th Dragoons could not furnish horses to carry the headquarter despatches and orders. The force assembled for this enterprise exceeded in strength any armament which had previously set sail from England; and the departure of the vast fleet of more than three hundred transports, with a division of the Royal Navy acting as its convoy, was a spectacle calculated to impress the mind with a lofty idea of British power and British wealth. The day was brilliantly fine, the wind favourable, and the whole of the ships were clear of the Isle of Wight by sunset, excepting an East Indiaman with 500 men of the Highland Regiment on board. The vessel had been in collision and was obliged to put back for repairs, an accident which probably averted from her more serious injury; for the fleet was dispersed and driven back by a severe storm, several ships were wrecked, and many hundred lives were lost.

The next attempt to put to sea was not made until December 9th, when a favourable breeze seemed to promise a prosperous voyage; but on the 13th, as the fleet was clearing the Channel, a violent storm set in and continued with unabated violence for several weeks. The greater part of the fleet was dispersed, and the admiral returned to Portsmouth in the end of January, 1796, with about fifty sail. The rest of the fleet was scattered in various ports, with the exception of seventy-eight ships which managed to reach Barbadoes in a straggling manner. The destinations were changed of several ships which had returned to port. Five companies of the Highlanders, under the command of Lieutenant-Colonel Dickson, were later sent to Gibraltar;

K

and other destinations were given to six of the infantry regiments which had originally belonged to the expedition. The troops were removed from the disabled transports, and along with those in the others which had been forced into harbour, sailed with the commander-in-chief on February 14th. He arrived at Barbadoes on March 14th; but it was not until the same day that the admiral sailed from Portsmouth. On February 2nd, the first of the ships which had sailed on December 9th arrived, and then others came straggling in. On the 9th the *Middlesex* arrived with 500 of the Highlanders, so healthy that only two men were on the surgeon's list. Part of the newly arrived troops were despatched to reinforce the garrisons of St. Vincent and Grenada, which had suffered much from the enemy as well as from the insalubrity of the climate. The 63rd Regiment was ordered to St. Vincent, and detachments of the 8th and 88th to Grenada.

Sir Ralph Abercromby gave earnest attention to the health of his troops, still confined in the transports and exposed to the heat of a vertical sun in a West India harbour. His success affords a strong proof of the efficacy of ventilation, exercise, cleanliness, and mental occupation in averting the pernicious effects which must result from negligence and too close confinement in such a climate. Because of the delays of the voyage much of the best of the season for action had been lost; and further delay was caused by the non-arrival of the admiral. The earliest enterprise was a descent on the Dutch settlements of Demerara and Berbice, which surrendered on April 22nd to a part of the Cork division under Major-General Whyte with three regiments. As it was deemed imprudent to attempt the reduction of Guadaloupe, preparations were made for a landing on the island of St. Lucia. The admiral having arrived on the 22nd, the expedition promptly sailed and on the 26th was off St. Lucia. A change of brigades now occurred. Colonel Macdonald retained in the reserve all the companies of Grenadiers which had arrived, but the five Highland companies were put under the command of Brigadier-General Moore. The troops landed in four divisions; at Longueville Bay, Pigeon Island, Chock Bay, and Ance la Raze. The Highlanders under General Moore landed in a small bay close under Pigeon Island, and on the 27th the divisions of the army closed in upon Morne Fortunée, the chief post in the island. Before this eminence could be fully invested, it was necessary to carry Morne Chabot, a strong and commanding position threatening the principal approach. Attacks were made on two different points by detachments commanded by Generals Moore and the Hon. John Hope. General Moore advanced at midnight, and an hour later General Hope followed by a less circuitous route; but coming suddenly on the enemy sooner than he had anticipated, General Moore, after a short but smart resistance, carried the post; the enemy fleeing so precipitately that they could not be intercepted by General Hope, who came up precisely at the appointed time. On the following day, General Moore occupied Morne Duchassaux, and Major-General Morshead advancing from Ance la Raze, Morne Fortunée was thus entirely invested; but not without resistance on the part of the enemy, who attacked the advanced post of Colonel Macdonald so fiercely that several officers and about fifty Grenadiers had been killed or wounded.

To dispossess the enemy from the batteries which they had constructed on the Cul-de-Sac, General Morshead's division was ordered to advance against two batteries on the left, while General Hope with the five companies of Highlanders, the light infantry of the 57th, and a detachment of Rangers, supported by the 55th Regiment, was to attack the battery of Secke, close to the works of Morne Fortunée. The light infantry and rangers quickly expelled the enemy from the battery, but the divisions of Brigadier-General Perryn and Colonel Riddle had been obstructed in their advance, and the light infantry and rangers retired in their turn from the battery which they had so gallantly captured. General Hope's detachment lost the brave Colonel Malcolm killed, and General J. J. Fraser of the 42nd and a few men wounded. The other divisions suffered severely. Colonel Malcolm was a most promising young officer. When a lieutenant in the 45th Regiment in 1794, he was appointed by Sir Charles Grey to discipline a small corps of coloured troops, who had entered our service in Guadaloupe and Martinique. On every occasion they conducted themselves with much valour, and he had so secured their attachment to him that when he fell they crowded round him loudly lamenting their loss, which had so great an effect that their spirit seemed to die with their gallant leader, for they never afterwards distinguished themselves.

Notwithstanding the zeal and strenuous exertions of the sailors in dragging the guns across the ravines and up the acclivities of mountains and rocks, it was not until May 14th that the first battery was ready to open. In the night of the 17th the 31st Regiment was ordered to seize upon the Vizie, a fortified ridge under the principal fortress. The attempt failed, and the regiment had to retire with heavy loss; but the Grenadiers pushed forward in support and compelled the enemy to retire. For six days a constant fire was maintained between the batteries and the fort At length the 27th Regiment went to the front, and after a sharp struggle formed a lodgment within five hundred yards of the enemy. A sally in force from the fort was repulsed, and a suspension of hostilities was demanded and obtained, which was presently followed by a capitulation and the surrender of the whole island. The garrison evacuated all the strong places and became prisoners of war on the 29th. The British loss was two field officers, three captains, five subalterns, and 184 men killed, and four field officers, twelve captains, fifteen subalterns, and 523 men wounded. Thus was accomplished the second conquest of this island within two years—a conquest of no great account in itself in comparison with the blood and money expended in its acquisition, but of importance to the future security of our colonies.

This expedition strikingly illustrated the influence of the mind on bodily health, and the effect of mental activity in the prevention of disease. "During the operations," wrote General Stewart, "which from the nature of the country were exceptionally harassing, the troops continued remarkably healthy; but immediately after the cessation of hostilities they began to droop. The five companies of Highlanders, for example, who had landed 508 strong, sent few men to the hospital until the third day after the capitulation; but immediately after this event, so sudden was the failure of their health that upwards of sixty men were laid up within seven days. This collapse may be partly ascribed to the sudden transition from incessant activity to idleness, but its principal cause must have been the relaxation of the moral energies, after the excitement which had stimulated the men had subsided."

The commander-in-chief lost no time in completing

his arrangements for the accomplishment of the ultimate objects of the campaign. The 27th and 57th Regiments were assigned to the reinforcement of the garrison of Grenada; and the Buffs, 14th, 42nd, and 53rd Regiments were ordered to St. Vincent, then under the command of Major-General Hunter, with the 63rd, recently arrived from home, the 34th, 54th, 59th, and the 2nd West India Regiment. All those regiments with the exception of the 63rd, had been reduced by climate and were weak in numbers.

Scattered detachments of the enemy still continued to harbour in the woods of St. Lucia, having refused to surrender in terms of the capitulation; and Brigadier-General Moore, with the 31st, 44th, 48th, and 55th regiments and the Rangers and German Jägers, was appointed to garrison that island. That zealous officer penetrated into the most difficult recesses of the woods and compelled the enemy to surrender; but so destructive was the climate and so unwholesome the constant subsistence on salt provisions, that three-fourths of the troops were carried off before the end of the first year. General Moore himself, persevering to the last extremity, was at length removed on board ship, where, after a severe illness, he at length recovered. During the whole of those trying operations Moore's exertions had been unremitting. At least once every fourteen days he visited in person every post, of which there were a great many in different parts of the island. He was, in fact, almost always in the woods, so careless of any comfort and so anxious to show an example of privation to his men that he fared as they did, on salt pork and biscuit, and slept on a cloak under a bush. Several officers had obtained leave to visit other islands for change of air, and so many were dead or disabled that there was not a sufficient number for duty. Moore therefore issued orders that none, except in the last necessity, should quit St. Lucia. At length he was himself attacked, and when informed that if he did not go on board ship he could not survive four days, he referred his advisers to his orders, expressing his determination to remain at all risks; and it was not until he had become insensible that he was carried on board.

The mortality among the troops was awful. The 31st Regiment was almost annihilated, and after losing twenty officers the remainder were ordered to Barbadoes. On the arrival there of the skeleton of the regiment in December, 1796, a return of men fit for duty was sent to General Morshead who commanded in that island. There were only seventy-four men alive. Seven months previously the regiment had landed in St. Lucia 915 strong.

In those days the lot of the soldier had many disadvantages. Among others there prevailed a practice destructive of all hope that he could ever return to his native country. When a soldier, in virtue of a good constitution and regularity of conduct, had survived his comrades, instead of being rewarded by removal to a better climate or being sent back to his native country, he was moved from one regiment to another while life or the ability to serve remained. The hospital or the grave was thus very often the only termination of his career of service. Thus the remains of the fine flank battalion which had accompanied Sir Charles Grey to the West Indies in 1794, were drafted *en masse* into the 45th Regiment, which continued for sixteen years on the West India station. In the garrison of St. Lucia the men fit for duty of the 44th and 48th were drafted into the 55th, which was to remain in St. Lucia for an indefinite period. This practice of compulsory drafting was soon after this period abolished, thanks to the regulation established by the Duke of York, that no soldier should be removed from his regiment without his consent; so that he had a chance of returning to his native country. Experience showed that soldiers, when their feelings were consulted and the proper means adopted, were quite ready to remain in any climate or country where their services were required. An illustration of this willingness occurred at this very time. The 79th Highlanders, then in Martinique, were allowed to volunteer into the 42nd about to embark for England, with permission to such as wished to remain in the West Indies to volunteer into any corps on that station. A considerable number chose to remain, although they had the immediate prospect of returning home. Later, in 1802, the 14th Regiment, then quartered in Barbadoes, was ordered home, with directions that none should be drafted, but that liberty should be given to such as chose to remain to volunteer into any corps stationed in that island. General Greenfield, then commanding in the West Indies, ordered the regiment to parade and informed the men that they were to have their choice whether they would remain in the West Indies or embark for England. Standing in front, watch in hand, he gave them half an hour to make up their minds. Twenty-five minutes lasted without a man moving, when the general repeated that all were at liberty either to remain or to return home. Upwards of 500 men stepped out of the ranks and announced their determination to continue to serve in the West Indies. Had those men been ordered to leave their regiment and to be drafted in reinforcement of some other regiment, or to garrison the West India stations, they would have considered the measure as a harsh and unjust banishment; but when an option was given them, content reigned.

The next enterprise was against the island of St. Vincent. The expedition, consisting of the Buffs, 14th, 34th, 42nd, 53rd, 54th, 59th, and 63rd regiments, landed on June 8th, and on the 10th the enemy were attacked. They were in position on a lofty ridge called the Vizie, on which they had erected four redoubts which could be assailed only by a difficult approach. The troops, when within a short distance of this fortified ridge, were formed in two divisions, under Major-Generals Hunter and Morshead. Lieutenant-Colonel Dickens, with detachments of the 34th and 40th, took post on the opposite side of the ridge. Some field-pieces had been brought up and a fire was opened on the redoubts, which, however, continued with little result for some hours. Meanwhile, the Highlanders, with some Rangers, pushed forward up the wooded steep and got close to the nearest redoubt. The Buffs were then ordered up, when the whole force attacked, and in less than half-an-hour the enemy were driven from the first three redoubts in succession. Some of the Highlanders had got up close under the last and principal redoubt, and were ready to storm it when supported in more force; but the general, finding that he had the enemy in his power and wishing to spare the lives of his troops, recalled them, and offered terms of capitulation which were accepted, the conditions being that the enemy should embark as prisoners of war. The following night, however, several hundred of them broke the capitulation, made their escape into the woods, and joined their friends in the farther end of the island. The British loss was two captains, one ensign, one volunteer, four sergeants, one drummer, and thirty-one rank and file killed; two majors, one captain, four lieutenants, one ensign, one volunteer, fifteen sergeants, six drummers, and 111 rank and file wounded. The Highlanders had one sergeant and twelve rank and file killed; Lieutenant Simon Fraser, two sergeants, one drummer, and twenty-nine rank and file wounded. Among the wounded was a lieutenant of the 40th. A musket-ball had passed through his body, entering below his left breast, and coming out at his back. He fell at the top of a steep hill, which he had mounted with a small party but from which he was forced back. A sergeant who was much attached to the officer, anxious to carry his body away but unable to do so, took hold of a leg and dragged it after him more than a mile down the declivity, leaving it at the foot with the intention of returning at night to inter it. When he returned he found his officer alive and able to speak. The officer recovered, and in six weeks returned to England in perfect health.

The enemy who had retreated to the woods were immediately pursued. Lieutenant-Colonel Brent Spencer of the 40th, with 600 men, was detached to Mount Young; Lieutenant-Colonel Gower of the 63rd, with 200 men, to Owia; Lieutenant-Colonel Stewart of the 42nd, with the 42nd, to Colonarie; and Lieutenant-Colonel Samuel Graham to Rabaca. The enemy, though poor soldiers, were numerous, and military posts were established in regions possessed by the Caribs and brigands. On one occasion the men of a scouting detachment began to drop and continued to do so, till at length it was discovered that the fire came from the tree-tops immediately above. A handful of Caribs had run up the trees, and, lurking in the thick foliage, had commenced a fire which for a time was unperceived amidst the noise and constant firing kept up by the troops. As soon as it was discovered, a volley fired into the tree-tops brought down seven men, and the rest soon followed. A somewhat similar incident occurred during the Indian Mutiny. When the slaughter in the Secundrabagh was almost over, many of the soldiers lay down under a large peepul tree with a very bushy top, to enjoy its shade and quench their thirst from the jars of cool water set round the foot of the tree. An exceptional number of dead and wounded also lay under the tree, and this attracted the notice of an officer. Carefully examining the wounds, he found that in every case the men had evidently been shot from above. The officer called to a soldier to look if he could see anyone in the tree-top. The soldier had his rifle loaded, and stepping back, he carefully scanned the top of the tree. He almost immediately called out: "I see him, sir!" Cocking his rifle, he immediately fired, and down fell a body dressed in a tight-fitting red jacket and tight-fitting rose-coloured silk trousers; and the breast of the jacket bursting open with the fall, showed that the wearer was a woman. She was armed with a pair of heavy old-pattern cavalry pistols, one of which was in her belt still loaded, and her pouch was still half full of ammunition. From her perch in the tree, which had been carefully prepared before the attack, she had killed more than half a dozen men.

On another occasion a detachment commanded by Lieutenant-Colonel Graham, perceiving nothing through the thick foliage, advanced close up to a line of trees in luxuriant leafage. In an instant a fire was opened which laid the Colonel senseless and wounded several of his party. Some men returned in search of him, and carried to camp what was believed to be his dead body. But Graham survived, and his recovery from his wound was attended with an uncommon circumstance. The people, believing him to be dead, rather dragged than carried him over the rough channel of the river till they reached the sea-beach. Observing here that he was still alive, they put him in a blanket and proceeded in search of a surgeon. After travelling in this manner for four miles, they carried him to a military post occupied by a party of the 42nd. All the surgeons were out in the woods with the troops. Colonel Graham was still insensible. A ball had entered his side three inches from the back-bone, and passing through the body had come out under his breast; two fingers were shattered. No assistance was available but that of a soldier's wife who had been long in the service and who was in the habit of attending sick and wounded soldiers. She washed the Colonel's wounds and bound them up in such a manner that when the surgeon came and saw how the operation had been performed, he said that he could not have done it better and would not unbind the dressing. The Colonel soon afterwards opened his eyes, and though unable to speak for some hours seemed sensible of what was passing around him. In this state he lay nearly three weeks, when he was carried to Kingston and thence conveyed to England. At home, during a violent fit of coughing, he threw up a piece of cloth, and from that day recovered rapidly. In Holland in 1799 he lost an eye by a bullet; but a good constitution again triumphed, and he lived to be a Lieutenant-General and Governor of Stirling Castle.

The soldier's wife who was of so great service to Colonel Graham in his extremity was a woman of an uncommon character—a sister-Amazon to the Scotch wife spoken of by Kinglake, who on the day of Balaclava belaboured the fleeing Turks with tongue and frying-pan. The soldier's wife of the 42nd in the West Indies had long been a follower of the camp and had acquired some of its manners. While she was so good and useful a nurse in quarters, she was also bold and fearless in the field. General Stewart thus wrote of her:—" When the arrangements were made previous to the attack on the Vizie on 10th June, I directed that her husband, who was in my company, should remain behind to take charge of the men's knapsacks, which they had thrown off to be light for the advance up the hill, as I did not wish to have him exposed to danger on account of his wife and family. He obeyed his orders and remained with his charge, but his wife, believing herself not to be included in those injunctions, pushed forward to the assault. When the enemy had been beaten from the third redoubt, I was standing giving some directions to the men and preparing to push on to the fourth and last redoubt, when I found myself tapped on the shoulder and turning round I saw my Amazonian friend standing with her clothes tucked up to her knees; and seizing my hand, 'Well done, my Highland lads!' she exclaimed. 'See how the brigands scamper like so many deer! Come,' added she, 'let us drive them from yonder hill.' On inquiry I found that she had been in the hottest fire cheering and animating the men, and when the action was over she was as active as any of the surgeons in assisting the wounded."

The mortality this year among the troops in the West Indies was lamentably great. From May, 1796, to June, 1797, the deaths amounted to 264 officers and 12,387 soldiers. No one maintained a more vigorous state of health than the venerable commander-in-chief, who, although in the sixty-fourth year of his age, generally slept in his clothes—indeed, always when in the field. He was on horseback every morning an hour before daybreak, and was ever found where his presence was necessary. He returned to England in September, when the temporary command of the army devolved upon Major-General Charles Graham, who was this year promoted from the lieutenant-colonelcy of the 42nd to be colonel of the 5th West India Regiment. Born in the regiment in which he had served all his life, General Graham intimately understood the character and peculiar dispositions of the men. An admirable disciplinarian, strict but judicious, just and humane, with a fine voice and a clear and distinct manner of communicating his orders, he was excellently suited for his situation as commander of the Highland Regiment. His promotion to the rank of general officer, which removed him from its command, was a severe loss to the corps. He went out second in command to Sir Ralph Abercromby to the West Indies in 1795, and died at Cork in 1800. Major James Stewart succeeded to the lieutenant-colonelcy, and Captain Stirling to the rank of major. Some time previously Captain Alexander Stewart had succeeded Major Christie who died of fever, and Lieutenant David Stewart became captain-lieutenant.

The commander-in-chief returned from England early in February, 1797, and immediately brought together a force for an attack on Trinidad, which surrendered without opposition. Having received intelligence of the favourable disposition of the inhabitants of Porto Rico, he determined to make an attempt on that island. A force consisting of the 26th Dragoons dismounted, and the 14th, 42nd, 53rd, and 60th regiments, was assembled at St. Kitts, whence it sailed on April 25th and anchored off Congregus' Point on the 17th. The enemy made some slight opposition to the landing, but retired when the troops debarked. The town and Moro, or citadel, of Porto Rico, are built on an island separated from the mainland by a narrow arm of the sea. The Moro was strongly fortified and all but inaccessible. From the further shore of the lagoon the distance was too great for the batteries of the assailants to produce any effect, and no symptom was shown of any inclination to surrender. A number of French privateers had taken shelter in the harbour, the crews of which had landed and manned the batteries, determined to protect to the last their vessels and prizes. As the British force was insufficient to blockade more than one face of the castle, or to prevent a free communication with the main island, the commander-in-chief resolved to abandon the attempt and re-embark. There were lost in this futile enterprise one captain killed, one lieutenant-colonel and one captain wounded, and ninety-eight rank and file killed or wounded. A lieutenant and 121 foreigners in British service were missing, supposed to have deserted. The troops returned to their stations, and the Highlanders were sent to Martinique, where they embarked for home free from sickness, and in consequence of copious volunteering into their ranks, actually stronger than when they embarked at Portsmouth in October, 1795. At that same port the regiment disembarked in perfect health on the 30th July, and marched to Hillsea Barracks. The spectacle of a body of 500 men landing from the West Indies and promptly setting forth on march without leaving a man behind, was unique. Prior to the landing an account of the troops was sent ashore according to custom. It was returned with directions to correct the assumed mistake in omitting to fill up the "sick" column. But there were no sick.

After remaining at Hillsea for a few weeks the five companies embarked for Gibraltar, where they joined the other five companies, whose destination had been changed by their return to port after the sailing of the expedition to the West Indies. The regiment was now 1,100 strong, but the character of the troops was sensibly deteriorated under the temptation of drink. A soldier, in a paroxysm of passion and intoxication, stabbed a civilian to the heart with his bayonet. Two men deserted to the Spaniards. Fortunately for the regiment it was soon removed to Minorca, where its old habits and conduct were in a measure restored by the discipline exercised by Brigadier-General Oakes, who was in command for several months. In November, 1798, a small armament intended for the reduction of Minorca was prepared, the command of which was entrusted to Lieutenant-General Sir Charles Stuart. Four regiments were employed, of which the 42nd was one. Those regiments which had been quartered at Gibraltar sailed from that fortress on October 24th, and reached Minorca on 6th November. A landing in the Bay of Addaya was next morning effected without opposition. The British troops having invaded Citadella, the principal place of arms on the island, on November 14th, the Spanish commander, who had concentrated his forces in the fortress, surrendered on the following day, the prisoners considerably outnumbering the invaders. The prize-money for this capture was paid with exceptional promptitude. Sir Charles Stuart directed everything to be sold and converted into money as soon as possible, and the shares to be apportioned on the spot where the prize-money was earned. An agent wished to send the proceeds to England to be lodged in security; but General Stuart held that it could not be in better security than in the pockets of those to whom it belonged; and with characteristic generosity he gave his own share to the wives and families of the soldiers, although his private fortune was very modest. The possession of Minorca was of considerable importance as being the rendezvous of a large force to be employed in the Mediterranean in support of the allies of Great Britain. The command of this army was declined by Sir Charles Stuart, and it was given to Sir Ralph Abercromby, who reached the island on June 22nd, 1799, accompanied by Major-Generals Hutchinson and Moore. The interval previous to active operations the commander-in-chief devoted to a strict examination into the internal economy and discipline of the respective corps. It was at this time that the system was first suggested to General Moore of marching, firing, and general discipline which he afterwards carried to so high perfection in the 43rd, 53rd, and 95th Regiments, and which afterwards was followed by all light cavalry corps. Major Kenneth Mackenzie of the 90th Regiment had practised this mode of discipline for several years, and while he commanded his regiment in Minorca had brought the men to great perfection in it. One morning as he was superintending the exercise on the glacis of Fort St. Philip, General Moore, who was present, was so struck with its excellence and simplicity that, with his usual frankness, he expressed his surprise that an evolution so simple and so admirably adapted to its purpose had not already suggested itself to his mind. Major Mackenzie was next year promoted to the 44th Regiment, from which he was removed, on General Moore's recommendation, to the 52nd, his own regiment. The new system of discipline and field tactics was now taken up, and Lieutenant-Colonel Mackenzie being supported by the influence, assiduity, and zeal of

L

General Moore, was speedily brought to a high state of perfection.

In the month of August despatches were received from England in consequence of which the army immediately sailed for Gibraltar, where it arrived on September 14th. On October 2nd the fleet sailed for Cadiz, with the object of taking possession of that city, and seizing the Spanish war-ships in the harbour of Carracas. The British fleet from Gibraltar was joined by a force from Ferrol under the command of Sir James Pulteney; but while the Highlanders and part of the reserve were about to land in the boats in waiting for the signal to make for the shore, a gun from the city announced the approach of a flag of truce. Cadiz was suffering under the ravages of a pestilence which had already carried off thousands, and which threatened destruction to the whole population. The commanders yielded to the appeal, and signals were made for the return of the troops who were already under way in the boats. After undergoing a violent gale, which compelled the fleet to shelter under Cape Spartel, it returned to Gibraltar. On October 29th Sir James Pulteney with the regiments whose service was limited to Europe, received orders for Portugal, while the commander-in-chief with the rest of the forces, proceeded to Malta. This measure was the first intimation of an extended field of service.

Up to the beginning of the present century, the Royal Highland Regiment was in certain respects by no means fortunate. During the long period from 1739 until 1801 it had taken part in but one pitched battle, that of Fontenoy; and Fontenoy was a defeat — a glorious one, yet a defeat. More glorious than Fontenoy, Ticonderoga also was yet, in a technical sense, a defeat; although there the regiment earned an immortal renown.

The Havannah, Brooklyn, and Brandywine were successes, but none of those were battles—they were merely actions, more or less bloody, but none of them memorable in the annals of war. It was the misfortune of the regiment, not its fault, that it should have been for the most part skirmishing and bush-whacking on and beyond the confines of civilisation, when more fortunate comrades were stirring the nations by such memorable victories as Minden, Louisbourg, and Quebec. Until Alexandria the colours of the regiment seem to have been virgin of a single honour. During all those long years was the Black Watch so haughty in its self-concentration as not to be solicitous for honours on its colours, while other corps were straining successfully to have blazon on blazon on their standards. The regiment fought at St. Lucia, as did the Royal Scots, the Inniskillings, the Shropshires, and the North Staffordshires, all of whom carry the honour of "St. Lucia" on their colours; but no "St. Lucia" is woven on the silk of the Black Watch banners. It fought time and again in Martinique shoulder to shoulder with the Royal Fusiliers, the King's Liverpool Regiment, the Somerset Light Infantry, the East Yorkshires, the Scottish Borderers, the Cameronians, the Manchester Regiment, all of which have "Martinique" on their colours; but there is no "Martinique" on the colours of the Black Watch. "Guadaloupe" floats over the East Yorkshires, the Cameronians, the East Surreys, and the Manchesters. The kilted soldiers of the Black Watch fought and died along with those regiments in the pestilential islands of the West Indies, but no trophy of "Guadaloupe" shines on the list of honours on the colours of the old Highland Regiment.

L 2

# CHAPTER XVII.

### ALEXANDRIA. 1801.

December 20th, 1800, sailed from Malta for Bay of Marmorice. The Scottish Turk. Fleet anchored in Aboukir Bay, March 1st. Details of Abercromby's army. On morning 8th, landing accomplished in face of enemy with considerable loss. Enemy driven back from beach, after short but decisive combat. On 12th, British army advanced to proximity of Fort of Mandora. On morning 13th, advanced to attack. Gallantry of 92nd Highlanders. Sir Ralph Abercromby's escape. Enemy driven back, but difficulties unsurmountable. Deception of the mirage. Folly of young officers. British position carefully strengthened. Relative positions of British and French armies. Regnier, "the spoiled child of defeat." Opening of battle of Alexandria, early morning of 21st. First fighting in darkness. Advance of 42nd. Fierce struggle in ruined palace. The advance of French "Invincibles." Their heroic resistance. Ultimate destruction—remnant surrender with standard. Fighting in the open. Charges of French cavalry. Exhaustion of British ammunition. Long strain until its arrival—ordeal of fire and iron. Final attack of French cavalry, which was broken up and destroyed. French retreat pursued by British cannon shots. Abercromby wounded, after hand-to-hand fight. Disregarded wound, which, however, proved fatal. His death on board *Foudroyant*. Estimate of his character. Succeeded by General Hutchison. Surrender of French army and its embarkation for France. Baird's voyage from India with fine little army in reinforcement of main army, too late to participate in campaign.

THE brilliant victory won by Nelson in the Bay of Aboukir imprisoned the army of France amid the arid sands of Egypt; but nevertheless in 1799 Napoleon led it across the desert to Palestine. He stormed Jaffa and laid siege to Acre, where he was repulsed by the British and Turks under Sir Sidney Smith. Soon after his return to Egypt alarming information caused him to hurry back to France, leaving his troops behind. With his departure they began to lose heart about the time when the British expedition to that country was projected for the purpose of driving them out of it. That Egypt was the object of attack was divulged in Malta, and the information was joyfully received. All were excited by the prospect of release from the monotony of life in transports and of a debarkation in an interesting country with the object of meeting a brave and hitherto invincible enemy. On December 20th and 21st, 1800, the fleet sailed for the Bay of Marmorice, on the coast of Greece. The first division arrived on December 28th and the second on January 1st, 1801, to await a reinforcement of men and horses to be furnished by our Turkish allies. Among the numbers who came to see the British armament was an unexpected visitor in the dress of a Turk. This gentleman gave his name as Campbell, and was a native of the district of Kintyre in Argyleshire. Early in life he had been so deeply affected by the death of a schoolfellow who had been killed by accident when they were at play together that he had fled the country and joined the Turkish army. He had served for forty years under the standard of Islam, and had risen to the rank of a general of artillery. He went on board the ship on which was the 42nd, to make inquiries about his family. When he saw the dress to which he had been accustomed in his youth, he was so much affected that he could not restrain his tears. The astonishment of the Highland soldiers may be imagined when they were addressed in their own language, which he had not forgotten, by a Turk in his full costume with a white beard flowing down to his girdle.

The Turkish supplies, which were in every way deficient and unsatisfactory, having been embarked, the fleet at length put to sea, and on the morning of Sunday, March 1st, the coast of Egypt was descried. The fleet anchored the same evening in Aboukir Bay, in the proximity of the spot where the battle of the Nile had been fought nearly three years before. The delay at Marmorice while waiting for the junction of the Turkish ships and forces permitted the safe arrival from Toulon of two French frigates having on board troops, guns, ammunition, and much general military stores. One section of the reinforcement which the enemy so opportunely received consisted of nearly 700 artillerymen, a number more than equal to the whole artillery of the invading army. That army consisted of the following regiments:—Guards, commanded by Major-General the Hon. J. Ludlow; the 1st Royal Scots, both battalions of the 54th, and the 92nd (Gordon) Highlanders, under Major-General Coote; the 8th King's, 13th, 19th, and 90th Perthshire Light Infantry (the Greybreeks), under Major-General Cradock; the 2nd Queen's, 50th, and 79th (Cameron) Highlanders, under Major-General Lord Cavan; the 18th Royal Irish, 30th, 44th, and 89th, under Brigadier-General Doyle; and the regiments of Minorca, De Rolle, and Dillon, under Major-General John Stuart, the future hero of Maida. The reserve, under the command of Major-General Moore (the fated victor of Coruña) consisted of the 40th flank companies, the Welsh Fusiliers, 28th, Black Watch, 58th, the Corsican Rangers, a squadron of the 11th Light Dragoons; a detachment of Baron Hompesch's mounted riflemen, under the command of Sir Robert Wilson; 12th and 26th Light Dragoons dismounted, under Brigadier-General Finch; and artillery and engineers under Brigadier-General Lawson. The total force under the command of Lieutenant-General Sir Ralph Abercromby amounted to 15,330 men at the date of the landing.

The first tidings received by the commander-in-chief on anchoring in Aboukir Bay were that two brave and intelligent officers, Major Mackerras and Major Fletcher of the Engineers, who had been despatched to examine the line of coast, had fallen into the hands of the enemy, the former dead, the latter alive. Scarcely had the fleet anchored when a gale sprang up so violent and unremitting that no landing was possible, nor could the general venture to reconnoitre the coast and decide on the most eligible place of debarkation. The task before him was such as severely tested his well-known strength of mind. He had to force a landing in an unknown region in the face of an enemy at least double his own strength—an enemy, moreover, in full possession of the positions and of the country, having a powerful artillery and a numerous and well-appointed cavalry inured to the climate; an enemy conversant with every point where a landing might be attempted, who had taken advantage of the delays of the adversary to erect batteries and bring guns to the points where the attempt seemed most likely.

On the evening of the 7th the wind at length moderated; and the general, accompanied by Sir Sidney Smith with three armed launches, went close in shore. A naval officer landed from one of the launches, drove in a picquet stationed on the beach, boarded a guard-boat, and brought back to the shipping some prisoners, in the shape of an officer, a donkey and his driver. The preparations to resist the debarkation were found very formidable. The sand-hills, stretching in a semicircular form from the castle of Aboukir for a mile to the leftward, were held by strong bodies of cavalry and infantry. Along the ridge were planted twelve pieces of artillery, so as to throw, with the cannon of Fort Aboukir, a cross-fire on every approach; and several mortars, half concealed by the inequalities of the ground, promised some variety of peril in the nature of the missiles to be encountered. The weather continued moderate, and at two o'clock on the morning of the 8th the first detachments, consisting of the 40th flank companies and Welsh Fusiliers in the right; the 28th, 42nd, and 58th Regiments in the centre; and on the left the brigade of Guards, Corsican Rangers, Royals and 54th, the whole amounting to 5,230 men, manned the boats and pushed off for the general rendezvous under the lee of the *Mondovi* brig anchored out of reach from the shore. So well conceived and executed was this arrangement that before the signal to start for the beach, every brigade, every regiment, and every company found itself in its proper station. Such a combination, however, required time; and it was eight o'clock before the dispositions were completed and the troops ready to act promptly on the signal. That was given at nine o'clock, and the boats sprang forward under the orders of Captain the Hon. Alexander Cochrane, the seamen straining every nerve but rowing with strokes so regular that the line was perfectly kept. In light marching order and closely packed, each man with his loaded musket between his knees, the soldiers sat in silence while the sailors bent to their oars and for a time the rattle of them in the rowlocks and the striking of the blades into the water alone were heard; but in a few moments later the artillery and mortars from the beach and the castle of Aboukir opened fire, and the sea began to hiss and boil ahead, astern, and around the frail armada, as round shot, grape, and shells were showered on the face of the water. Three boats, each containing sixty men, were sunk by the enemy's fire within a hundred yards of the land. Many were saved, but nearly all the wounded inevitably perished. Reprisals were made by the light-armed vessels and from the bomb-ketches and gun-brigs moored broadside to the beach, but with little effect owing to the superior weight of the enemy's fire.

Undaunted by this hot reception given by the enemy, the seamen pulled steadily on. Ere long a hail shower of musketry fire was added to the hostile cannonade. But the troops leaped into the surf, forming line as they gained the beach with fixed bayonets and colours flying, while loud cheers rang from flank to flank. "Forward!" was the word, and forward all went with a will, led by the gallant Moore.

The flank companies of the 40th and the Welsh Fusiliers on the extreme right charged vigorously up the steep slope; then advancing towards the two sandy knolls farther back, "they rushed up the heights," wrote Sir Robert Wilson, "with almost preternatural energy, never firing a shot, but charging with the bayonet the two battalions crowning the summit, breaking and pursuing them till they reached and carried the two knolls commanding the plain to the leftward, taking at the same time two cannon." "The Royal Highlanders on the right centre," wrote Mr. Cannon, himself a soldier of the regiment, "leaped ashore, formed on the beach, and rushing up the steep ascent rendered difficult by the loose sand in the face of the fire of a battalion of infantry and two guns, speedily gained the summit, and instantly closing on their numerous opponents with the bayonet, drove them from their position before they had time to fire a second volley. Scarcely had the Royal Highlanders driven back the French infantry when a squadron of cavalry galloped forward to charge them, but it was immediately repulsed with the loss of its commanding officer." The French rallied in rear of a second line of sand-hills, from which they maintained a straggling fire; but the British troops pressed on and soon drove the enemy from the field, thus achieving a victory "almost without parallel in the annals of war." The Guards on their landing were attacked by the same cavalry, which had rallied; but a flanking fire from the 58th enabled them to form and advance against the enemy. Before this the French cavalry had actually ridden into the sea, and in some instances killed in the boats men so densely crowded as to be unable to use their arms. The engagement at Aboukir was short but decisive. The French troops posted to oppose the landing having been repulsed on all points, the British troops advanced to support the column commanded by General Moore, who had obtained complete possession of the commanding ground in his front, with the loss, however, of 700 men killed and wounded, including seamen and marines. Covered by swarms of tirailleurs, the French were now in full retreat along the road to Alexandria. No attempt was made to follow them, for the general and staff had ample occupation in getting the stores conveyed from the ships to the beach and thence to the bivouac, and in having wells dug in the sand wherever the appearance of date-trees gave promise of water. The old castle of Aboukir still held out, but was blockaded by the 2nd Queen's and the 26th Light Dragoons dismounted.

The British loss in landing in the Bay of Aboukir was four officers, four sergeants, and ninety-four rank and file killed; twenty-six officers, thirty-four sergeants, five drummers, and 450 rank and file wounded. Of those the Highlanders had thirty-one killed, and Lieutenant-Colonel James Stewart, Captain Charles Macquarrie, Lieutenants Alexander Campbell, John Dick, Frederick

Campbell, Stewart Campbell, Charles Campbell, Ensign Wilson, seven sergeants, four drummers, and 140 rank and file wounded. The loss of the French did not exceed one-half of that of the British. The principal loss of the latter was incurred while in the boats and when mounting the slope. In both instances they were exposed to the fire of the enemy without being able to make any rejoinder. As soon as they had gained a position where their courage and firmness were available, the loss sustained was trivial. Four-fifths of the loss of the Highlanders were incurred before they reached the summit of the eminence.

By the exertions of the navy the whole army was landed the same evening. General Stewart tells that "when the men had lain down to rest after the action, observing some men digging a hole and a number of dead bodies lying around, I stepped up to one of them, and touching his temples, felt that they still retained some warmth. I then told the soldiers not to bury their comrade, but to carry him to the surgeon as he did not appear to be quite dead. 'Pho!' said one of them, 'he is as dead as my grandfather, who was killed at Culloden'; and taking the man by the heels, proceeded to drag him to the pit. I caused him to desist, but the wounded man was so horribly disfigured as to justify his comrade in the judgment he had formed. He was carried to the hospital, where he revived from his swoon, and he recovered so rapidly that in six weeks he was at duty."

The delay rendered necessary in landing stores and provisions had enabled the enemy to reinforce themselves to some extent, so that when on the 12th the British encamped near the Fort of Mandora, they found that the strength of the adversary was increased to over

5,000 infantry, 600 cavalry, and 300 pieces of cannon, well appointed. By the helpful and judicious arrangement of the admiral, Lord Keith, a large body of troops were landed to serve as pikemen and gunners under Sir Sidney Smith and several other captains, and to act in concert with the movements of the army. The French now began to perceive that they had no longer Turks and Mamelukes to contend with; they felt that the soldiers of another great European nation were confronting them on Egyptian soil, and that now the ultimate possession of the country was problematical.

On the morning of the 13th, the British troops advanced through a forest of date-trees to attack the French under General Menou, then in possession of some ridges in front. Beyond those ridges were visible gloomy Alexandria, with its surrounding ruins, its Pharos jutting into the sea, Cleopatra's Needle, the domes of many mosques, with the masts of the shipping in the harbour, and the Tricolour waving on Fort Crétin. During the whole of this march the light troops of the enemy skirmished with the flanking parties of the British army, which advanced to the attack in three columns of regiments, the 90th Light Infantry forming the advance of the first column, and the 92nd Gordon Highlanders that of the second; the third column, being the reserve under General Moore, marching on the right, covering the movements of the first line, and moving parallel with it. When the army had cleared the date forest of Mandora, the enemy were visible drawn up along a line of sand-hills extending from the canal of Alexandria to the Lake Maadieh. They quitted the heights, and with great boldness moved down upon the 92nd, which had formed in line. Although that gallant regiment, being far in advance of the rest of the column, was exposed to a heavy fire of artillery and musketry and at the same time was attacked by the 61st French demi-brigade, it continued its advance up to the very muzzles of the hostile guns, maintained its ground until the line came up, and captured two field pieces and a howitzer, completely routing their defenders. Their Perthshire comrades, who, acting as light infantry, then wore brass helmets, were mistaken by the enemy for dismounted dragoons, and were charged with great impetuosity down a declivity by French cavalry. The Scottish regiment, holding its ground with cool intrepidity, allowed its adversaries to approach within fifty yards, when by a well-directed fire it so completely broke the hostile charge that only a few got within striking distance and most of those were instantly bayoneted; the rest swerved away to their left and retreated in utter confusion. During the *mêlée* Colonel (afterwards Lord) Hill received a blow on his helmet which brought him to the ground. Sir Ralph Abercromby also had a narrow escape; his horse was shot under him, but he was rescued by the devoted bravery of the Perthshire Regiment.

The conduct of the 92nd—the commanding officer of which, Colonel Erskine, was killed, and which lost many officers and men—was on this day most conspicuous. It was its first battle; the regiment was but seven years old; in its ranks were a number of young soldiers whose constitutions had suffered from long confinement on board of a transport during a Mediterranean summer, and from unaccustomed food; it had suffered much from sickness while on the passage from Minorca to Egypt—everything, it may be said, was against it; yet it had distinguished itself in this its earliest battle, perhaps with more fire than if it had been a regiment of war-accustomed veterans. "Opposed to a tremendous fire," wrote Sir Robert Wilson, "and suffering severely from the French line, the regiment never receded a foot, but maintained the contest alone, until the marines and the rest of the line came up to its support." So conspicuous was the gallantry of the regiment that it was afterwards ordered to bear the honour "Mandora" on its colours and appointments.

The two divisions now formed line, the reserve remaining in column to cover the right flank. The whole force moved forward in this order, suffering from the enemy's flying artillery, which, having six horses to each piece, could execute its movements at a gallop; whereas the British, with only a few badly appointed cavalry and no artillery horses, had their guns dragged by sailors occasionally assisted by the soldiers, through sands so loose and so deep that the wheels sank almost to the axle. The enemy fell back into an entrenched position which they had prepared with great care in front of Alexandria, and those works Sir Ralph Abercromby was determined to force. He continued to advance till the line had come within point-blank range of the hostile batteries. A halt was then commanded and the troops stood fast under a murderous fire of skilfully handled cannon, while the commander-in-chief with his staff rode forward to reconnoitre. At length the difficulties of carrying out the attack were recognised as insurmountable; the troops were ordered to retire and to occupy that position which was later, on the 21st, so well maintained, and in which they avenged themselves for their present disappointment.

"The difficulties under which Sir Ralph Abercromby laboured at this time, through the absence of all information as to the plans and dispositions of the enemy, were," wrote his biographer, "very great." It was found impossible to make the Arabs comprehend the object of such questions as were put to them; while from their own statements voluntarily offered, no conclusions could be drawn on which the general considered that he ought to place the slightest reliance. The face of the country was also in many respects deceptive to the eye of a stranger, and on the present occasion led such as had attempted to examine it into the commission of several glaring errors. There was, for instance, a plain on the enemy's right covered by a species of nitrous salt, which dazzled the visual organs and presented on its smooth and shining surface a striking resemblance to a sheet of water. No man in the army was aware at that time of the now well-known effect of mirage; and thence the weakest point of the enemy's position—a point by traversing which they might have been taken in reverse —was regarded as impregnable. In like manner the fiery brightness of the atmosphere acting on a white and glittering sand, gave to the gentle undulations along which the French had ranged their batteries an overcharged semblance of height and strength. The consequence was that, after examining with the closest attention what he believed to be a position of extraordinary difficulty, Sir Ralph Abercromby came to the resolution of suspending his attack; and the troops were directed to fall back into the positions from which they had dislodged the enemy in the morning.

The losses of the day were by no means slight. The killed amounted to 156. The ordinary proportion is one man killed to five wounded; but in the combat of Mandora seven men were wounded to one killed. Only six officers were killed, an exceptionally small number in proportion to the total strength engaged; but on the other hand, no fewer than sixty-six officers were wounded, a remarkably great proportion. With good troops such as Abercromby commanded the ordinary ratio of wounded officers to wounded men in the smooth bore and flint-lock period was one officer to thirty men; whereas at Mandora the proportion was one officer to fifteen men. Notwithstanding that the Royal Highlanders were not engaged and were exposed only to distant fire, their loss was far from being insignificant. Only three privates were killed; but Lieutenant-Colonel Dickson, Captain Archibald Campbell, and Lieutenant Simon Fraser, three sergeants, and twenty-four rank and file were wounded. Lieutenant-Colonel James Stewart, who had been wounded at the landing in Aboukir Bay, nevertheless commanded the regiment at the battle of Alexandria. The loss of the regiment on this day was the more to be regretted because—apart from the wounds received by Colonel Dickson, by Captain Campbell, who was severely wounded in the arm and side, and by Lieutenant Fraser, who lost a hand—all the casualties might have been avoided but for the idle curiosity of three young officers of the regiment. During an interval in the fighting General Moore had ordered the 42nd up to the right, to form in the closest possible order immediately under a steep hill, which would effectually conceal the regiment, while it should be ready on the first signal to dash forward on the enemy. It accordingly lay close under the hill unperceived by the enemy; the most positive orders were given that every man should sit down with his musket between his knees, on the alert to start up at a moment's notice; and that on no account was any person to quit the column, lest the position should be discovered by the enemy who had covered with guns the hill-top directly above.

In this attitude the regiment lay in perfect silence until three young men, seized with an irresistible curiosity to see what the rest of the army was doing, crept out unperceived by Colonel Stewart. They were descried by the enemy, who quickly brought their guns to bear on the regiment and in an instant round shots were plunging in among the Highlanders. Before the regiment could be removed beyond the line of hostile fire thirteen men were left on the ground, either killed or wounded. Thus a foolish and unpardonable curiosity caused death or serious injuries to several officers and soldiers.

As the ground now occupied by the British army afforded few natural advantages, no time was lost in strengthening it by art. The flanks were securely covered, on the right by the sea, on the left by Lake Maadieh. The reserve as a whole was pushed forward on the right as an advanced post. The 58th Regiment occupied a ruin of great extent, supposed to have been the palace of the Ptolemies. On the outside of the ruin, close to the left of the 58th, but advanced a little distance, was a redoubt occupied by the 28th. Five hundred yards rearward was posted the 23rd, the flank companies of the 40th, the 42nd, and the Corsican Rangers, in position to support the two corps in front. To the left rear of the redoubt a sandy plain extended and then dipped into the valley wherein was the cavalry of the reserve. Still further to the left were the Guards posted on rising ground with a redoubt on their right, a battery on their left, and an epaulement with ditch connecting the two. Left of the Guards, were posted in echelon formation, the Royals, 54th (two battalions) and the 92nd; then the 8th King's, 18th, 90th, and 13th; facing the lake at right angles to the left flank were drawn up *en potence* the 27th, 79th, and 50th Regiments.

On the right of the second line were the 12th and 26th Dragoons, dismounted; on its left the 30th, 89th, 44th, Dillon's, De Roll's, and Stuart's regiments. The right flank was covered by four cutters anchored near the shore. There was a considerable interval between the right of the Guards and the rearward regiments of the reserve. Such was the position of the army from the 14th until the evening of the 20th; the whole force being during this period in constant employment, in performing military duties, erecting batteries, and bringing forward artillery, stores, and provisions. At intervals along the front were in position two twenty-four pounders and thirty-two field guns; and a third twenty-four pounder was in the redoubt occupied by the 28th.

The enemy held a corresponding position opposite to that of the British. It was very formidable, owing to the steepness and command afforded by the ridge of hills extending from the sea to beyond the left of the British line, and having the town of Alexandria, Fort Caffarelli, and the Pharos in the rear. Of General Menou's army the disposition was as follows: General Lanusse's force on the left extended from the sea to the centre, with four demi-brigades of light infantry, and two regiments of cavalry, commanded by General Roize. Generals Friant and Rampan led the centre, which consisted of five demi-brigades. General Regnier was posted on the right with two demi-brigades and two regiments of cavalry. General D'Estain commanded the advanced guard, consisting of one demi-brigade, some light troops, and a detachment of cavalry. In Menou's general orders he announced grandiloquently his intention of "driving the British into Lake Maadieh." That, not to put too fine a point on it, was scarcely a genial intimation. But it was not against General

Menou that the wrath of the British army waxed hot. The disparaging remarks regarding that army made in General Regnier's work on the expedition to Egypt, and his attempts to diminish the credit and honour of that conquest are generally known. It may be recollected that Regnier stated in his account of the battle of Alexandria that the Highland soldiers took shelter from their opponents under the bellies of the French horses. A better expedient for obtaining personal safety might have been devised than that of creeping under horses in a state of high excitement; indeed, it must have required some courage to adopt it, considering that well-armed dragoons were on the backs of those novel safeguards. When Regnier left Monte Leone to engage in battle against Sir John Stuart at Maida, he invited the inhabitants to a grand fête which he was to give them in honour of his victory. That fête did not come off; Regnier did not win his victory, but very much the reverse. Indeed, he never won a victory, and he got beaten with a consistent monotony. He was beaten at Maida by Sir John Stuart, at Ximena by Ballasteros, at Kalisch by Winzingerode. Regnier might have been styled the " spoiled child of defeat."

The fort of Aboukir, which had been blockaded by the Queen's Regiment, had been surrendered to Lord Dalhousie on the 18th, and to replace the Gordon Highlanders who had been much reduced by sickness and the action of the 13th, the Queen's was ordered to the front on the evening of the 20th. The same evening Sir Ralph received intelligence that General Menou had reached Alexandria with a large reinforcement from Cairo, and was preparing for the impending struggle.

An hour before daybreak of the 21st the French were in motion; but the British were not taken by surprise, as it was the invariable custom of the commanding general to have his troops under arms every morning by three o'clock. Amidst the intense silence and darkness a single musket-shot was suddenly heard; the explosion of three pieces of cannon immediately followed; and all held their breath in suspense, till a volley of musketry fired by the enemy's dromedary corps far away on the British left, gave notice that the battle of Alexandria had begun. General Moore, who was the general officer of the night, galloped towards the left on the sound of the firing. But almost momentarily impressed with the conviction that what had been heard from the left indicated merely a false attack he wheeled in his tracks and had but a moment returned to his brigade, when a wild, broken hurrah rising from out of the plain beneath warned him of the approach of the enemy. The sound of the first shot had brought Sir Ralph to the front. There he found the right of his army already fiercely engaged; for the French, after driving in the picquets, assailed with incredible fury the redoubt, the ruins, and the left wing of the 42nd, which under Major Stirling had been sent forward to take post on the open space previously occupied by the 28th, now ordered within the redoubt. While the left wing of the Highlanders was thus formed up, its right supported by the redoubt, Lieutenant-Colonel Alexander Stewart with the right wing was ordered to remain two hundred yards in rear, but exactly parallel with the left wing. The Welsh Fusiliers and the flank companies of the 40th moved forward in support of the 28th and 58th in the ruins. At every point the foe was gallantly met. The 28th poured in on the enemy a fire which nothing could withstand, while the 58th under Colonel Crowdjye, manned the breaches in the ruined walls, and after three rounds of musketry rushed on the enemy with the bayonet, supported in its charge by the Welsh Fusiliers. The attacks on the ruins, the redoubt, and the wing of the Highlanders on its left were made simultaneously and with the greatest impetuosity; but the return fire quickly checked the ardour of the enemy, and the 40th companies rendered more complete their repulse by a steady and well-directed fire which cut down whole sections of the now disordered foe. Lieutenant-Colonels Paget of the 28th and Houston of the 58th allowed the adversary to come quite close, when they reopened a fire so heavy and effective that he was compelled to retire precipitately to a hollow in his rear. Meanwhile, out in the open on the left of the redoubt, Stirling's wing of the Highlanders repulsed a very superior force.

The darkness was still intense, and the smoke that curled along the ranks rendered all objects at arm's length from the eye totally invisible. Favoured by this gloom and obscurity a fresh column of French infantry, all grenadiers who on account of their past exploits bore the name of the "Invincibles," stole silently with a six-pounder at its head along the interval between the left of the 42nd and the right of the Guards, and calculating its distance and line of advance correctly notwithstanding the darkness, wheeled suddenly to the left and penetrated unseen between the two wings of the 42nd which were drawn up in parallel lines. The instant that the "Invincible" column was discovered, Colonel Stewart, in command of the right wing of the Highlanders, instantly charged to his proper front and captured the enemy's six-pounder, while the rear rank of Major Stirling's wing faced to the right about and charged with the bayonet to its new front. Maddened by this double assault the "Invincibles" pressed on in the face of a murderous fire from the 28th in the ruins; and dashing at the shattered walls made good their entrance, closely followed by the Highlanders. Following the example of the 28th, the 58th and the 40th companies poured volley after volley on the bewildered Frenchmen as they entered. A desperate *mêlée* now occurred with bayonet and butt-end within the ancient ruins. The 58th and 40th received the "Invincibles" in front; the Highlanders slaughtered them in the rear. The combined assaults proved decisive of the fate of this gallant but unfortunate body of French veterans. The "Invincibles" resisted heroically; and the officer who bore their embroidered standard was heard to shout again and again "Vive la République!" before he fell pierced by a shot. Of those brave men 650 had fallen, when the survivors, about 250 in number, threw down their arms, and a French officer delivered their standard after a struggle to Major Stirling of the 42nd, who gave it in charge to a sergeant of his regiment, directing him to keep charge of it and stand by a gun which had been taken from the enemy. The sergeant was overthrown and stunned by cavalry charging to the rear. When he recovered the standard was gone, and he could give no account of its loss.

General Moore had followed the enemy's column into the ruins, where he and General Oakes were wounded; but those officers, disregarding wounds which did not altogether disable them, continued to perform their duties. The former, on the surrender of the "Invincibles," left the ruins and hurried to the left of the redoubt, where part of the left wing of the 42nd was hotly engaged with the enemy after the rear rank had followed the corps into the ruins. The enemy were now seen in great force advancing on the left of the redoubt, apparently with the intention of making another attempt to turn it. General Moore immediately ordered the Highlanders out of the ruins, and directed them to form line in battalion on the flat on which Major Stirling had originally formed, with their right supported by the redoubt. This extension of the line enabled the Highlanders to present a greater front to the enemy, who pressed forward so rapidly that it was necessary to check their advance even before the Highland battalion had completed its line formation. The order was therefore given at once to repulse the enemy, which was promptly performed with complete success.

Here the commander-in-chief had taken his station, and he called out, " My brave Highlanders, remember your country! Remember your forefathers!" The Highlanders pursued the fleeing enemy along the plain. They had not followed far when Moore's keen eye perceived in the growing daylight fresh hostile columns formed on the plain beyond, with three squadrons of cavalry seemingly ready to charge through the intervals of the retreating French infantry. Without losing a moment, Moore ordered the Highland Regiment to withdraw from its advanced position and to re-form on the left of the redoubt. This order, although repeated by Colonel Stewart, was heard only in part because of the noise of the firing; and while the companies which heard it retired on the redoubt, the others followed at a considerable interval and gained no support from the redoubt. The opportunity was promptly seized by the enemy, fully aware of the advantage afforded by the interval between the wings of the Highland Regiment; and they advanced in great force. Broken as was the line by reason of the separation of the companies and thus ill-calculated to resist an impetuous charge of cavalry, yet every man stood firm. Many of the enemy were struck down in the advance. The French horsemen who charged on the compact rallying squares of the Highland companies were invariably beaten back with heavy loss. The squadrons which passed through the intervals in the ragged Highland line and wheeled to the left, as the infantry column had done in the early darkness, were met by the 28th Regiment, which, facing to its rear, poured on the French troopers a fire so effective that most were killed or taken. Strange to tell, only thirteen men of the Highlanders were wounded by the sabres of the hostile cavalry. That the casualties were so few in the 42nd was owing to the staunchness of the men, who, as they stood, first endeavoured to bring down the horse before the rider came within sword-length, and then despatched him with the bayonet before he had time to recover from the fall of the horse.

General Menou, exasperated by the disaster which had befallen the flower of his cavalry, ordered forward a column of infantry supported by cavalry to make a second attempt on the position; but although the formation of the Highlanders was not completely restored, they repulsed the enemy's infantry at all points. Another body of cavalry then dashed forward as the former had done, with great ardour and impetuosity, and met with a similar reception, many falling in the charge, others passing through the line only to be overpowered by the 28th. It was now on the part of the Highlanders a question of personal firmness and individual courage, every man fighting for his own hand and on his own ground, regardless how he was supported, facing his enemy wherever the latter presented himself and resolute to maintain his post while strength or life remained. The enemy seemed struck with this situation: a body of men broken—cavalry charging through them—attacked in flank—with an enemy in rear; yet still stoutly resisting, either in groups or as individuals as necessity required. This they did not expect. Probably they regarded this species of fighting as contrary to the ordinary custom of service, and therefore their charges were presumably made with greater boldness and in fuller confidence of success, believing that no broken, disjointed body of men could in such circumstances attempt to resist their impetuous attacks. But finding, instead of a fugitive enemy, every individual man standing firm and ready to receive all comers, their assaults were delivered with less vigour and assurance.

But this condition of affairs could not endure. The Highland Regiment was now greatly reduced and had it not been supported, must ere long have been annihilated. From this fate it was saved by the opportune arrival of the foreign brigade commanded by Major-General Sir John Stuart, who, advancing from the second line, formed his three regiments on the left of the Highlanders, occupying, as far as his line extended, part of the vacant space on the right of the Guards. No support could have been more seasonable. The enemy were now again advancing in great force both of cavalry and of infantry, with an apparent determination to overwhelm the scanty body which had so long stood its ground against their reiterated efforts. To their surprise they found opposed to them a fresh and more numerous body of adversaries, who withstood their assault with so great spirit and firmness that they were driven back with great precipitancy.

It was now eight in the morning; but as yet, although from the repulse of the enemy at all points the indications seemed favourable to the British, the situation was still far from free from doubt. The French continued a heavy and constant cannonade from their great guns, and a straggling fire was maintained by their sharpshooters, who lurked in hollows and behind some sandhillocks in front of the redoubt and the ruins. By this time the fire of the British had ceased, in consequence of the expenditure of the whole of their ammunition during the early and hottest period of the contest. An immediate replenishment was not to be looked for owing to the distance of the ordnance stores. While this unfortunate cessation of hostilities on the part of the British astonished the enemy—who probably ascribed it to some dark design which they could not comprehend—the British forces suffered greatly from the fire of the enemy; in particular the Highlanders and the right of General Stuart's brigade, who were exposed to its full effect, being posted on a piece of level ground over which the cannon-shot rolled after striking the ground and carried off a file of men at every successful ricochet. This ordeal of fire and iron was more trying to the courage and discipline of the troops than had been the preceding assaults, but the long strain was supported with perfect steadiness. Not a man moved from his position, except to close up the gap made by the shot when his right-hand or left-hand man was struck down. During the cessation of the fire on the right Menou made a last attempt to carry the position by a furious charge of cavalry led by Brigadier Roize, and supported by General Regnier with the divisions of Lanusse, Rampan, and Friant; but the brigadier was killed with many other gallant officers, and the French cavalry was completely broken and destroyed. The enemy's sharp-shooters had advanced close up to the redoubt, but just then the fresh ammunition arrived. At the first shot fired from the twenty-four pounder in the redoubt, the enemy began to retreat, and before a fourth round was fired they had fled out of range. Their retreat was hastened by the admirable precision with which the big gun was pointed by Colonel Duncan of the Artillery. With his first shot he took aim at the sixth file from the right angle of the enemy's close column, and it levelled with the ground all that were outward of the file, either killing or overthrowing them by the force of the concussion; the second shot plunged into the centre of the column; the third had less effect, as the column opened out in the retreat; and before the fourth was ready the enemy was nearly covered by the sand-hills.

What occurred in the centre may be told in comparatively few words. Before dawn a heavy column of infantry advanced on the position occupied by the British Guards. General Ludlow allowed it to approach very close to his front, and then he ordered his fire to be opened. This had an effect so great that the enemy was driven back with great speed. When later they endeavoured to turn the left of the British position, they were repulsed so spiritedly by the Royals and the right wing of the 54th that they desisted from all further attempts to carry the position. They still, however, continued an irregular fire from their cannon and skirmishers, the former of which did more execution in the second line than further to the front. The left of the line was never engaged, as General Regnier, who commanded the French right, never advanced to the attack, but contented himself with keeping up a heavy cannonade from which several corps on the British left suffered considerably. The retreat was general throughout the whole French line, and by ten o'clock the enemy were back in their positions in front of Alexandria. The strength of this position, the numerical superiority of its defenders, and the fatigue already undergone by the British army, rendered it judicious to act with caution. In addition to those considerations, another strong reason for desisting from any further attempt on that day was the sad loss of the loved and honoured commander-in-chief. Early in the day he had taken his station in the front, between the Highland right and the left of the redoubt. Standing there he had a full view of the field, and here, having detached the whole of his staff on various duties, he was left alone, with the result that two hostile cavalrymen dashed forward, drew up on either side of the gallant old chief, and attempted to carry him off as a prisoner; but the gallant Abercromby refused to yield. In the unequal contest one of his assailants made a thrust at his breast, and passed his sword with great force under the arm of the general. Though severely bruised by the guard of the weapon, with the strength of arm for which he was distinguished he grasped his adversary's sabre and wrenched it from his antagonist. At the moment a corporal of the 42nd ran up to his assistance and shot one of the assailants, on which the other retired. A Highland soldier, noticing that Sir Ralph had some difficulty in dismounting from his horse, assisted him and asked if he should follow with the horse. The general answered that he would not require him any more that day. No officer was then near him; and the first one whom he met was Sir Sidney Smith. Observing that Sir Sidney's sword was broken, Sir Ralph presented him with the weapon which he had recently wrested from the French trooper. He betrayed no symptom of personal suffering, nor did he relax for a moment the intense interest he took in the state of the field; and it was not perceived that he had been wounded till he was joined by some members of his staff, who noticed the blood trickling down his thigh. Even between the time of his being wounded and the final cavalry charge, he walked with a firm and steady step along the front of the Highlanders and General Stuart's brigade, back to the position of the Guards in the centre of the line, where, from its elevated position, he had a full view of the whole field. Here he remained regardless of his wound, giving his orders so much in his usual manner that the officers who came to receive them perceived nothing indicative of pain or anxiety. A musket-ball, however, had entered his groin and lodged deep in the hip joint. The ball was so firmly fixed in the joint that it required considerable force to extract it after his death. He was soon surrounded by the generals and a number of officers. The soldiers crowded around the group, anxious for tidings as to the state of their honoured and beloved commander. He was carried on board the *Foudroyant*, where he lingered for some days, still maintaining his wonted serenity and composure. On the morning of the 28th his breathing became difficult, and a few hours later he expired.

The *Gazette* commemorated the dead warrior in appropriate and truthful expressions: "As his life was honourable, so his death was glorious. His memory will be recorded in the annals of his country, will be sacred to every British soldier, and embalmed in the memory of a grateful posterity." The respect and affection with which he was universally regarded were the best tribute to Sir Ralph Abercromby's talents and integrity. Though a rigid disciplinarian when rigour was necessary, such was the general confidence in his judgment and in the high character of his measures that in the numerous armies which at different periods he commanded not a complaint was ever heard that his rigour bordered on harshness, or that his decisions were influenced by partiality, prejudice, or passion. No methods for embalming the dead chief were practicable on the spot, and the body for the sake of preservation was immersed in a hogshead of rum to be conveyed to England. Leakage occurred during the voyage; and all that was mortal of Abercromby lies in Malta—interred appropriately in one of the bastions of the Fort of St. Elmo at the mouth of Valetta harbour.

As a soldier Sir Ralph Abercromby displayed a strong and vigorous intellect, with a military genius which overcame the disadvantages of inexperience. Yet it was not until the age of sixty-one that he first took the field in 1793, after having seen service only as a subaltern of dragoons during a short time in Germany in the course of the Seven Years' War. At the age when many men are retiring from the fatigues of active life, he began an honourable and successful career of military service, in which from the outset he displayed great capacity. The family was a remarkable one. The father, all but a centenarian at his death, lived to see his four sons honoured, respected, and at the head of their respective professions. When his eldest son Sir Ralph was commander-in-chief in the West Indies, his second son, Sir Robert, held the same station in the East; Lord Abercromby, the third son, was an eminent, learned, and just judge; and the fourth son died possessed of a great fortune acquired in the service of the East India Company. Summoned once to active service at a moment's notice in his sixty-eighth year, Sir Ralph had some difficulty in procuring the consent of his venerable parent. "They will wear him out too soon," complained the brisk nonogenarian, "and make an old man of him before his time, with their expeditions to Holland one year, and to the West Indies the next. If he would but follow my advice he would settle down at home for life." When his mother Lady Abercromby observed that her soldier-son must go abroad because of duty, the old gentleman said, "Then he will never see me more!" This prediction was verified when, a few months later, the father died at the age of ninety-seven.

The reader perchance may remember the story of the winning of the "red heckle," as set down in his simple, soldierly phrases on dingy paper a century old by " Rowland Cameron, pensioner, 42nd Regiment," who was himself present in the skirmish for which the "Forty-Twa" received that cherished trophy of ready valour. Such another record is now before me in the strange history of the standard of the French "Invincibles" in and after the battle of Alexandria, as told by Private Andrew Dowie of the Black Watch, who, as at Gildermalsen, was himself a participator in the dangers and glory of that fierce and heady fight. Worthy Andrew, as he has good right to do, differs in some points from the accepted versions of the incident. Andrew may tell his story in his own words:—

"On the morning of March 21st, an hour before daylight, the French made a grand attack upon our line; in making a feint upon our left the real attack was made upon our right. The 28th Regiment went into a battery on our right, and we occupied the ground in front of their tents. We warmly engaged a column in front. The morning being very calm, and not a breath to carry the smoke away, a French regiment passed our right and formed in our rear. This being observed by Major Stirling, who, hearing the officers dressing their line in the French language, instantly ordered the right wing to the right-about, gave them a volley, and charged. We pushed them forward at the point of the bayonet, and in spite of every effort on their part, we forced them towards the ruins of Cleopatra's Palace, where they made for a breach of the wall and chocked themselves like cattle forced in at a gate; we were obliged to force forward to get at those in the inside. By this time it was daybreak; the carnage was dreadful—in fact they were almost annihilated. While I was inside the ruins I observed an officer with a stand of colours, surrounded by a groupe of some thirty men. On looking round I noticed Major Stirling coming in at another breach, accompanied with a number of men. I ran and told him what I saw, and followed him to the French groupe. He advanced towards the French officer, having his sword concealed by his right thigh; he grasped the colours and carried them off with little resistance. Major Stirling then called Sergeant Sinclair of the grenadier company, and handed the colours to him. Sinclair asked if he should take them to headquarters. 'No,' replied the major, 'take them to the rear of the left wing and display them there and show the villains what you have got!' The left wing then closely engaged, Lieutenant Hillas was left with a guard to escort this groupe of French to the boats. The major then ordered all out of the ruins to support the left wing, which was done as quickly as possible, and commenced firing. The general commanding the French cavalry, seeing our irregular formation, made a charge on us. Sir Ralph Abercromby seeing the cavalry coming, called us to come to the rear of the tents; in proceeding thither my foot got entangled with a cord, and I was prisoner for nearly a quarter of an hour. During that time I saw Sir Ralph engaged with three of the French cavalry, cutting behind and before just like a youth of twenty. One of our grenadiers named Barker, having spent his ammunition, charged his piece with the loose powder from his cartouch, fired his ramrod, and killed one of Sir Ralph's assailants while Sir Ralph struck down another; the third made off. Sir Ralph thanked Barker for having saved his life and asked his name, and when taken to headquarters, ordered his son to remember Barker. During that charge, some of the French, seeing Sinclair with the colours, made after him and attacked him, who defended himself to the utmost, until he got a sabre-cut on the back of the neck. He fell with the colours among the killed and wounded. The German regiment, commanded by Sir John Stuart from the rear line, came to our support, and in passing through the killed and wounded one Anthony Lutz picked up the colours and stripped them off the staff and wound them round his body, and in the afternoon carried them to headquarters and delivered them to Sir Ralph's son; and I heard that he received some money for them.* In 1802 the German regiment arrived at Winchester Barracks, where this Anthony Lutz, in a quarrel with one of his comrades, stabbed him with a knife, was tried by civil law, and sentence of death passed upon him. His officers, to save his life, petitioned the proper authorities, stating that it was he who took the 'Invincible' colours. Generals Moore and Oakes (who commanded our brigade in Egypt), then in London, wrote down to Lieutenant-Colonel Dickson, who was then with the 42nd in Edinburgh Castle, and a Court of Inquiry was held. Sergeant Sinclair was sent for from Glasgow, and was examined in the matter, and I likewise underwent an examination, and the result of this examination was in substance what I have narrated. How Lutz's business ended I do

* *Vide* page 200.

not remember. The following were among the officers on this Court of Inquiry in Edinburgh Castle in 1802:— Major Stirling, Major Alex. Stewart, Lieutenant Robert Campbell, Lieutenant Rose, Captain Mutter, etc. Sergeant Sinclair—the last time I saw him was in Sicily in 1810—was then captain in the 81st Regiment."

Andrew Dowie states that the 42nd did not know at the time of the battle of Alexandria that the French Grenadiers with whom the Highland Regiment fought on that day were styled the "Invincibles." The 42nd heard them called "Bonaparte's Bons Grenadiers"; and it was not until the regiment returned to England that the term of "Invincibles" first became known to it.

On the 21st the weight of the fighting on the British side was sustained by the reserve on the right, the Guards, two regiments of the first brigade in the centre, and the brigade of Sir John Stuart, which gave to the Highlanders a support at once so timely and so effectual; so that the sum total of the British force actually engaged was somewhat less than 6,000 men. While at Mandora, on the 13th, the French losses were less by one half than those of the British, on the 21st they were so much greater that 1,700 Frenchmen were left on the field, either killed or desperately wounded. While the total number of British killed was 243, there were buried on the field of the enemy 1,040 men. The total loss of the enemy on the day of Alexandria must have been upwards of 4,000 men, exclusive of prisoners. The British lost: killed, ten officers, nine sergeants, and 224 rank and file; wounded, sixty officers, forty-eight sergeants, three drummers, and 1,082 rank and file; total losses, 1,193 men. The Highlanders lost Brevet-Major Robert Bisset, Lieutenants Colin Campbell, Robert Anderson, Alexander Stewart, Alexander Donaldson, and

Archibald McNicol, and forty-eight rank and file killed; Major James Stirling, Captain David Stewart, Lieutenants Hamilton Rose, J. Milford Sutherland, A. M. Cuningham, Frederick Campbell, Maxwell Grant, Ensign William Mackenzie, six sergeants, and 247 rank and file wounded. The six officers killed were promising young men, and their death was a serious loss to the regiment. Few officers equalled Major Bisset in professional accomplishments. With a keen and penetrating mind, great application, and a retentive memory, his information was general and extensive, and equally fitted him to adorn the character of the soldier, the gentleman, and the man of the world. Ensign Maxwell Grant was wounded by a bayonet which entered one side of his stomach and came out at the other. Lieutenant Stewart was wounded in the same region by a musket-ball. After the action they lay together in the same tent. Grant, vomiting and throwing up blood, was considered in immediate danger. Stewart complained only of a dull pain in the lower abdomen, and his wound was regarded as comparatively trivial. Yet Stewart died the same evening, whereas Grant was quite well within a fortnight.

The conquest of Egypt might now be considered as virtually complete. General Hutchinson, on whom the command of the British army now devolved, remained before Alexandria for some time, during which a detachment commanded by Colonel Brent Spencer took possession of Rosetta. General Hutchinson then removed his headquarters to that place, whence he moved on Rhamanieh, an important position commanding the passage of the Nile, preserving the communication between Alexandria and Cairo, and defended by 4,000 infantry, 800 cavalry, and thirty-two guns. During the advance there was considerable skirmishing and cannonading, in the course of which the British lost thirty men killed and wounded, including six officers; but as General Hutchinson approached the French position on May 5th it was found to be evacuated. He then moved forward towards Cairo, and on June 16th encamped four miles from the capital. Belliard, the French commander, waited until the approaches of the British were so forward as to allow him to capitulate with honour; and on June 22nd he offered to surrender on the condition that his army should be sent to France with its arms and baggage.

Alexandria still remained to be reduced; and on his return from Cairo General Hutchinson proceeded to invest it. Detaching to the westward of the city General Coote with nearly half the army, he himself advanced from the eastward. General Menou, finding himself surrounded on two faces by an army 14,500 strong, hemmed in by the sea on the north, cut off on the south by a lake which had been formed by the destruction of the dyke on the canal from the Nile to Alexandria, and already forced to feed his troops on horse-flesh, could delay a surrender only for the sake of effect. Yet the French general played his part well and disputed every advance until 26th August, when he applied for an armistice for three days in order to frame conditions of capitulation. The armistice was agreed to, and on 2nd September the capitulation was signed and was ratified by the respective commanders. Early in July the British army had been reinforced from England and Minorca by a cavalry regiment, a detachment of Guards, five regiments of the line, and two foreign regiments. A little army of some 5,000 men, which was sent from India under the command of Major-General

Baird to reinforce and act in conjunction with the army already in Egypt, reached Kosseir on the Red Sea in June. It had marched across the Nubian desert to Keneh, whence it descended the Nile to Rosetta and encamped there in August. This little army was in high discipline and bore full ranks. It consisted of the 10th and 61st Regiments, with large detachments of the 80th, 86th, and 88th Regiments, two Bombay regiments, a corps of Bengal volunteers, and a full proportion of artillery. Its only regret was that it had not reached Egypt in time to take part with its comrades in fighting for king and country. The French troops were the first to embark; their departing strength was 27,500 men. The grand total of British troops in Egypt at this time was 22,350 men. During the campaign in Egypt, the killed and wounded of the British army amounted to 3,592; 550 killed, and 3,042 wounded. The number of dead from dysentery, the plague, and other diseases, was very considerable.

## CHAPTER XVIII.

#### HOME SERVICE. 1801-1805.

Landed at Southampton, December, 1801. Vote of thanks from the Highland Society of Scotland, January 12, 1802. Misunderstanding between the Highland Society and the Forty Second regarding a French standard captured in the battle of Alexandria. Interruption of communication between them. Friendly relations restored in 1817. Presentation to the regiment by the Duke of York of a superb piece of plate on behalf of the Society. Parade of the regiment at Armagh Barracks for the occasion. In May, 1802, the regiment reviewed at Ashford by the King. Return to Scotland. Presentation of new colours at Edinburgh December 1, 1802. Moved to Weeley Camp, Essex.

WHEN the destinations of the troops in Egypt were finally arranged, the three Highland regiments (42nd, 79th, and 92nd) were included among the corps ordered home. The 42nd landed at Southampton, and marched to Winchester. With the exception of those affected with ophthalmia, all the men were healthy.

Soon after the arrival of the regiment at Winchester the following document was received by the commanding officer :—" At a general meeting of the Highland Society of Scotland, on 12th January, 1802, when upwards of one hundred noblemen and gentlemen were present, the EARL OF EGLINTON, Vice-President, in the chair,

" RESOLVED unanimously, and with the greatest applause, to vote the thanks of this Society to the British Army in Egypt for their gallant achievements, in which our countrymen the Highland regiments maintained in so conspicuous a manner the warlike character of their ancestors, and more especially to that old and long-distinguished corps, the FORTY - SECOND or ROYAL HIGHLAND Regiment; and recommends to the Secretary to transmit this resolution to the commanding officer, in order to be communicated to the regiment in such manner as to him shall seem proper."

Lieutenant-Colonel Dickson inserted this vote in regimental orders, with directions for it to be read at the head of each company; and added that he felt himself "highly flattered by the distinguished mark of approbation bestowed upon the officers and soldiers of the ROYAL HIGHLANDERS by their countrymen for their brave and gallant behaviour in Egypt which they so justly have merited; and he is confident that whenever an opportunity may again occur, they will be equally conspicuous in maintaining that national character of bravery hitherto experienced by their enemies and, which they so gloriously evidenced in their late campaign in Egypt."

At this period an event occurred which caused some interest and controversy regarding the standard of the French captured in the battle of Alexandria. The Highland Society of London, deeply gratified by the accounts given of the conduct of their countrymen in Egypt, resolved to bestow on them some mark of their esteem and approbation. The Society being composed of men of the first rank and character in Scotland and including several members of the royal family, it was considered that such a tribute would be honourable to the corps and agreeable to all true Highlanders. It was proposed to begin with the 42nd as the senior of the Highland regiments, and to continue with the others in succession as their service offered the opportunity of distinguishing themselves. Fifteen hundred pounds was immediately subscribed for this purpose. Medals were struck with a head of Sir Ralph Abercromby and some emblematic figures on the obverse. A superb piece of plate was also ordered. While the medals and plate were in preparation the Society held a meeting, in which Sir John Sinclair with the warmth of a clansman, mentioned his namesake Sergeant Sinclair, as having taken or got possession of the French standard, which had been brought home and is now in the Chapel Royal at Whitehall. The captured standard bore several "honours" gained by the "Invincibles" in Italy, and in its centre was a bugle-horn wreathed with laurel. Sir John, being at that time ignorant of the circumstances, made no mention of the loss of the standard which had been given in charge to Sergeant Sinclair. This called forth the production of it on the part of the German soldier Lutz already alluded to,* accompanied by some strong remarks by Cobbett, the editor of the work in which the claim by Lutz appeared. The Society then desired an explanation on the part of the officers of the 42nd. To this very proper request a reply was given by the officers then present with the regiment. The majority of those happened to be young men, who expressed in warm terms their surprise that the Society should imagine them capable of countenancing any statement implying that they had laid claim to a trophy to which they had no right. This misapprehension of the Society's meaning brought on a correspondence which ended in an interruption of further communication for many years. From 1811 to 1817 endeavours had been frequently made to establish a better feeling between the Highland Society and the officers of the

* *Vide* p. 188.

42nd who had served in Egypt, but in vain. The latter would not yield, and in the meantime the vase remained at the maker's.

However, as a prelude to a fresh correspondence and the restoration of relations between the Society and the Highland regiments, a communication with the 42nd was renewed in 1817. General Stewart, who was himself one of the vice-presidents of the Highland Society, was requested by some of his brother members to use his good offices in a matter which had originated in mistake and misapprehension. A complete understanding was the happy issue; and on 17th March, 1817, the anniversary of the battle of Alexandria, the Duke of York, then President of the Highland Society, being in the chair, presented the Marquis of Huntly on behalf of the 42nd Regiment, with a superb piece of plate, in token of the respect of the Society for a corps which for more than seventy years had contributed to uphold the martial character of the Highlanders of Scotland. This presentation his Royal Highness accompanied with an impressive speech, in which he recapitulated the various services of the regiment from its first battle at Fontenoy down to the recent victories of Quatre Bras and Waterloo. It was at Armagh Barracks on Wednesday, the 18th June, 1817—the second anniversary of the battle of Waterloo—that the Duke of York's gift of a "superb piece of plate" which took the form of a massive and graceful vase on a pedestal, was presented to the Old Highland Regiment on its own parade ground.

At the time four companies were detached to Newry and several other detachments were absent from Armagh, so that not more than about three companies were present at the ceremony. The parade was in review order with side-arms, and a square of two deep was formed. On a table in the centre of the square was the vase, still covered; and there were also several small kegs of Highland whisky brought from Scotland for the express purpose of the occasion. A portion of the correspondence with the Highland Society was read by the adjutant; Lieutenant-Colonel Robert Henry Dick addressed the regiment; the casks of whisky were broached and the cup was filled. The colonel drank to the officers and men, the staff officers followed, and afterwards the captains and subalterns drank to the health of their respective companies, and the cup, held by both hands and kept well replenished, went three times along the ranks. All was happiness and hilarity, not only on parade but during the remainder of the day. Thus was presented to the regiment the beautiful vase, which is of great elegance and beauty. Of the officers present on the occasion, the last remaining one, the late Lieutenant-Colonel Wheatley, recently died.

The day of "the Cup" was long remembered among the men of the regiment, and the quality and quantity of the whisky distributed on the day of the presentation were ever spoken of with enthusiasm. The vase was renovated in 1869, when the regiment was quartered at Aldershot camp towards the close of that year; and it was then placed on an ebony stand which has enhanced its elegant and imposing aspect.

The intention of granting medals was abandoned by the Society on the ground that military men could receive medals for war services only from the Sovereign. When the Prince Regent became Chief of the Highland Society one of those medals with an address from the Society was presented to his Royal Highness by Sir Archibald Macdonald, accompanied by a deputation which was most graciously received. As those medals commemorated the heroic death of Sir Ralph Abercromby, one was presented to each of his sons.

In May, 1802, the King being desirous to see the 42nd, the regiment marched to Ashford, where it was received by his Majesty, accompanied by the Prince of Wales and the Duke of York. The King expressed himself satisfied with the appearance of the regiment; but although the men bore themselves with a martial air, there was a distinct falling-off in size and long service in hot climates had left its mark on the physique of the regiment.

Soon after this review the regiment marched northward to Edinburgh. During the long march the men were everywhere received with kindness; and as the regiment approached the northern metropolis, thousands met it at some distance from the city, congratulated it with acclamation on its return to Scotland, and escorted it to the Castle.

New colours had been prepared bearing the lately-won distinctions—the *Sphinx* with the word *Egypt*—granted to the regiment for its services in Egypt; and they were presented to the regiment on parade at Edinburgh on 1st December, 1802, when the following address was delivered by Lieutenant-General Vyse, commanding the forces in North Britain:—

"Brother Soldiers of the Forty-Second Regiment! Let me earnestly exhort you most sincerely to reflect on the invaluable deposit now committed to your protection, and which is rendered doubly sacred by the solemn benediction of this reverend minister, Principal Baird, of our holy faith.

"Remember that the standards which you have this day received are not only revered by an admiring world, as the honourable monuments and trophies of your recent heroism, but are likewise regarded by a grateful country as the sacred pledges of that security which, under protection of Heaven, it may expect from your future services.

"Should the restless ambition of an envious and daring enemy again call you to the field, think, then, that you behold the spirit of those brave comrades who so nobly fell in their country's cause upon the plains of Egypt, hovering round these standards; think that you see the venerable shade of the immortal Abercromby leading you again to action, and pointing to that presumptuous band whose arrogance has been humbled and whose vanity has been compelled by your intrepidity and courage to confess that no human force has been 'invincible' against British valour, when directed by wisdom, conducted by valour, and inspired by virtue."

While the regiment remained quartered in Edinburgh Castle, the men in some degree deteriorated temporarily by the temptations to which too great and indiscriminate hospitality exposed them. Fortunately for the reputation of the regiment, a change of quarters occurred in the spring of 1803, when in consequence of the disruption of the Peace of Amiens in May, the regiment embarked at Leith, landed at Harwich, and marched to the camp of Weeley in Essex, where it was incorporated in the brigade commanded by Major-General Sir John Hope. Under his firm command all the bad effects of the too great hospitality of Edinburgh soon disappeared. The regiment was at this time low in strength, not exceeding 400 men, in consequence chiefly of the discharge of 470 men in the preceding year. In 1803 the regiment was recruited in a novel manner. As a means of ensuring the internal defence of the kingdom, and of recruiting the regular army, an Act had been passed for the raising of a body of men by ballot, to be styled the "Army of Reserve." The service of this army was to be confined to Great Britain and Ireland, but with liberty to volunteer into the regular—the active—army, on a certain bounty. In Scotland the men availing themselves of this liberty were in the first instance to be formed into second battalions of line regiments. The quota furnished by the counties of Perth, Elgin, Nairn, Cromarty, Ross, Sutherland, Caithness, Argyle, and Bute, destined to form the second battalion of the 42nd, which had been placed on the establishment on July 9th, 1803, amounted to 1343 men. The second battalion, consisting of those quotas, embarked in November, 1803, at Fort George, to join the first battalion in the Weeley camp, when upwards of 500 men had already volunteered into the regular army. In April, 1804, Captain David Stewart of Garth became major of the regiment, and Lieutenants Robert Henry Dick and Charles McLean were promoted captains in the second battalion of the 78th Regiment. In the following September, Colonel Dickson was made a Brigadier-General; when Lieutenant-Colonels James Stewart and Alexander Stewart retired, and were succeeded by Lieutenant-Colonels Stirling and Lord Blantyre. Captains McQuarrie and James Grant became majors; Lieutenants Stewart Campbell, Donald Williamson, John McDiarmid, John Dick, and James Walker, captains; and Captain Lord Saltoun was promoted to the Foot Guards. Lieutenant-Colonel Stirling was a very gallant officer. He joined the 42nd as a volunteer in 1774, served in the regiment for forty-two years, and was present in every engagement in which the 42nd took part during that long period. During his protracted regimental service he had only six months' leave of absence; he was twice wounded, once taken prisoner at sea, and once shipwrecked. All his service until he attained general rank, was in the 42nd, the left wing of which he commanded at the battle of Alexandria, where with his gallant Highland soldiers, he defeated Napoleon's famous "Invincibles," took prisoners the survivors of that body, and captured their standard with his own hand. He commanded the 42nd Regiment through the Peninsular war; and at length in 1813 he retired into private life, where, cultivating the virtues which adorn the Christian character, he died full of years and honours at his villa of Eskbank on 12th December, 1834. General Stirling was in possession of the Egyptian medal and a medal with two clasps for Coruña, Salamanca and the Pyrenees. Before entering the 42nd, Lord Blantyre had been in several regiments—the Foot Guards, the 12th, and 7th Light Dragoons; he became colonel in 1813, major-general in 1819, and lieutenant-general about 1827. He had served on the staff in Portugal in 1798; in the Helder expedition in 1799; on the staff of Sir John Stuart, in Egypt, 1801-2; as Assistant Adjutant-General to Lord Cathcart, in the Baltic, 1807; commanded second battalion 42nd in the Peninsula, from 1809 to 1812. Medal for Fuentes d'Onoro, Knight of the Tower and Sword (Portugese), and C.B. Lord Blantyre died 22nd September, 1830.

## CHAPTER XIX.

### GIBRALTAR. 1805—1808.

Ordered to Gibraltar. Death of Sir Hector Munro. Arrival in Portugal after Vimiera. Sir John Moore's march into Spain.

THE two battalions remained together in Lieutenant-General Hope's brigade until early in October, 1805, when the first battalion of the 42nd and the second of the 78th embarked for Gibraltar, which was reached in November. Since its former stay on "The Rock" the moral habits of the garrison had experienced a marked improvement. It must always be difficult to prevent soldiers from drinking somewhat to excess when wine can be bought at threepence the quart and when they have money to pay for it; but the quantity now consumed did not materially affect discipline and in no degree health. That this was so was evidenced by the fact that during the three years of 1805, 1806, and 1807 the number of deaths in the 42nd amounted to only thirty-one in this regiment of 850 men.

In the end of 1805 Sir Hector Munro died. A fine soldier, he did not interest himself greatly in the regiment, of which he had been colonel since 1787, nor did he seem to regard it with the concern and feeling which might have been expected on the part of a fellow-countryman and a fellow-Highlander, who, with an affluent fortune and the influence which it commanded, might have materially contributed to the welfare and furtherance of the Black Watch. Although the first and second battalions of his regiment were for a considerable time quartered at Fort George in the neighbourhood of his country seat, he never came near them except once, when he stopped in the garrison for a few minutes to change horses on his way to London. He was succeeded in the colonelcy of the Highland Regiment by the Marquis of Huntly, on January 3rd, 1806. The Marquis had not undergone a great range of service, but he was a good soldier and took considerable interest in his regiment. He accompanied a detachment of Foot Guards to Flanders in the spring of 1793, and was present at the action of St. Amand on 8th May. He was subsequently engaged in the siege of Valenciennes, and later at Lincelles and at the siege of Dunkirk. In 1794 he raised a regiment of Highlanders, which was numbered the 100th and afterwards the 92nd, of which he was appointed lieutenant-colonel commandant. He accompanied his regiment to Gibraltar, and on the return voyage to England was captured by a French privateer. During the Irish rebellion of 1798 the Marquis was appointed a brigadier-general, and was actively employed against the rebels in Wexford. He accompanied the expedition to Holland in 1799, and was wounded at the battle of Bergen on 2nd October. In 1809, he commanded a division in Holland. In 1820, he was nominated a Knight Grand Cross of the Order of the Bath, and on acceding to the dignity of Duke of Gordon in 1827, was appointed Governor of Edinburgh Castle and Keeper of the Great Seal of Scotland. His Grace died 28th May, 1836; and his remains, by order of King William, were escorted by a battalion of the Scots Fusilier Guards from London to Greenwich, where they were placed on board ship for conveyance to Scotland. By his decease the dukedom of Gordon became extinct, the vast properties going to his maternal kinsman the fifth Duke of Richmond. The titles of Duke of Gordon and Earl of Kinrara were revived in 1876 in the person of the present Duke of Richmond, who is now Duke of Richmond and Gordon.

The period had now arrived when the Royal Highland Regiment was soon to participate in the long, bloody, and ultimately successful military operations which began in the Spanish peninsula in 1808, and lasted until the glorious conclusion of the war in 1814.

The regiment had not the good fortune to share in Sir Arthur Wellesley's short but brilliant campaign in August, 1808, on the coast of Portugal, which terminated in the victory of Vimiera. It was not until after that success that the Royal Highlanders joined the army in Portugal, coming from Gibraltar with a strength of 826 men. The regiment was almost exclusively Scottish, for it contained but seven Englishmen and five Irishmen; but it no longer consisted entirely of Highlanders, although they were greatly in the majority. Of Highlanders it numbered 583 men; of Lowland Scots, 231.

It was not until 6th October, 1808, that a despatch from England containing the first determinate plan of campaign arrived at Lisbon. Thirty thousand infantry and 5,000 cavalry were to be employed in the north of Spain; of those numbers 10,000 were to be sent direct from England, and the remainder was to consist of regiments drafted from the army then in Portugal. Lieutenant-General Sir John Moore was to be commander-in-chief; and he was authorised at his discretion to effect a junction of his forces by a voyage round the coast, or by a march through the interior. Sir John chose the latter procedure, for several reasons which need not be detailed. He was directed to take the field immediately; but he had much to execute, and that with scarcely any means. He was to organise an army of raw soldiers, and in a poor and unsettled country he had to procure the transport necessary for his stores, ammunition, and even for the conveyance of the officers' baggage. He was unacquainted with the views of the Spanish Government, nor was he informed of the numbers, composition, and localities of the troops with which he was to act, as well as those with which he was to contend; £25,000 in his military chest and his own genius, constituted the resources for a campaign which would probably lead his army far from the coast and from all its means of supply. Believing it impossible to convey his artillery by the road through the mountains, he resolved to divide his army and to march into Spain by different routes. One brigade of guns he retained with headquarters; the rest of his artillery, the cavalry, and four infantry regiments, of which the 42nd was one, moved by the road of Talavera under the command of Sir John Hope, an officer of great talents, firmness, and zeal. The rest of the army marched in three divisions; the first by Alcantara and Coria, the second by Abrantes, and the third by Coimbra. Those divisions, amounting altogether to 18,000 infantry and 900 cavalry, were to form a junction at Salamanca. With such energy did Moore overcome all obstacles that his army had quitted Lisbon by 26th October, just twenty days after the receipt of the despatch appointing him to the chief command. "The army," to use his own words, "ran the risk of finding itself in front of the enemy with no more ammunition than the men carried in their pouches; but had I waited," he added, "until everything was forwarded, the troops would not have been in Spain until the spring."

## CHAPTER XX.

#### THE RETREAT AND BATTLE OF CORUÑA. 1809.

Sir John Moore's tactics. Bad conduct of the troops when ordered to retreat. Movements of Lord Paget. General Craufurd and Sir David Baird. The march to Coruña. Preparations for the battle. Disposition of the forces. Soult's arrival. The Forty Second's share in the fighting. Napier's account. The death of Sir John Moore.

MEANTIME Sir David Baird arrived with his forces at Coruña; he came destitute of money and Moore could supply him with only £8,000. When Moore reached Almeida on November 8th, he found the whole of the infantry there instead of being on the road to Salamanca. The condition, however, of the troops was superb; but it was evident that no considerable force could be brought into action before the end of the month. While awaiting the junction with Sir David Baird and the division of Sir John Hope, which was the last of Moore's force to come up, he received information of the utter defeat and dispersion of Blake's army on 10th November, as well as of the fate which subsequently befell Castaños at Tudela. No Spanish army now remained in the field except the corps of Romana, which tended rather to obstruct than to forward the plans of the British commander. After the defeat of Castaños at Tudela, Sir John Moore had resolved to fall back on Portugal; but he was now informed of the enthusiasm in Madrid, and the emissary impressed on him that propriety and policy alike demanded an immediate advance of the British to support the ardour of the capital and aid it to make a vigorous resistance against Napoleon. There seemed no doubt that Madrid was resolved on resistance, and that the spirit and energy of the country were awakening. The fire essential to the salvation of the nation seemed to be kindling, and Moore, feeling conscious of ability to lead a British army to success, hailed the appearance of an enthusiasm which promised success in a just cause, and a brilliant career of glory to himself.

The situation of the army was also improved; Hope's junction was accomplished, and there was no doubt that Baird's junction could likewise be effected. A chivalrous soldier and an enterprising commander, Moore adopted the boldest and most generous side. He ordered Baird to stand fast, while he himself prepared for an advance. It was mortifying to find that Madrid should have held out but a single day. The precipitancy of its surrender diminished the hope of arousing the Spanish nation: but so long as there was any hope the resolution of the English general was fixed not to abandon the cause, even when the Spaniards themselves were abandoning it. Intelligence, however, received through Colonel Graham, and an intercepted letter of Marshal Berthier to Marshal Soult, laid open to him the real posture of affairs. In consequence Moore resumed his original intention of retiring, not to the south but to the north of Spain, where he would be able to effect a junction with General Baird. Accordingly the army advanced to Toro on the 21st and there united with Baird's force, making altogether a total of 26,311 infantry and 2,450 cavalry. It was then determined to attack Soult at Saldana. The order operated on the troops like a charm, and as they flew to arms all privations and disappointments seemed forgotten. Fortunate is the general who commands troops whom the prospect of attacking the enemy inspires. But while the hopes of the army were at their height, intelligence poured in that the enemy were advancing in force from several directions to concentrate on one and the same point, the British army. No time was to be lost if it was to escape from the toils which encompassed it. The retreat was forthwith begun on the 24th, the same day as that on which the French advanced guard passed through Tordesillas. General Hope with two divisions fell back by the road of Mayorga, and General Baird by that of Valencia de San Juan. The enemy's dragoons arrived the same day at Frechilla, and the division of Laborde at Paredes. Next day (the 25th) the general-in-chief with the reserve and light brigades, followed the route of Hope's column to Valderas, and on the 26th Baird crossed the Esla at Valencia.

In proportion to the ardour of the troops when they were expecting to meet the enemy were their depression and disappointment when ordered again to retreat; and their discontent soon broke out in acts of turbulence and depredation hitherto unexampled in a British army. How disgraceful were those scenes and how evil were the consequences resulting from the inconsiderate reflections made by officers on the measures of their commanders, was evident from the tone of an order issued at Benevente, on December 27th: "The Commander of the Forces has observed with concern the extreme bad conduct of the troops at a moment when they are about to come into contact with the enemy, and when the greatest regularity and the best conduct are most requisite. The misbehaviour of the troops in the column which marched from Valderas to this place exceeds what he could have believed of British soldiers. . . . He can feel no mercy towards officers who neglect at such a time essential duties, or towards soldiers who injure the country they are sent to protect. It is impossible for the General to explain to the army his motives for the movements which he directs. When it is proper to fight a battle he will do so, and he will choose the time and place he thinks most fit. Meantime he begs the officers and soldiers of the army to attend diligently to discharge their part, and to leave to him and to the general officers the decision of measures which belong to them alone."

The indiscipline of the troops was occasionally relieved by brilliant and successful encounters with the advanced parties of the enemy, who now hung close on the rear and flanks of the British army. Lord Paget, after passing Mayorga, was intercepted by a strong body of horse belonging to Ney's corps, drawn up on a rising ground close to the road. The soil was deep and soaked with snow and rain, but two squadrons of the 10th Hussars reached the summit, and notwithstanding the enemy's advantage in number and position, killed twenty men and captured a hundred. From Mayorga Lord Paget proceeded to Benevente; but Soult, with great judgment, pushed for Astorga by the Mancilla road, whereupon Romana fell back on Leon. By a critical march Moore had recovered his communications with Gallicia; but his position was neither safe nor, indeed, tenable. The town of Benevente is situated in a plain through which winds the river Esla, but the right bank was completely commanded from the further side and there were many fords. In this exposed position the general desired to remain no longer than was necessary to empty his magazines at Benevente and to cover the march of his stores; and he requested and obtained Romana's consent to leave to the English army the Astorga-Leon road. A remarkable instance of courage and discipline occurred at the bridge of Castro Gonzales. John Walton and Richard Jackson, private soldiers of the 43rd, were posted beyond the bridge with orders on the approach of an enemy, the one to stand firm, the other to fire and run back to the brow of the hill to give notice whether the enemy advancing were many or few. Jackson fired, but was overtaken and received twelve or fourteen sabre-cuts in an instant; nevertheless he came staggering in and gave the signal; while Walton, with equal resolution, stood his ground and wounded several of his assailants, who then retired leaving him unhurt; but his cap, knapsack, belts, and musket were cut in about twenty places, his bayonet was bent double and notched like a saw.

On the 27th, when the cavalry and stragglers had all crossed the Esla, General Craufurd set about the destruction of the bridge, half the troops working while the other half kept the enemy at bay from the heights on the left bank. Two arches had been destroyed, and at midnight the troops descended, and passing in silence by single files over planks laid across the broken arches, gained the right bank without the loss of a man. The mine was sprung with good effect, and Craufurd marched to Benevente where the cavalry and reserve still remained. Soon after daybreak of the 29th, General Lefebre-Desnouettes crossed the river with 600 horsemen of the Imperial Guard, and advanced into the plain beyond. General Charles Stewart took the command on the British side, and a sharp contest ensued. Lord Paget ordered the 10th Hussars to mount and form under cover; he desired to draw the enemy well out into the plain before he attacked. Presently the signal was given, when the 10th galloped forward and charged. In an instant the enemy were fleeing at full speed towards the river, the British troopers in close pursuit, until the French squadrons without breaking ranks plunged into the stream and gained the opposite bank. During the pursuit in the plain, an officer was observed to separate himself from the main body and make towards another part of the river. He was followed, and refusing to stop when overtaken, he was cut across the head and brought in a prisoner. The fugitive officer turned out to be General Lefebre-Desnouettes, the commander of the cavalry of Napoleon's Imperial Guard.

On the 31st the flank brigades separated from the main army, and marched by cross roads towards Orense and Vigo, being thus detached to lessen the pressure on the commissariat and cover the flanks of the army. The divisions of Fraser and Hope entered Villa Franca; Baird's division was at Bembibre, whither, too, came the reserve in the course of the night. On January 1st, 1809, the Emperor took possession of Astorga, where 70,000 French infantry, 10,000 cavalry, and 201 guns were now united, after many days of incessant marching. Recalled to France by tidings of imminent war elsewhere, Napoleon left Soult to continue the pursuit, for which duty he had in the immediate advance about 25,000 men with fifty-four guns. In all, nearly 60,000 men and ninety-one guns were put on the track of the British army. Soult's main body followed the route of Foncevadon and Ponteferrado ; and Moore, after having twice baffled Napoleon's combination, was still being pressed in his retreat with a hot energy that seemed to increase every moment. The separation of his light brigades weakened him by 3,000 men ; but he had still

19,000 men of all arms, good fighting soldiers—none better, but severely shaken in their discipline by their earlier disorder. Nineteen thousand British soldiers could confront greatly superior numbers, it was true; but of what advantage could it be to fight an enemy who in Spain alone had 300,000 soldiers under arms?

On the arrival of the reserve at Bembibre Baird's division moved forward to Calcabellos, but hundreds of men remained behind intoxicated by the wine in the cellars of Bembibre; and notwithstanding the utmost exertions of the general, when the reserve marched next morning the number of the inebriated wretches was undiminished. Leaving a small guard for their protection, Sir John Moore went forward to Calcabellos; but scarcely had the reserve quitted Bembibre when some French cavalry rode into the place. "In a moment," wrote the historian Napier, who himself endured the sufferings of the retreat, " the road was filled with the miserable stragglers, who came crowding after the troops, some with loud shrieks of distress and wild gestures, others with brutal exclamations; while many, overcome with fear, threw away their arms; those who preserved them were too stupidly intoxicated to fire, and kept reeling to and fro, alike insensible to their danger and to their disgrace. The enemy's horsemen, perceiving this confusion, bore down at a gallop, broke through the disorderly mob, cutting to the right and left as they passed, and riding so close to the columns that the infantry were forced to halt in order to check their audacity."

In Villa Franca, to which the general-in-chief went forward, great excesses had been perpetrated by the earlier-passing divisions; the magazines had been plundered, the bakers had been driven away from the ovens, and the wine-stores broken open, so that the commissaries were prevented from making the regular distributions; and the gross insubordination of the soldiers made it evident that a discreditable relaxation of discipline had occurred on the part of the officers. The general promptly corrected this disorder, hanged a man caught in the act of plundering, and issued stern and stringent orders for the prevention of a recurrence of such conduct. The transports were ordered round from Vigo to Coruña; and meanwhile orders were sent to the leading division to halt at Lugo, Moore's intention being to rally the army there and to offer battle to the enemy. Those orders were sent to Sir David Baird by an aide-de-camp, but Sir David forwarded them by a private dragoon who got drunk and lost his despatches; and General Fraser went on towards St. Jago de Compostella and had to return without food or rest, losing on the way some four hundred stragglers. Of the main army the followers were dying fast from cold and hunger and the soldiers were dropping to the rear by hundreds, while broken carts, dead cattle, and the piteous plight of women with children falling exhausted in the snow completed the picture of misery. It was on the march near Nogales where dollars to the amount of £25,000, to prevent the treasure from falling into the hands of the enemy, were rolled down a precipice into the ravines beneath. At Lugo, where the general had resolved to make a stand, 19,000 British soldiers were in position under arms on the 7th when the French columns came in sight, and the greatest alacrity and animation now prevailed. The laggards, the lame, and the sick no sooner heard the firing than their misery and weakness instantly vanished; they seized their arms and joined their comrades.

At daybreak of the 8th the two armies still confronted each other. Soult had in line 17,000 infantry, 4,000 cavalry, and fifty guns, but he refrained from an attack. The British force — 16,000 infantry, 1,800 cavalry, and forty guns — impatiently awaited the assault; but darkness fell without a shot having been fired, and with it ended the English general's hope of engaging the adversary on equal terms. There was not another day's bread in the Lugo magazines; it was impossible to remain in that position, and useless if it had been possible. The general prepared to decamp in the night of the 8th, leaving the fires to be kept up and exhorting his troops to make a final exertion. At ten o'clock the regiments retired in excellent order; but ill fortune pursued the British army. A terrible storm of wind, rain, and sleet began as it moved from its positions; the divisions lost their way in the darkness, and at daylight the rear columns were still near Lugo. The loss of men from Lugo to Betanzos was greater than in all the previous part of the retreat; yet 14,000 infantry were still in column on the 12th, and an orderly march to Coruña directed by the commander-in-chief in person proved that the inattention and want of experience of the officers were the true causes of the previous disasters. Moore's ill fortune still dogged him; contrary winds detained the fleet at Vigo. The troops were put into quarters, and their leader awaited the course of events.

The inhabitants of Coruña cheerfully joined in the labour of repairing and strengthening the land front of the walled town. Two great magazines of powder on a hill were blown up on the 13th with a terrible explosion. At length the transports arrived, and all the impedimenta of the army were shipped in the night between the 15th and 16th. The enemy had been gradually coming up, and about two o'clock on the afternoon of the 16th a general movement along the French line gave notice of the approaching battle. The French occupied the superior ridge enclosing the British position, their right on the intersection of the roads from St. Jago and Betanzos, their left on a rocky eminence overlooking both lines, their cavalry in extension further left, supported by some light troops in and about an intervening valley. During the previous night the French had established a battery of eleven heavy guns on the rocky eminence just mentioned. The French force, on the outer and loftier ridge, had a strength of about 20,000 men. The British infantry, 14,500 strong, occupied the inner and inferior ridge already spoken of. The right was formed by Baird's division, which, because of the oblique direction of the ridge, lay nearest to the enemy; while the centre and left slanted away so that the great French battery on the rocky height enfiladed the whole British line. General Hope's division prolonged Baird's line leftward into the strong ground abutting on the marshy bank of the Mero. Each division had a brigade in rear behind the respective outward flanks. General Paget's reserve was posted near the village of Airis in rear of the main centre, and looked along the valley which separated Baird's right from the upper ground held by the French cavalry. Fraser's division held the heights immediately in front of Coruña.

Soult lost no time in preliminaries. He promptly opened fire from his heavy battery on the rocky eminence on his left, and simultaneously his infantry descended the ridge in three great columns. The village of Elvina, beyond Baird's extreme right, was carried by the first French column, which then divided and attempted at once to turn Baird's right by the valley and to break his front. The second French column struck at the British centre, and the third attacked Hope's left. Soult's artillery fire dominated utterly the fire of the few British six-pounders, and swept the position; but Sir John Moore, noting that the enemy showed no infantry save the body which was outflanking Baird's right, ordered General Paget to turn the French left and threaten the great battery. He himself threw back *en potence* the 4th Regiment forming Baird's extreme right, and opened a heavy fire on the flank of the French troops penetrating up the valley, while the 50th and 42nd Regiments met those breaking into and through the village of Elvina. It was intersected by stone walls and hollow roads, and a fierce irregular fight ensued in which the French were forced backward with great loss. The 50th entered the village along with them, and after a second struggle drove them from it.

There is a discrepancy in the narratives of an episode in this period of the battle which has occasioned some controversy, and in which the Royal Highland Regiment was concerned. William Napier writes, "The General ordered up a battalion of the Guards to fill the void in the line made by the movements of those regiments [the 4th and 50th],* when the 42nd, with the exception of its Grenadiers, mistaking the General's intention, retired, and at that moment the enemy, being reinforced, renewed the fight beyond the village; the officer commanding the 50th [Major Charles Napier, afterwards the conqueror of Scinde] was wounded and taken prisoner, and Elvina then became the scene of a second struggle,

---

* Baird's right brigade consisted of the 4th, 42nd, and 50th Regiments, commanded by Lieutenant-General Lord William Bentinck.

which being observed by the commander-in-chief, he addressed a few animating words to the 42nd, and caused it to return to the attack."

The following letter from Major-General James Stirling, who commanded the 42nd Regiment at the battle of Coruña on 16th January, 1809, appears in the Regimental Record of the regiment.

"MUSSELBURGH, 30*th March*, 1830.

"SIR,—In the Annals of the Peninsular Campaigns it is stated that from some misapprehension the FORTY-SECOND Regiment had retired at the battle of Coruña. Having had the honour to command the FORTY-SECOND in that action, I feel it incumbent on me to state to you, that what relates to the FORTY-SECOND is very inaccurate. The FORTY-SECOND never retired, as therein stated, nor evinced occasion for a brief but animated address from the General. On the advance of the French to the village of Elvina, Sir John Moore allowed the enemy to deploy, and to form their line at half musket-shot from us. He then gave me the order to advance and charge with the FORTY-SECOND, accompanying that order with the words, 'HIGHLANDERS, Remember Egypt!' which was the only address they received from him or anyone else. As soon as the regiment had given their fire and driven the enemy with the bayonet to the bottom of the ravine, Sir John directed me to halt the corps and defend that position; and turning myself round to him when he gave the order, I saw him, at the moment, struck to the ground from off his horse, and I immediately sent a party to carry him from the field. The Grenadiers and First Company not hearing my word of command to halt, continued the charge a little in advance, as did the Light Company also; when I was ordered by Lord William Bentinck commanding the brigade to recall them and form them in line with the regiment; and in that position, as directed by Sir John Moore, the corps continued in close action with the enemy till night put an end to the contest. . . . I have, etc.

(Signed) "J. STIRLING, Major-General.

"To the Editor of *The Edinburgh Magazine*."

The Historical Record of the regiment differs to some extent from General Stirling's statement. It is to the following effect:—"The 4th met that part of the French column which attempted to turn General Baird's right by the valley; and the FORTY-SECOND and 50th encountered the French battalions breaking through Elvina. The ground round the village was intersected by stone walls and hollow roads, and a severe contest ensued. Sir John Moore was on the spot, and as the FORTY-SECOND advanced to meet the enemy he called out, 'HIGHLANDERS, remember Egypt!' . . . The General applauded this brilliant success, and ordered up a battalion of Guards to fill the void occasioned by the advance of the two regiments, when the light infantry* and two or three other companies of the FORTY-SECOND, which had expended their ammunition, mistook his intention and retired, thinking they were to be relieved by the Guards. At this moment the enemy renewed the fight beyond the village, and Elvina became the scene of another struggle. Sir John Moore, observing this, turned to the companies which had retired, and said, 'My brave FORTY-SECOND, join your comrades; ammunition is coming, and you have your bayonets!' At the well-known voice of their General, the Highlanders instantly sprang forward and closed on the enemy with their bayonets."

Major Charles Napier, who commanded the 50th and who was left for dead, wrote a most graphic account of his regiment's share in the battle of Coruña. "Neither," he wrote, "did I receive an order from Lord William [Bentinck], nor from anybody else, unless Sir John Moore's permission to move my grenadiers forward may be called one; neither did I see a single staff officer during the

* Clearly should be "company."

battle, except Sir John and Lord William. . . . The men were falling fast, and seemed uneasy at standing under fire. The colours were lowered by the advice of Mr. John Montgomery, a brave soldier who had risen from the ranks. Soon the 42nd advanced in line, but no orders came for me. 'Good God! Montgomery, are we not to advance?' I asked. 'I think we ought,' he said. 'But,' said I, 'no orders have come.' 'I would not wait,' said Montgomery. The 4th did not move, the 42nd seemed likely to want our aid; it was not a moment for hesitation, and John Montgomery, himself a Scotsman, said laughingly, 'You cannot be wrong to follow the 42nd.' Many of the men cried, 'Major, let us fire!' 'Not yet,' was my answer; for having advanced without orders, I thought to have them more under command if we were wrong, since if firing once began we could not charge. At that moment the 42nd checked a short distance from a wall and commenced firing, and though a loud cry of 'Forward! forward!' arose, no man, as I afterwards heard, passed the wall. This check seemed to prove that my advance was right, and we passed the 42nd. Then I said to my men, 'Do you see your enemies plain enough to hit them?' Many voices shouted out, 'By Jasus, we do.' 'Then blaze away!' I cried; and such a rolling fire broke out as I have hardly ever heard since."

The conduct of the Royal Highland Regiment at Coruña was conspicuous; in effect the battle was won by the three regiments of Lord William Bentinck's brigade of Baird's division. In general orders issued on 18th January, Lieutenant-General Hope congratulated the army on the victory of Coruña; and after stating that, "On no occasion has the undaunted valour of British troops been more manifest," he added that "his acknowledgments are in a peculiar manner due to Lieutenant-General Lord William Bentinck, and *the brigade under his command, consisting of the Fourth,* FORTY-SECOND, *and Fiftieth Regiments,* which *sustained the weight of the attack.*" In the account of the battle addressed by General Hope to Sir David Baird, it is stated, "The first effort of the enemy was met by the commander of the Forces, and by yourself, at the head of the FORTY-SECOND Regiment," etc.

Sir John Moore, while watching the result of the fighting about the village of Elvina, was struck on the left breast by a cannon shot. The shock threw him from his horse with violence; but he rose in a sitting posture, his steadfast eye still fixed on the regiments engaged in his front. When he was satisfied that the British troops were gaining ground, his countenance brightened. His aide-de-camp Captain Henry Hardinge — afterwards Lord Hardinge—wrote describing his fall: "The violence of the shock threw him off his horse on his back. Not a muscle of his face altered, nor did a sigh betray the least sensation of pain. I dismounted, and taking his hand he pressed me forcibly, casting his eyes very anxiously towards the 42nd Regiment, which was hotly engaged, and his countenance expressed satisfaction when I informed him that the regiment was advancing. Assisted by a soldier of the 42nd, he was removed a few yards behind the shelter of a wall. He consented to be taken to the rear, and was put into a blanket for that purpose." Captain Hardinge attempted to unbuckle his sword from his chief's wounded side. It had got entangled, and the hilt had entered the wound; but the dying man said in his usual tone and manner, "It is as well as it is; I had rather it should go out of the field with me." "He was borne," continued Captain Hardinge, "by six soldiers of the 42nd and Guardsmen, my sash supporting him in an easy manner. I caught at the hope that I might be mistaken in my fear that the wound was mortal, and I remarked that I trusted that when the surgeons had dressed his wound he might recover. He turned his head, and looking steadfastly at the wound for a few moments, said, 'No, Hardinge; I feel that to be impossible.' I wished to accompany him to the rear, but he said, 'You need not go with me; report to General Hope that I am wounded and carried to the rear.'" A sergeant of the 42nd and two spare files, in case of accident, were ordered to conduct their beloved general to Coruña. As the soldiers were carrying him slowly along, he made them turn round frequently to view the field of battle and to listen to the firing; and he was well pleased when the sound grew fainter, judging that the enemy were retiring. Colonel Winch, who was wounded, was passing in a spring waggon and he wished the General to be removed into the vehicle. Sir John asked the Highland sergeant whether he thought the waggon or the blanket the better. The soldier thought the blanket best. "I think so, too," said the general; and the soldiers bore him to Coruña, shedding tears all the way.

Colonel Anderson, his friend and aide-de-camp for twenty years, thus describes Moore's last moments.—
"After some time he seemed very anxious to speak to me, and at intervals got out as follows: 'Anderson, you know that I always wished to die in this way. I hope the people of England will be satisfied! I hope my country will do me duty! Anderson, you will see my friends as soon as you can. Tell them everything—say to my mother——' Here his voice quite failed, and he was excessively agitated." At the thought of his mother

the firm heart of this brave and affectionate son gave way, a heart which no danger could shake till the sorrow which his death would bring to his mother broke down his fortitude. He died a few minutes later, that sacred name on his lips; and his corpse, wrapped in his "martial cloak," was interred by his staff officers and a few soldiers of the Black Watch on a bastion of the citadel of Coruña; the guns of the enemy paid him funeral honours; and his adversary Soult, with a noble sentiment of respect for his valour, raised a monument to his memory.

Napier's tribute to Moore is very fine:—"Thus ended the career of Sir John Moore, a man whose uncommon capacity was sustained by the purest virtue, and governed by a disinterested patriotism more in keeping with the primitive than the luxurious age of a great nation. His tall graceful person, his dark searching eyes, strongly defined forehead, and singularly expressive mouth indicated a noble disposition and a refined understanding. The lofty sentiments of honour habitual to his mind, adorned by a subtle playful wit, gave him in conversation an ascendency that he always preserved by the decisive vigour of his actions. He maintained the right with a vehemence bordering upon fierceness, and every important transaction in which he was engaged increased his reputation for talent, and confirmed his character as a stern enemy to vice, a steadfast friend to merit, a just and faithful servant of his country. The honest loved him, the dishonest feared him; for while he lived he scorned and spurned the base, who, with characteristic propriety, spurned at him when he was dead."

## CHAPTER XXI.

### HOME SERVICE AND WALCHEREN.

The 42nd return to England. Arrival at Plymouth. Death of Major Campbell, the only officer of the Black Watch lost during the retreat on Coruña. Losses during retreat and in battle. The regiment brigaded at Shorncliffe with the Rifle Corps. The Walcheren Expedition.

THE embarkation of the army was completed on the 18th and 19th of January, 1809, when it sailed for England. One division landed at Portsmouth, another, in which was the 42nd, landed at Plymouth. In the retreat to Coruña the soldiers had suffered more from want of shoes than from any other privation; marching over mountains deeply covered with snow, their feet were torn by the ice, and their toes were frost-bitten. Their shoes were contract articles, and, as was but too common, became unserviceable after a few days' marching. Colin Campbell, afterwards Lord Clyde, used to relate how for some time before reaching Coruña he had to march with bare feet, the soles of his boots being completely worn away. He had no means of replacing them, and when he got on board ship he was unable to remove them, as from constant wear and his inability to take them off, the leather had adhered so closely to the flesh of the legs and ankles that he was obliged to steep them in water as hot as he could bear, and have the leather cut away in strips—a painful operation, as in the process pieces of the skin were brought away with it.

The soldiers soon recovered from their wounds, and from the hardships of the retreat to Coruña. No officer of the Highland Regiment died except Major Campbell, who sank under the severity of the weather during the retreat. In general orders, Lieutenant-General Hope congratulated the army on its victory at Coruña, and added, "On no occasion has the undaunted valour of British troops been more manifest. At the end of a severe and harassing march, rendered necessary by the superiority which the enemy had acquired, and which had materially impaired the efficiency of the troops, many disadvantages were to be encountered. These have all been surmounted by the conduct of the troops themselves; and the enemy has been taught that whatever advantage of position or numbers he may employ, there is inherent in British officers and soldiers a bravery that knows not how to yield—that no circumstances can appal, and that will ensure victory when it is to be obtained by the exertion of any human means."

The regiment on its return to England was brigaded at Shorncliffe with the Rifle Corps, under the command of Major-General Sir Thomas Graham, who after many years' denial of army rank, notwithstanding that he had raised two battalions at his own expense, had now at length attained general rank as the result of the dying entreaties of the generous and chivalrous Moore. The second battalion, which had been quartered in Ireland since 1805, was now under orders to embark for Portugal, and therefore could spare no men to supply the losses suffered by the first battalion in the retreat to Coruña and the battle fought there. Those losses were considerable. The regiment had one sergeant and thirty-six men killed; and six officers—Captains Duncan Campbell, John Fraser, and Maxwell Grant, and Lieutenants Alexander Anderson, William Middleton, and Thomas MacInnes—one sergeant, and 104 men, wounded. The British loss in the battle amounted to 800 men, that of the enemy, upwards of 3,000; a remarkable disproportion, especially when it is considered that the British troops fought under many disadvantages.

The regiment next took part in the disastrous Walcheren expedition, the principal memorial of which now extant, apart from the desolating Walcheren fever, is the well-known doggrel:—

> "The Earl of Chatham, with sword drawn,
> Stood waiting for Sir Richard Strachan,
> Sir Richard Strachan, longing to be at 'em,
> Was waiting for the Earl of Chatham."

From this pestilential region the 42nd returned to Dover in September, having only 204 men fit for duty out of 758, who about six weeks previously had marched through the same town for embarkation to Holland. The Highland soldiers recovered very slowly from the Walcheren fever, and many of them suffered long under its baneful influence. The regiment remained at Canterbury until July, 1810, when it was removed to Scotland and was quartered at Musselburgh. The ranks of the regiment, notwithstanding its prestige as the senior Highland regiment in the service, were not now to be filled with the old facility and enthusiasm, and neither recruiting in the country nor volunteering in the Scottish Militia was successful. Those altered circumstances were so sadly conspicuous when the second battalion embarked for Portugal, that the commanding officer, Lieutenant-Colonel Lord Blantyre, recruited from the Irish Militia 150 men to be transformed into Scottish Highlanders. During the stay of the 42nd at Musselburgh the men unfortunately indulged to excess in the use of ardent spirits, and it was fortunate that a change of scene ere long occurred.

# CHAPTER XXII.

### WELLINGTON'S PENINSULAR CAMPAIGNS. 1810—8114.

The first battalion moved to England in August, 1811. Ordered to Portugal April, 1812. Meets with the second battalion and consolidated with it after the reduction of Ciudad, and Badajos. Service of the second battalion in the war prior to the time. Rodrigo share in the honour of Busaco. Wellington at Salamanca. His entry into Madrid. The 42nd before Burgos. Abandonment of the siege. The retreat. Demoralisation of the army. Wellington's strictures. Winter quarters taken up in Portugal. Wellington's advance on Vittoria. Fierce fighting at Gamara Mayor. Victory of Vittoria. Rout of French army. Royal Highlanders not actively engaged in campaign of Pyrenees. Capture of St. Sebastian. Passage of Bidassoa. Entrance of British army into France. The combat of the Croix des Bouquets. Battle of Nivelle—gallant bearing of Royal Highlanders. Five days' fighting on the Nive. Honours of "Nivelle" and "Nive" awarded to Royal Highland Regiment. Medals to officers. German troops join British ranks. Battle of Orthez—defeat of Soult. French loss estimated 8,000 men. Advance on Toulouse. Final battle of Peninsular War, triumphant victory of Toulouse. Severe losses of Royal Highland Regiment. Its conduct in battle narrated by Mr. Malcolm. Cessation of hostilities. Peninsular army broken up. Highland brigade quartered in Ireland until May, 1815. Shipped to Belgium on return of Napoleon from Elba.

IN August, 1811, the first battalion moved to England and was quartered at Lewes, until it embarked for Portugal in April, 1812. It joined Wellington's army in May, after the reduction of Ciudad Rodrigo and Badajos. The capture of those fortresses under the circumstances of difficulty to which the besieging forces were exposed, and defended as they were by a brave and disciplined enemy, gave the nation a marked earnest of its great commander's career of brilliant skill and ultimate triumph. At this auspicious period the first battalion met the second, which had already been nearly three years in the Peninsula, and the two battalions were now consolidated. The second battalion had seen considerable service when in the Peninsula. The Royal Highlanders were in position on the long lofty ridge of Busaco when Massena assailed it so furiously on September 27th, 1810, while the valour of Wellington's soldiers repulsed the vehement charges of the gallant and stubborn French troops. Major Henry Robert Dick received a medal for this battle. The battalion served during the winter season of 1810-11 in the famous lines of Torres Vedras. When Wellington blockaded Almeida the French advanced to attempt the relief of the fortress; and on May 3rd, 1811, they fell upon the five battalions of chosen British troops which occupied the position of Fuentes d'Onoro. Very severe fighting took place; but the French were repulsed, and the British regiments held the village in the midst of the killed and wounded of both sides. Massena attacked again on the 5th in far greater strength. The British cavalry withdrew behind the light division. Houston's division, thus entirely exposed, was charged with great impetus, and Captain Norman Ramsay's troop of horse-artillery was cut off and surrounded. Presently a great commotion was observed among the French squadrons; men and officers closed in confusion towards one point, where a thick dust was rising, and where loud cries, the sparkling of blades, and the flashing of pistols indicated some extraordinary occurrence. "Suddenly," in Napier's burning words, "the multitude was violently agitated, a British shout arose, the mass was rent asunder, and Norman Ramsay burst forth at the head of his battery, his horses breathing fire, and stretching like greyhounds along the plain, his guns bounding like things of no weight, and the mounted gunners in close and compact order protecting the rear." But while this brilliant action was in progress, it was nevertheless abundantly evident that the battle would soon be lost if the original position was not immediately regained. Craufurd retired slowly over the plain in squares, followed by the enemy's horse, which near the wood surprised and sabred an advanced post of the Guards, making Colonel Hill and fourteen men prisoners. They then continued their charge, but suddenly found themselves in front of the Royal Highlanders. They charged with great fierceness, but before that day the Highlanders had learned how to deal with charging cavalry. With signal gallantry Lord Blantyre and his battalion repulsed the efforts of the French troopers. It fared not so well with the brother-Highland regiments of the 71st and 79th; two companies of the latter corps were taken prisoners, and its colonel, the gallant Cameron, was mortally wounded. The fighting lasted until evening; both sides claimed the victory, but Wellington's principal object, the covering of the blockade of Almeida, was attained, with, however, a loss of 1,500 officers and men, 300 of whom were prisoners. Lord Blantyre received a gold medal; and the "honour" of "Fuentes d'Onoro," displayed by royal authority on the regimental colour, commemorates the steadfast resolution of the second battalion of the Royal Highlanders in this fierce conflict. Its loss on May 3rd was two soldiers killed; Captain McDonald, one sergeant and five rank and file wounded. On the 5th, the loss was one sergeant and one private killed; one sergeant and twenty-two rank and file wounded. Major H. R. Dick received a medal for the battle of Fuentes d'Onoro, where he commanded a flank battalion.

The recapture of Ciudad Rodrigo and Badajos had long occupied Wellington's attention. On January 9th, 1812, the former strong place was invested; with such rapidity and skill was the siege pressed that on the 19th a breach was practicable. Wellington's orders were peremptory and curt. "Ciudad Rodrigo must be carried by assault this evening at seven o'clock." The difficulties and horrors of that assault can be but feebly described; but the breach was carried, and the great fortress of Castile was in the hands of the allies. In twelve days in the depth of winter, 40,000 men had been gathered round the fortress with such secrecy and celerity that before the great hosts of the enemy could arrive to its succour, the fortress had fallen; and with a loss of about 1,300 men, the stores, the artillery, and the *matériel* of Marmont's army had been captured, and a severe blow struck at the power of France. The Cortes granted to the victor the dukedom of Ciudad Rodrigo; the Portuguese gave him the marquisate of Torres Vedras. In England, too, clamour became silent, the Crown granted the ever-successful chief another step in the peerage, and the nation settled £2,000 a year on the new earldom of Wellington.

On the 17th March Badajos was invested with 30,000 men, while Hill covered the siege which Wellington conducted with 22,000 picked troops. For twenty days, in spite of the murderous inventions of Philippon the French engineer, the siege made slow but sure progress in favour of the allies; the outlying fort of the Picurina had fallen and already the walls of the Trinidad bastion were crumbling beneath the besiegers' fire. By the morning of 6th April three breaches in its walls were pronounced practicable. The following day was named for the assault; for Marmont was already concentrated at Salamanca and threatening Ciudad Rodrigo, and Soult was moving up from Andalusia. Three attacks were ordered: on the right, Picton led against the castle; in the centre, General Colville assaulted the breaches; on the left, Leith's division menaced the outwork of Pardaleras and the San Vincente bastion. In the three breaches the defences were unsurmountable : sharpshooters, each provided with four loaded muskets, commanded every inch of the ground; heavy guns flanked the ditches; hundreds of shells were ready to be rolled down on the assailants, and an immense beam of wood studded with sword-blades barred all entrance to the great breach. Still the soldiers struggled to ascend the ruins, and a conflict too awful to be depicted stretched 2,000 killed and wounded in the crowded ditches at the foot of the breaches. Success, nevertheless, eventually crowned the exertions of Picton's and Leith's divisions, and from San Vincente and the castle the men soon streamed in force to the rear of the long-continued breaches. Still the contest raged; but the great defences before which so many had fallen and given away their lives were turned in the rear and rendered nugatory. The bugles sounded an English air in the heart of Badajos, Philippon hastily retreated to the fort of San Christoval, and on his surrender on the following morning the second great border stronghold was in the possession of the allies. Again rapine and debauchery disgraced the victory, and it was not until some of the worst of the marauders were gibbeted in the marketplace that the horrors ceased, and that on the third day order was restored in Badajos. The loss had been immense; 5,000 men had suffered during the siege, of whom 3,500 had been killed or wounded during the assault.

The second battalion of the Royal Highlanders certainly had a good claim to the "honour" of "Busaco" —a battle in which it was under fire in the ridge, for which one of its field officers, Major Dick, received a gold medal, and in which it lost six men killed and wounded. It did receive the "honour" of "Fuentes d'Onoro," where it suffered some considerable loss. It was engaged at the siege of Ciudad Rodrigo and also that of Badajos, but on neither occasion is loss recorded. That circumstance, however, goes for nothing, except that it seems to indicate with great force that those who ought to have upheld the prestige of the regiment, and to have asserted and sustained its just claims to the "honours" and "distinctions" fairly due to it, must have been singularly careless in regard to this almost sacred duty. The officers and staff of the second battalion were ordered to England, leaving the first upwards of 1,160 rank and file fit for service, and included in Lieutenant-General Sir Thomas Graham's division. The second battalion had suffered with exceptional severity on the banks of the Guadiana; and when the first battalion received its full complement, the few men who remained were ordered to Scotland to be stationed there at the peace in 1814.

Early in June the indefatigable Wellington moved towards Salamanca. The forts which the French had constructed there, and some 800 men in them, fell prisoners into his hands; and Marmont retreated towards the Douro closely followed by his antagonist. Then began a series of movements, when for days the army of Wellington moved parallel with that of Marmont over an open country within cannon-shot, each commander waiting for the opportunity to make the long-expected attack. By the 21st both armies had drawn towards Salamanca, and Marmont's left wing was so far advanced that the communication with Ciudad Rodrigo seemed menaced. At this critical juncture, when the respective armies were close to each other on the rocky eminences of the Arapiles, the over-confidence of Marmont and his anxiety to strike a blow before being superseded by a senior marshal, precipitated his fate.

The movement of the allied baggage deceived Marmont. It was about two o'clock in the afternoon when he began his manœuvres, and in less than two hours he had fallen into the very trap which he had laid for Wellington. No sooner was the British general informed of his opponent's movement than he hastened to the summit of the English Arapiles, and with his field-glass surveyed Marmont's line of march. "At last," he said, as he looked down on the French left, already separated from the centre by more than a league of distance—"At last I have them!" In an instant the orders were issued; and when he saw that they were already being executed he grasped the arm of the Spanish General Alava, who stood by him as he said, "Mon cher Alava, Marmont est perdu."

With the additional advantage of moving on the chord of the arc round which the French were toiling, Wellington could collect his troops with the utmost rapidity. In a few moments his right was strengthened; one portion ordered to move so as to take Thomiere in front; while the other, moving perpendicularly on the French line of march, should interpose between the left and Brennier's division. The movement of the British army revealed his error to Marmont, and he did his best to retrieve it. But now nearly two leagues of distance lay between the division of Thomiere and that of Brennier; and at the moment when the latter was hastening to its appointed place, the red-coats burst in between it and Thomiere, while the extreme British right met and enveloped that general at the moment when he was expecting from the next rising ground to see the British in full retreat on Ciudad Rodrigo with Marmont on their track. Enveloped on every side and surprised during their march, the French in vain struggled against their opponents, and performed deeds worthy of their reputation. But rapidly their array became confused, their cavalry was routed and driven back upon their infantry, while the allied horse broke through the openings unresistedly. Bravely fighting to the last, Thomiere fell at the head of his bewildered troops, and then they were driven in a huddled mass towards the division of Clausel, which was hurrying to their assistance. Three thousand prisoners attested the thoroughness of their defeat.

The divisions of Leith and Cole attacked Clausel in front, while the heavy dragoons and light infantry threatened his flank. For a time his gallant men bore up against the storm; but when the mass of the British cavalry suddenly burst on the already wavering lines of the French infantry, the rout was immediate, and so complete, that of a small division 2,000 prisoners were made, and every gun fell into the hands of the assailants. The French left was totally discomfited.

In the centre and left the tide of war was turning against the British. Pack's Portuguese had been suddenly assailed and driven in confusion down the sides of the French Arapiles. This advance of the French brought their fresh and victorious troops on the flank of the British fourth division, then abreast of the French Arapiles in its steady progress against Bonnet, with whose division it was engaged in front. The effect was decisive. The soldiers of the fourth division staggered, both their generals fell wounded, and at last they fled in utter confusion. At this critical moment the sudden movement of a division made by Beresford arrested the imminent danger; and soon afterwards Wellington restored the combat with his reserves and by dint of hard fighting regained the long-contested ridge.

Bonnet had succeeded Marmont, and now Clausel succeeded Bonnet. For the French it had become a struggle for safety—no longer for victory. His right wing was affording means for saving the remnants of the broken French army; with great skill Clausel gathered the *débris* of his left and centre into a compact body, and covering it with the yet intact divisions of the right retreated to the heights behind the Ciuba brook, and there maintained his ground until his reserve and baggage had effected their retreat towards Alba de Tormes.

Forty-four thousand men had collected round Marmont's eagles on the eventful morning of June 21st; hardly half that force could be numbered in their retreat behind the Douro. Above 130 officers and 7,000 soldiers had been made prisoners. Eleven guns, two eagles, and six standards were the trophies of the battle. Such a victory could not be gained without a heavy loss on the side of the conqueror. Above 5,000 had suffered, including many officers of high rank. Of that number 3,000 were British, 2,000 Portuguese, and just eight Spaniards. While leading the pursuit with the light division, Wellington overtook a squadron of French dragoons. Quick as thought they fled but discharged their pistols in bravado. One shot hit the holster of the British commander and struck him sharply on the thigh. Happily momentary pain was the only result.

In forty minutes, as a French officer remarked to Lord Wellington, 40,000 men had been utterly defeated, and no fewer than 20,000 were in retreat towards the Douro. Neglecting this discomfited mass, Wellington, who had been appointed generalissimo of the whole Spanish armies, marched with his army towards Madrid and on August 12th entered that capital. Crowding around his horse the impulsive Madrilĕnos kissed his coat-skirts, hung on his stirrups, and blessed him as the deliverer of their country. The palace and fortress of the Buen Retiro still held a garrison of 2,000 French veterans, but it offered but a feeble resistance and within two days a capitulation placed Madrid in possession of the allies. At home the victory of Salamanca and the reduction of Madrid were followed by additional substantial honours to the commander of the forces; the Prince Regent granted him another step in the peerage as Marquis Wellington, and an augmentation of his coat of arms commemorative of his services, to which the nation added a grant of £100,000 to maintain adequately his increased rank in the peerage.

Clausel evacuated Burgos on the night of September 18th, and on the 19th Major Somers Cox, supported by Pack's Portuguese, drove in the French outposts on the hill of San Michael. The same night the same troops, reinforced by the 42nd Regiment, stormed the horn-work. The conflict was murderous. The Highland soldiers who bore the ladders under the command of the engineer Pitt, placed them very well, splicing them together to meet the great height of the scarp. The soldiers of the 42nd ascended with signal gallantry, heading the column of Portuguese troops intended for the storming of the left salient; but the French were numerous and prepared, a severe fire was opened by them on the attacking troops; every man who reached the top of a ladder was instantly bayoneted and in his fall he knocked down several others. The gallant engineer Pitt with his men descended the ditch, reared the ladders, and actually mounted them in the endeavour to persuade the Portuguese to follow the Highlanders, but in vain. Nothing would induce them even to enter the ditch, and the attempt had to be abandoned. The stormers were beaten back with great loss, and the assault would have failed if the gallant Cox had not forced an entrance by the gorge with the 79th. The garrison of the horn-work was thus cut off and must have surrendered if Cox had been well supported; but he was followed only by the 42nd, and the French, being still 500 strong, broke through and escaped. A most welcome capture of seven French field-pieces was made on this occasion. The conduct of Major Dick of the Royal Highlanders was commended in the Marquis of Wellington's public despatch.

Jones (afterwards Sir Harry), in his "Memoirs," is very bitter on the arrangements for this attack. He writes: "The siege (of the castle) was preceded by the assault of an outwork under an arrangement which no commander but Lord Wellington would have dared to order, and which no troops in the world but British troops would have dared to execute. The men behaved like heroes, but in a few minutes were nearly all annihilated. An officer, as he fell, heard his own funeral dirge from the mouth of an Irish sergeant: 'Arrah, be Jasus, there is the colonel of engineers gone who brought us here, an' good luck to him—may his sowl be aisy!'" Five successive assaults were made on the Castle of Burgos, and all in succession failed. Wellington pressed the siege with every effort in his power; but after five weeks of bootless expenditure of life and limb, the retreat of the allied army became inevitable, so rapidly were the

French forces concentrating in its rear. Burgos was Wellington's only failure. The loss sustained by the 42nd in the abortive siege of Burgos, chiefly in the attempt on the San Michael horn-work, was three officers, two sergeants, and forty-four rank and file killed; and six officers, eleven sergeants, one drummer, and 230 rank and file wounded. The officers killed were Lieutenants D. Gregorson and P. Milne, and Ensign David Cullen; those wounded were Captains Donald Williamson (who died of his wounds), Archibald Menzies, and George Davidson, Lieutenants Hugh Angus Fraser, James Stewart, and Robert Macintosh.

After the abandonment of the siege of Burgos on 21st October, the allied army, when darkness had set in, left its positions without beat of drum; the artillery, its wheels thickly muffled with straw, passed the bridge over the Arlanzon immediately under the guns of the castle, with such silence and celerity that Du Breton the governor though ever alert and suspicious, knew nothing of the departure until some of the Spanish *partidas*, beginning to lose nerve, broke into a gallop. As the clatter of the hoofs were heard the red flashes from the cannon broke from the castle walls, and a storm of round shot and grape was poured down at random till the range was lost. On the 23rd the infantry passed the Pisuerga; but while the main body was making this long march Souham, who had passed through Burgos on the preceding night, vigorously attacked the rear-guard under Sir Stapleton Cotton. On the 25th the bridges over the Carrion and Pisuerga were blown up to hinder the progress of the enemy. Those on the Duero at Tudela and Puente del Duero shared the same fate; but many of the French swam the river at Tordesillas, so eager were they in the pursuit that followed the abandonment of Burgos. During the retrograde movement the troops suffered severely from the inclemency of the weather and the badness of the roads; but far more than even from the lack of regular supplies did they suffer from their own irregularities in discipline and disorganisation, which were worse even than during the retreat to Coruña. The demoralisation into which the army fell during the retreat from Burgos called forth the severest rebukes from the commander of the forces. Regardless of the murmurs which his stern conduct and equally stern and bitter reproaches evoked, Wellington did not hesitate to attribute the disasters to their true cause— the habitual inattention of his officers to their orders and their duties. His most stringent orders had been habitually neglected and violated, either from carelessness or wilfulness; and he openly charged on the disregard or incapacity of his officers the sufferings and losses to which his willing and ready soldiers had been subjected. The severity and publicity of a rebuke conveyed in a general order drew down on the commander much abuse and slander. But little did the discontented know the man if they thought that he would be moved by unmerited censures. Able to appeal to his own acts for the principles on which they were performed, he left the malignants to their devices, and calmly ordered the officers to act on the methods which actuated their commander.

The allied army retired to Frenada and Coria on the frontier of Portugal, where winter quarters were taken up in a wide area. The enemy followed the example, apparently "unwilling to advance, unwilling to retire, yet renouncing the hope of victory." Subsequent events proved that this view of the situation was accurate, "for every movement on the part of the enemy after the campaign of 1812 was retrograde, every battle a defeat."

While the 42nd lay in winter quarters a melancholy instance occurred of unbridled passion. Lieutenant Dickenson was quartered in the village of Villatora, a short distance from headquarters. He had sent Corporal Macmorran, an Irishman, on some duty in the neighbourhood. The corporal did not attend evening parade; the lieutenant reprimanded him and ordered him to get under arms. He did so and returned to the officer. When within a few paces the corporal shot the officer through the heart. They had no previous difference, nor had the corporal any apparent cause for his ungoverned action, except the affront of having been ordered to parade by himself. He was tried by courtmartial and executed.

Augmented in strength, improved in organisation, and confident in the skill of the allied army, Wellington again took the field in May, 1813, and advanced into Spain for the final campaign, 70,000 strong; sweeping onward on a broad front, turning the positions of the French, and driving them before it towards the Pyrenees The three corps constituting the British army, with the glories of twelve victories encircling their colours, marched forward full of ardour; and so proudly confident was their great leader of all that they would achieve that on the morning his march to the front began, he raised himself in his stirrups, and waving his hands cried, "Adieu, Portugal!"

Sir Thomas Graham had the left; in his corps marched the first battalion of the 9th, to the light company of which young Colin Campbell belonged. In Graham's corps also marched the Royal Highland regiment, brigaded with the 79th and 91st. Graham's march through the difficult mountain region of Tras-os-Montes and onward to Vittoria was exceptionally arduous; but the obstacles were skilfully surmounted. On the 20th June Wellington's army moved down into the basin of Vittoria. Graham, moving southward from Murguia by the Bilbao road, was to attack General Reille commanding the French right, and to attempt the passage of the Zadora at Gamara Mayor, and Ariaga; should he succeed, the French would be turned, and in great part enclosed between the Puebla mountains on one side and the Zadora on the other by the corps of Hill and Wellington.

Graham approached the valley of the Zadora about noon on the 21st—the day of the battle. Before moving forward on the village of Abechuco, it became necessary to force across the river the enemy's troops holding the heights on the left, and covering the bridges of Ariaza and Gamara Mayor. This was accomplished after a short but sharp fight, in which Colin Campbell participated. He thus describes the sequel: "While we were halted, the enemy occupied Gamara Mayor in considerable force, placed two guns at the entrance into the village, and occupied with six pieces of artillery the heights immediately behind the village on the left bank. About 5 p.m. an order arrived from Lord Wellington to press the enemy in our front. The left brigade moved down in contiguous columns of companies, and the light companies covered the right flank of this attack. The regiments, exposed to a heavy fire of musketry and artillery, did not take a musket from the shoulder until they had carried the village. The enemy brought forward his reserves, and made many desperate efforts to retake the bridge, but could not succeed. The attempts were repeated until the bridge became so heaped with dead and wounded that they were rolled over into the river below. After three hours' hard fighting, the enemy retired, leaving their guns in British possession. Crossing the Zadora in pursuit, we followed them about a league, and encamped near Metanco." The French left and centre had been driven in, and Graham had closed to the enemy their retreat by the Bayonne Road, so that there remained to the French only the road leading to Pampeluna, which was all but utterly blocked by vehicles and fugitives. "Never was there a defeat more decisive; the French were beaten before the town, and in the town, and through the town, and out of the town, and behind the town." In the words of one of themselves, " the French at Vittoria lost all their equipages, all their guns, all their treasure, all their stores, all their papers, so that no man could prove even how much pay was due to him; generals and subordinate officers alike were reduced to the clothes on their backs, and most of them were barefooted."

During the long and fierce fighting in the Pyrenees, the 42nd and 79th Highlanders did not belong to the brigades whose good fortune it was to be more actively engaged. Nevertheless, the Royal Highlanders had the opportunity of gaining another honourable inscription for their regimental colours, on which the words " Pyrenees" was displayed by royal authority to commemorate their gallantry. Lieutenant-Colonel Stirling received the addition of a clasp to the medal previously acquired, and Lieutenant-Colonel Robert Macara also received a medal. St. Sebastian was captured in the early part of September, and the passage of the Bidassoa was effected on 7th October, when the British troops entered France and a division sprang up the slopes beyond the river to assail the key of the position, the Croix des Bouquets. To that French stronghold reinforcements were hurrying and attacks on it had already been made in vain. "But," in Napier's words, "at this moment Cameron arrived with the 9th, and rushed with great vehemence to the summit of the first height. The French infantry opened ranks to let the guns retire, and then retreated themselves at full speed to a second rise, where they could only be approached on a narrow front. Cameron quickly threw his men into a single column and bore against this new position, which, curving inwards, enabled the French to pour a concentrated fire upon his regiment; nor did his violent course seem to dismay them until he was within ten yards, when, appalled by the furious shout and charge of the 9th, they gave way and the ridges of the Croix des Bouquets were won as far as the royal road."

From the Pyrenees the British troops looked down on a formidable line of fortifications along the river Nivelle, stretching from Ainhoe to the sea; but they descended the mountains in the night, forded the river at daybreak of November 10th, and carried the French fortifications by storm, capturing thirty-one guns and 1,300 prisoners. The gallant bearing of the Royal Highlanders in this battle is commemorated by the word "Nivelle" on their regimental colours. The allies had twenty-one officers and 244 soldiers killed; and 120 officers and 1657 soldiers wounded. Of the 42nd, Captain Mungo Macpherson and Lieutenant Kenneth Macdougal were wounded; one private killed, and two sergeants and twenty-three rank and file wounded. The commanding officer of the regiment, Lieutenant-Colonel Macara, received the addition of a clasp to his medal; Major William Cowell also received a medal for commanding a light infantry battalion. On December 9th the allied army crossed the river Nive and attacked the enemy's positions beyond that river with success. The French quitted their entrenched camp at Bayonne and attacked the British divisions on the 9th, 10th, 11th, 12th and 13th, but were steadily repulsed. For its conduct in this long and stubborn contest the 42nd received the honour of bearing the word "Nive" on its colour; and its commanding officer, Lieutenant-Colonel Macara, was rewarded with an additional honorary distinction. Its losses were Captain George Stewart, Lieutenant James Stewart and ten rank and file killed; one sergeant and fifteen rank and file wounded.

Thus every object of the recent advance had been gained. Soult was driven from the Nive and cooped up in Bayonne; the courses of the Nivelle, the Nive, and the Adour, were in the power of the allies, who, well supplied through St. Jean de Luz and the other coast towns, enjoyed comfortable quarters in the valley of the Adour; whilst the French were compelled to throw their left on its right bank and leave their right within the entrenched camp of Bayonne. Thus they had little command beyond their lines, while the allies threatened their communications and supplies.

The effects of those discomfitures were increased by the defection of the German contingent in the French army. On the evening of February 10th the commandant of the Frankfort and Nassau battalions found himself in front of the British 4th division. He had just learned the truth of the news from Germany that his country had thrown off the yoke of France; and drawing his sword he informed his men of the fact and bade them follow him into the British ranks in order to be sent to fight their country's battles in their own land. With loud cheers the Germans abandoned the French ranks and marched into the allied position. This defection not only weakened Soult's army by so many men but effectually embarrassed the movements of Suchet in Catalonia, and compelled him to disarm his German troops who formed some of his best soldiers.

Driven by a succession of skilful movements from the Gave d'Oleron across the Gave de Pau, the French fell back towards Orthez with the intention of making a final stand in that strong position. The semicircular range of heights which begins at the church of Baights and runs through the village of St. Boes to Orthez was occupied by the French army, mustering still nearly 40,000 men of whom 7,000 were conscripts and the rest veteran soldiers. Reille held the extreme right at St. Boes, with the divisions of Taupin and Rognet. Foy and D'Armagnac occupied the centre, and Clausel with the left defended Orthez and its ancient bridge, which had defied even the mines of the French engineers. Crossing by a pontoon bridge the British left under Beresford threatened St. Boes and the road to Dax; the centre under Picton moved against Foy and D'Armagnac; whilst Hill with the right endeavoured to force the bridge of Orthez or gain any other passage over tne Gave de Pau in that direction. Immediately opposite the French centre a lofty hill surmounted by an old Roman camp commanded a view of the entire field and served in particular as a shelter to the allied light division, which there acted as a reserve and as the connecting link between Picton and Beresford. The allied army mustered rather more than 37,000 combatants, and the artillery of the contending forces was nearly equal.

By nine of the morning of the 25th the battle began by the advance of Beresford against St. Boes and that of Picton against the French centre. For a time the advance of the allies was irresistible; St. Boes was taken, and the troops hastened to deploy on the heights in its rear in order to sweep the French right. But this manœuvre was impossible. Commanded by the great central battery of the enemy and assailed on all sides in the narrow pass behind the village, the British soldiers recoiled from the hostile fire and then again and again tried in vain to carry the deadly ridge The crisis of the battle had arrived; and already Soult was moving up his reserves, while Picton for the moment was retiring from his attack on the centre. Pressing on through St. Boes, the French right with loud shouts followed the retiring allies, and in doing so gradually lengthened its own distance from Foy's division. This error Wellington marked from the Roman camp, and he took immediate advantage of it. Rapidly moving up the right division he sent the 52nd Regiment across the marsh, and hurled it into the interval between the French centre and left, while fresh divisions moved to aid the British left and to renew the combat in front of St. Boes. Picton, too, renewed his attack with success, and while Reille was met in front by Beresford and taken in flank by the 52nd Foy was too hard pressed by Picton to be able to detach any troops to his aid; and already Hill, who had crossed the river at the ford of Souars, was threatening the French left by the road of St. Sever.

From that moment the battle was lost to Soult, and his operations were wisely concentrated on securing a good retreat. From every side his troops fell back in splendid order, and each division in turn defended the ridges behind the original position, while the rest of the French army retreated by the St. Sever road to the banks of the Luy de Bearn running about five miles in the rear. So long as the French were on the ridges, the retreat was most orderly; but when the plain was entered and Hill was seen moving rapidly on the French left, the French troops fell into disorder, were charged by the British cavalry, and were driven in haste and confusion to the river over which they passed in scattered parties. Here the chase ceased; for Wellington himself had been struck by a spent ball which prevented him from urging the pursuit with his usual vigour. The victory, if judged by its trophies, was of little import. By the loss of less than 2,000 men on the side of the allies the enemy had been weakened by nearly double that number and six guns had fallen into the hands of the victors. If judged by its effects, the victory was of the utmost importance; it led thousands of the French conscripts, who cared but little for Napoleon, to throw away their arms and to desert their standards; it broke the spirit of French resistance, opened the road to Bordeaux, and drove Soult to retreat from the coast towards Toulouse. The loss of the enemy in the battle of Orthez was estimated at 8,000 men in killed, wounded, and prisoners. The loss of the allies in killed and wounded amounted to about 1,800. Of the 42nd Lieutenant John Innes was the only officer killed, with a sergeant and three men. Major William Cowell, Captain James Walker, Lieutenants Duncan Stewart and James Brander, five sergeants, and eighty-five men were wounded.

When, after the rains, the rivers had fallen in during the first week of March, the allies were in full march after the enemy in the direction of Toulouse. General Fane took possession of Pau de Bearn and Marshal Beresford moved with 12,000 men towards Bordeaux. Deprived by his late defeat of his magazines, Soult retired towards Toulouse. Several gallant stands were made and many a gallant soldier had fallen before the entire French army was compelled to concentrate round the works of Toulouse. By March 25th Soult was there in position; while Wellington, encumbered with heavy artillery and a pontoon train, did not arrive in the vicinity until three days after the French had assembled round the city.

On the morning of April 10th the preliminary manœuvres in anticipation of the battle began, and the last victory of the long Peninsular war hung in the scale. The numbers were approximately equal. On the side of the allies Wellington had nearly 40,000 Anglo-Portuguese available, besides 12,000 Spanish troops and eighty-four pieces of cannon. On the side of the French between 38,000 and 39,000 men were in line, besides the national guard of the city; and eighty guns crowned the formidable works at which the townsfolk had so long laboured. Sending Hill to menace the suburb of St. Cyprian, Picton to threaten the bridge-head of Jumeau, and Alten with the Light Division to occupy the defenders of the bridge and works of Minimes, Wellington prepared to engage his real battle on the extreme right of the Mont Rave. Compelled by the destruction of the bridges on the Ers to cross that river at the Croix d'Orade, Wellington sent the Spanish troops against the hill at Pugade, while Beresford with 13,000 men moved along the bank of the river in the hollow between its waters and the fortified heights. With great courage the Spaniards rushed on, and at first carried the outer works and drove the French back to their greater fortifications. But soon the scene changed; the carnage became too great to be endured by such troops as the Spaniards, and they fled in confusion down the slope until a rapid charge of English cavalry and aid from the light division enabled them to re-form on the lower height of Pugade. Nor was Picton more successful on the extreme right. Not content with merely menacing the bridge-head at Jumeau and thus engaging the attention of its defenders, he forced on his troops without the means of scaling its entrenchments, and suffered the loss of above 400 of his men.

Slowly Beresford marched along the valley, exposed to the fire of the heights and losing men at every step. At last the road to Lavaur was reached, and the troops deployed to the attack of St. Sypiére and the right of the Mont Rave. The attack was irresistible. One by one the heavy redoubts were stormed or turned; and when for a time the battle ceased, the combatants shared the heights between them and the French had fallen back to the Calvinet platform. Shortly after one Beresford resumed the attack, aided now by his artillery, which had just arrived; while Soult had sent enormous reinforcements from his posts, perceiving that the Mont Rave was the point to be lost or won. With the utmost violence the battle raged again for nearly four hours; and though there were times when the British were driven from the newly captured redoubts, yet in the end their progress was not to be arrested and the whole range of the fortifications of the Mont Rave was in their possession before the evening. Now on all sides Soult drew in his troops and retired to his second line of defence behind the canal, though still holding his advanced posts on the lower heights behind the Mont Rave at Sacarin and Cambon. Thus ended the last battle of the Peninsular war; 4,500 men had fallen on the side of the allies, of whom one half were British; while Soult was weakened of his strength by more than 3,000 men, including three general officers

The loss of the 42nd in the battle of Toulouse was four officers, three sergeants, and forty-seven rank and file killed; and twenty-one officers, fourteen sergeants, one drummer, and 231 rank and file wounded. The names of the officers killed were Captain John Swanson, Lieutenants William Gordon, John Latta, and Donald Macrummen; the wounded were Lieutenant-Colonel Robert Macara, Captains James Walker, John Henderson (died of wounds), Alexander Mackenzie, Lieutenants Donald Mackenzie, Thomas Munro, Hugh Angus Fraser, James Robertson, R. A. Mackinnon, Roger Stewart, Robert Gordon, Charles Maclaren, Alexander Strange, Donald Farquharson (died of wounds), James Watson, William Urquhart, Ensigns Thomas Macniven, Colin Walker, James Geddes, John Malcolm, and Mungo Macpherson.

The part taken by the 42nd in the battle of Toulouse was described so graphically by Mr. Malcolm, formerly of the 42nd, in his "Reminiscences of a Campaign in 1814," that readers cannot fail to be interested by the vigorous narrative which is here condensed:—

"Our division approached the foot of the ridge of heights on the enemy's right, and moved in a direction parallel to them, until we reached the point of attack. We advanced under a heavy cannonade, and arrived in front of a redoubt which protected the enemy's position, where we were formed in two lines—the first consisting of some Portuguese regiments, and the second of the Highland Brigade (the 42nd, 79th, and 91st).

"Darkening the whole hill, flanked by clouds of cavalry, and covered by the fire of their redoubt, the enemy came down on us like a torrent, their generals and field-officers riding in front and waving their hats amidst the shouts of the multitude, resembling the roar of an ocean. Our Highlanders, as if actuated with one instinctive impulse, took off their bonnets, and waving them in the air returned the greeting with three cheers.

"A death-like silence ensued for some moments, and we could perceive a visible pause in the advance of the enemy. At that moment the light company of the 42nd Regiment, by a well-directed fire brought down some of the French officers of distinction as they rode in front of their respective corps. The enemy immediately fired a volley into our lines, and advanced upon us amidst a deafening roar of musketry and artillery. Our troops only answered their fire once, and unappalled by their furious onset, advanced up the hill and met them at the charge. On reaching the summit of the ridge of heights, the redoubt which had covered their advance fell into our possession; but they still retained four others with their connecting lines of entrenchments upon the level of the same heights on which we were now established, and into which they had retired.

"Meantime our troops were drawn up along a road which passed over the hill, and which, having a high bank on either side, protected us in some measure from the general fire of our last line of redoubts. . . . Marshal Beresford's artillery having arrived, and the Spanish troops once more brought up, Major-General Pack (commanding the Highland Brigade), rode up to the front of the brigade, and made the following announcement: 'I have just now been with General Clinton, and he has been pleased to grant my request, that in the charge we are now about to make upon the enemy's redoubts, the 42nd shall have the honour of leading the attack. The 42nd will advance!'

"We immediately began to form for the charge upon

the redoubts, which were about two or three hundred yards distant, and to which we had to pass over some ploughed fields. The grenadiers of the 42nd, followed by the other companies, led the way, and began to ascend from the road; but no sooner were the feathers of their bonnets seen rising over the embankment, than so tremendous a fire was opened from the redoubts and entrenchments as in a very short time would have annihilated the regiment. The right wing, therefore, hastily formed into line, and without waiting for the left, which was ascending by companies from the road, rushed upon the batteries, which vomited forth a terrific storm of fire, grape, and musketry.

"The redoubts were erected along the side of a road, and were defended by broad ditches full of water. Just before our troops reached the obstruction, however, the enemy deserted them, and fled in all directions, leaving their last line of strongholds in our possession; but they still possessed two fortified houses close by, from which they kept up a galling and destructive fire. Out of about 500 men whom the 42nd brought into action scarcely ninety reached the fatal redoubt from which the enemy had fled.

"Our colonel was a brave man; but there are moments when a well-timed manœuvre is of more advantage than sheer courage. The regiment stood on the road with its front exactly to the enemy; and if the left wing had been ordered forward, it could have sprung up the bank in line and dashed forward on the enemy at once. Instead of this, the colonel faced the right wing to its right, counter-marched in rear of the left, and when the leading rank cleared the left flank, it was made to file up the bank, and as soon as it made its appearance the shot, shell, and musketry poured in with deadly destruction; and in this exposed position we had to make a second counter-march on purpose to bring our front to the enemy. Those movements consumed much time, and by this unnecessary exposure exasperated the men to madness. The word 'Forward—double quick!' dispelled the gloom, and forward we drove in the face of apparent destruction. The field had been lately rough-ploughed, and when a man fell he tripped up the man behind; thus the ranks were opening as we approached the point whence all this hostile vengeance proceeded; but the rush forward had received an impulse from desperation. 'The spring of the men's patience had been strained until ready to snap, and when left to the freedom of its own extension, ceased not to act until the point to which it was directed was attained.' In a moment every obstacle was surmounted; the enemy fled as we leaped over the trenches like a pack of hungry hounds in pursuit, frightening them more by our wild hurrahs than actually hurting them by ball or bayonet.

"Two officers (Captain Campbell and Lieutenant Young) and about sixty men of inferior rank were all that now remained without a wound, of the right wing of the regiment that had entered the field in the morning. The flag was hanging in tatters, and stained with the blood of those who had fallen over it. The standard, cut in two, had been placed successively in the hands of three officers, who fell as we had advanced; it was now borne by a sergeant, while the few remaining soldiers who had rallied round it, defiled with mire, sweat, smoke, and blood, stood ready to oppose with the bayonet the advancing hostile column, the front files of which were pouring in destructive showers of musketry fire among our confused ranks. To have disputed the post against

R

such overwhelming numbers would have been hazarding the loss of our colours, and could serve no general interest to our army, as we stood between the front of our advancing support and the enemy; we were therefore ordered to retire. The greater number passed through the cottage, now filled with dead and dying, and leaped from the door that was over the road into the trench of the redoubt among the killed and wounded.

"We were now between two fires of musketry; the enemy to our left and rear, the 79th and left wing of our own regiment in our front. Fortunately, the intermediate space did not exceed a hundred paces, and our safe retreat depended upon the speed with which we could perform it. We rushed along like a crowd of boys pursuing the bounding ball to its distant limit, and in an instant we plunged into a trench which had been cut across the road. The balls were whistling among us and over us; while those in front were struggling to get out, those behind were holding them fast for assistance; and we became firmly wedged together until a horse without a rider came plunging down on the heads and bayonets of those in his way. They on whom he fell were drowned or smothered, and the gaps thus made gave way for the rest to get out.

"The right wing of the regiment, thus broken down and in disorder, was rallied by Captain Campbell and the adjutant (Lieutenant Young), on a narrow road, the steep banks of which served as a cover from the showers of grape that swept over our heads. As soon as the smoke began to clear away the enemy made a last attempt to retake their redoubts, and for this purpose advanced in great force; they were a second time repulsed with great loss, and their whole army was driven into Toulouse."

The allies entered Toulouse on the morning after the battle, and were received with enthusiasm by the inhabitants. By a singular coincidence official accounts reached Toulouse in the course of the day of the abdication of Napoleon, and of the restoration of Louis XVIII.; but it was believed that the despatches had been intentionally detained on the way.

By this time the clothing of the army in general, and of the Highland Brigade in particular, was in a very ragged state. The clothing of the 91st had been in wear for two years; some had the elbows of the coats mended with grey cloth, others had the one half of the sleeves of a different colour from the body; their trousers were in as bad a condition as their coats. The 42nd, which was the only regiment in the brigade that wore the kilt, was beginning to lose it by degrees. Men falling sick and left in the rear frequently got the kilt made into trousers, and on rejoining the regiment no plaid could be furnished to supply the loss. Thus a great want of uniformity prevailed; but this was of minor importance compared with the want of shoes. As the march continued from day to day, no time could be found for their repair, until they were completely worn out and a number of men had to march with bare feet. Those men were occasionally permitted to straggle out of the ranks to select the soft part of the roads or the adjoining fields; and others who had not the same excuse to offer for this indulgence followed the example, until each regiment marched regardless of rank and sometimes mixed with other corps in front and rear.

Toulouse was the last battle and the final victory of the Peninsular war. Hostilities immediately ceased. Part of Wellington's army marched through France on its way to England, a large proportion was despatched to America and a third portion was sent home by sea. The Highland Brigade remained in Ireland until May, 1815, when it was shipped to Belgium, as Napoleon had returned from Elba. When the 42nd was in Ireland the first battalion was joined by the effective men of the second, which had been disbanded at Aberdeen in October, 1814

## CHAPTER XXIII

### QUATRE BRAS AND WATERLOO.

Napoleon's advance on Charleroi, June 15th, 1815. Wellington's orders for concentration on Nivelles. March of British troops from Brussels on Quatre Bras. The Highland soldiers great favourites in Brussels. Picton's orders to halt at Waterloo. Wellington's interview with Blücher. Five hours' fighting at Quatre Bras. Ney's superior strength. Allies reinforced later. Details of positions. Picton's rout of French columns, advance of British troops. Death of Duke of Brunswick. Wellington's narrow escape. The 42nd assailed by French lancers, who were all slaughtered. The 42nd had four commanding officers in succession in as many minutes, three of whom killed or wounded. Christie's gallantry. Destruction of 69th regiment. Kellerman's cavalry advance. His cuirassiers rode down 69th. Clarke, a volunteer, killed three cuirassiers and received twenty-two sabre cuts, but preserved the colour. Kellerman's discomfiture—on his fall his cuirassiers fled in wild confusion. English possession of Gemioncourt and field of battle. Losses of Royal Highland Regiment very severe. Wellington's encomiums. Not heavily engaged at Waterloo.

IT was not until three o'clock in the afternoon of June 15th, 1815, that the Duke of Wellington, then in Brussels, received the first tidings that in the early morning of that day Ziethen, the commander of the 1st Prussian Corps, had been attacked by the French advance before Charleroi and along the Sambre. Uncertain whether Napoleon's advance was by Charleroi or further to the west by Mons, the duke, in anticipation of further information, took no measures for some hours. At length, in default of later tidings, he determined on the precautionary step of assembling his divisions at their respective rendezvous points in readiness to march;

further specially directing a concentration of 25,000 men at Nivelles on his then left flank, as soon as it should have been ascertained for certain that the enemy's line of attack was by Charleroi. These orders were sent out early in the evening, between five and seven. Tidings from Blücher in the Ligny position caused Wellington to issue about ten p.m. a second set of orders, commanding a general movement of the army, not as yet to any specific point of concentration, but in prescribed directions towards its left. Towards midnight, writes Müffling, the Prussian commissioner at his headquarters, Wellington told him, " The orders for the concentration of my army at Nivelles and Quatre Bras are already despatched. Let us, therefore, go to the ball." Readers of the " Letters of the first Earl of Malmesbury " will remember the apparently authentic statement of Captain Bowles, that Wellington, rising from the supper-table during the famous ball, " whispered to ask the Duke of Richmond if he had a good map. The Duke of Richmond said he had, and took Wellington into his dressing-room. Wellington shut the door and said, ' Napoleon has humbugged me, by God; he has gained twenty-four hours on me. I have ordered the army to concentrate at Quatre Bras; but we shall not stop him there, and if so I must fight him *there*' (passing his thumb-nail over the position of Waterloo). The conversation was repeated to me by the Duke of Richmond two minutes after it occurred."

Facts, however, are stronger evidence than words; and this alleged confession on Wellington's part is inconsistent with the circumstance that he had not hurried to retrieve the time he is represented as having owned that Napoleon had gained on him—that, on the contrary, he had allowed his adversary to gain several hours more,

The men of the 42nd and 92nd Regiments had become great favourites in Brussels. It was no uncommon thing to see a Highland soldier taking care of the children, and even keeping the shop of his host. Those two regiments were the first to muster. They assembled with the utmost alacrity to the sound of the pibroch, "Come to me and I will give you flesh"—an invitation to the wolf and the raven, for which the coming day did, in fact, spread an ample banquet. About four o'clock on the morning of the 16th June the 42nd and 92nd Highland Regiments marched through the Place Royale and the Parc. One could not but admire their fine appearance—their firm, collected, military demeanour, as they went rejoicing to battle, with their bagpipes playing before them and the beams of the rising sun dancing on their glittering arms. Before that sun had set how many of that gallant band were laid low! Byron has sung:—

> "And wild and high the Cameron's gathering rose,
> The war-note of Lochiel, which Albyn's hills
> Have heard, and heard, too, have her Saxon foes;
> How in the noon of night that pibroch thrills
> Savage and shrill! But with the breath that fills
> Their mountain-pipe, so fills the mountaineers
> With the fierce native daring which instils
> The stirring memory of a thousand years,
> And Evan's, Donald's fame rings in each clansman's ears!"

The kind and generous inhabitants of Brussels assembled in crowds to witness the departure of their gallant friends; and as the Highlanders marched onwards with their martial tread the people breathed many a fervent expression for their safety.

The 42nd belonged to the gallant Picton's division, and it was brigaded with the 1st Royals, 44th, and 92nd

Regiments. Sir Dennis Pack was the brigadier. As the division quitted the city and entered the forest of Soignes, the stream of rank following rank moved on in silent but swift course, like a river confined within its banks. The Duke of Wellington left Brussels about half-past seven a.m. As he passed the column he gave orders to Picton to halt at Waterloo, where the roads to Nivelles and Quatre Bras branch off. Picton arrived there about ten, halted for a couple of hours, and about noon an order reached him for the continuation of the march of his division on Quatre Bras. It seemed that when the duke passed Picton on the march, he had not yet decided whether to order the latter to Nivelles or to Quatre Bras. He knew that the latter place was occupied by a brigade or more of Dutch-Belgian troops, but it was not he who had ordered it there; he had on the previous evening ordered it to Nivelles. It had, in fact, come to Quatre Bras and stayed there contrary to the orders which he had given. The brigade, under Perponcher and Duke Bernard of Saxe-Weimar, had done excellent service, and but for it Ney would have occupied Quatre Bras without opposition on the evening of the 15th; yet, apparently, judging from his order to halt Picton at Waterloo, the duke had not yet fully decided whether he would withdraw it or reinforce it.

Pending the coming up of his reinforcements Wellington, with rather a sanguine reliance on Ney's maintenance of inactivity, which, however, the event justified, rode over to Brye, and had a conversation with Blücher. There are contradictory accounts of its tenor, and Gneisenau certainly seems to have formed the impression that the duke gave a pledge of support to the Prussians. Wellington honestly believed that he would be able to co-operate with Blücher. Müffling, who was present, states that the duke's last words were, "Well, I will come, provided I am not attacked myself." That Wellington regarded as faulty Blücher's dispositions for battle in the Ligny position, is proved by his blunt comment to Hardinge, as he rode away: "If the Prussians fight here they will be damnably licked!"

The duke returned to Quatre Bras at 2.30 p.m., when the Prince of Orange's advanced troops were being driven back, and his artillery had retired on either side of the Gemioncourt enclosure, with a loss of two guns. Picton's division and the Hanoverian militia of the sixth division, came into position at Quatre Bras between 3 and 3.30 p.m. The third division came up soon after five, and the Guards arrived only at 6.30; thus the brunt of the fighting fell on Perponcher's, the Duke of Brunswick's, and Picton's troops.

The area of the five hours' struggle on the afternoon and evening of Quatre Bras, measuring from the southern edge of the Gemioncourt enclosure on the south of the fighting-ground to the buildings of Quatre Bras at the intersection of the Charleroi-Brussels, and the Namur-Nivelles chaussées on the north, is about three quarters of a mile, and from east to west about the same distance; and in this limited space and in the wood of Bossu, the fight was waged with alternating fortune. This wood, in some parts close and intricate, was generally passable by cavalry in extended order, and during the action French batteries had no difficulty in moving inside the enclosure and there coming into action. The fields in which the French cavalry charged—no English cavalry had as yet come up—were covered with wheat and rye grass, which were as high as the infantrymen's shoulders and concealed in the undulating ground the movements even of mounted troops.

At 2 p.m., when Ney moved forward and his artillery opened fire, he had 1,700 cavalry, 16,000 infantry, and thirty-eight guns; while the British force numbered but 7,000 infantry, with sixteen guns. Ney imagined that the allies were in much greater strength than was the case. He did not advance until Foy's division reached Frasnes, about 2 p.m. About 3, as Picton's division was approaching Quatre Bras, Bachelu's infantry seized the farm-house of Piermont. The 95th Regiment was sent forward to try to save that place while the 28th attempted to occupy Gemioncourt, but the French had previously gained both places. Up to 3.30 p.m. the French infantry strength was unchanged, but Guiton's cuirassier brigade, 800 strong, had arrived. The allies had now 18,000 infantry and 2,000 cavalry (Continental), which, as described by Sir Evelyn Wood in his "Cavalry in the Waterloo Campaign," were thus placed:—

Perponcher held the Bossu wood to within a hundred yards of the stream passing northward of Gemioncourt; the Duke of Brunswick, who, with 3,000 infantry and 1,000 cavalry, had arrived soon after Picton, was in the open, west of the road parallel with the Dutch front and about 600 yards south of Quatre Bras, near which stood the 92nd Highlanders. Immediately south of the Namur-Nivelles road and south-east of the Charleroi-Brussels road, was Picton's division; Pack on the right, Kempt on the left; Best's Havoverian Militia brigade was in support. Ney, from his centre at Gemioncourt, presently sent two heavy columns into the valley east of Gemioncourt; and Wellington, fearing for the safety of the raw Brunswick troops, ordered Picton, about 4 p.m., to advance. Both of his brigades moved forward in line, east of the Charleroi road. The heads of the French column, which had been concealed by the high rye grass until the

British columns opened fire, fell into disorder, and at Picton's command the British division charged, bayoneted, and routed the French columns, driving them through the hedgerows into the valley. On the extreme British left the 79th Highlanders crossed the valley, and pursued up to the main French position. But now their ranks were much broken, and they were recalled. On the right of the line the 42nd and 44th, crossing the hollow, nearly got possession of the Gemioncourt Manor House and outbuildings; but both were too strong to be carried, and the two battalions fell back and reformed in line with Kempt's brigade.

The Duke of Brunswick, finding that he had not space for two cavalry regiments between the road and the wood, sent his hussars back to Quatre Bras, while he at the head of his lancers charged the enemy's advancing infantry. But the French battalion repulsed the lancers, who galloped back to Quatre Bras, and when assailed by French squadrons the Brunswick troops gave way. While the duke was attempting to rally his infantry, he was mortally wounded, a little eastward of the isolated house on the road south of Quatre Bras. The Brunswick lancers, pursued by French chasseurs, galloped headlong on to the 92nd, then lining the ditch of the Namur road close to Quatre Bras. The Highlanders wheeled back a company, let the Brunswick horsemen through, and then fired with great effect on the pursuing French squadrons, which, however, soon re-formed and retired in good order. The Brunswick Hussar Regiment was now ordered forward to attack the French Chasseurs, but the raw troopers were fired on from the wood, and they wheeled about from before their opponents, who pursued them so closely that the mass was mistaken by the British for allied cavalry retiring.

The Chasseurs chasing the Hussars got through the 92nd men, behind whom the Duke of Wellington took refuge, escaping from the pursuit only by leaping the garden-fence lined by a company of the Highland Regiment. The Chasseurs cut down fugitives and stragglers in Quatre Bras until, recognising that they were unsupported, they tried to escape by breaking through the 92nd from the rear. Few of those daring French troopers eventually escaped. An officer, coming from the rear, attacked the Duke of Wellington; but he was shot through both legs by some soldiers who faced about just in the nick of time, and just as he reached the duke his horse fell dead.

To the 42nd and 44th Regiments, the two foremost regiments, which were posted in line on a reverse slope close to the left of the Charleroi Road, the advance of French cavalry was so sudden and unexpected — the more so as the Brunswickers had just gone to the front—that as both of those bodies whirled past them to the rear in such close proximity to each other, they were momentarily taken to be one mass of allied cavalry. Some of the old soldiers of both regiments were not quite satisfied on this point, and opened an oblique fire on the galloping troopers, which, however, was restrained; but no sooner had this fire been quelled than the French lancers of Wathier's lancer brigade wheeled promptly about and attacked the rear of both British regiments. The 42nd was in the act of forming square from line and all but the two flank companies had run in to form the rear face, when the leading squadron of lancers drove in the uncompleted square, carrying along with it by the impetus of their charge several men of those two companies, and by spearing several created a momentary confusion. But the other faces stood firm, and gradually closing in, the Highlanders bayoneted all the Frenchmen who had entered the square along with the flank companies of the regiment. The lancers died hard. They killed the commanding officer of the 42nd, Lieutenant-Colonel Sir Robert Macara, a lance having penetrated his chin until it pierced the brain; and within a few minutes the command of the regiment devolved on three other officers in succession: Lieutenant-Colonel Dick, severely wounded; Brevet-Major Davidson, mortally wounded; and Brevet-Major Campbell, who commanded the regiment during the remainder of the campaign.

Colonel Hamerton, commanding the 44th, perceiving the impossibility of any attempt on his part to form square, the thud of galloping horses having been his first premonition of the coming storm, faced both ranks about and reserved his fire until the French lancers were close up, when a volley destroyed many of the foremost. With reckless bravery, however, individual troopers dashed on with couched lance; and one grey-haired old lancer, riding straight at the colour-party of the 44th, severely wounded Ensign Christie, who carried one of the colours, driving the lance through his left eye to the lower jaw. The lancer then strove to seize the colour; but Christie, with marvellous disregard of pain, dashed the flag to the ground and threw himself upon it. The Frenchman succeeded in tearing off a fragment with his lance, but he was presently bayoneted by the nearest soldiers and thus the colour was saved. The brave Christie was a lieutenant on half pay of the 44th in the middle of 1827, but after that date nothing was known of him. The French lancers, repulsed from the rear of the 44th galloped away to the eastward, suffering severely from a volley poured in from the left company of the line, which had reserved its fire until now.

Piré's French cavalry division recrossed the Gemioncourt brook in a shattered state; and thus, shortly before 5 p.m., ended the first main attack. Pack's brigade lost during the day 800 out of 2,200 men; and the 42nd and 44th were so reduced that they re-formed in a single square. Soon after 5 p.m., the third division (Alten's) reached Quatre Bras, the men having marched twenty-two miles under a hot sun, and dinnerless. Halkett's brigade, on which fell the next French cavalry charge, had left Soignies at 2 a.m., and now took up the position whence the Brunswick troops had been driven. Half an hour later the Guards arrived, and they immediately gained ground in the northern section of the Bossu wood. Some guns were brought up between the wood and the Charleroi road, but before they could be unlimbered suffered severely; yet they persevered for some time, but being unsupported were ultimately withdrawn. As Halkett with his four battalions took up his position, he was begged urgently for support by Pack, whose men were out of ammunition. Halkett sent him the 69th Regiment. Halkett himself rode forward to observe the French dispositions. He saw Kellerman about to advance, and he sent back orders to the 69th to form square immediately, as he expected an early cavalry attack. He galloped back to the other battalions of his brigade and gave them similar orders.

Kellerman had trotted twelve miles without drawing rein from Charleroi to Frasnes, where he arrived with his leading division at 2.30 p.m., from which time it had remained dismounted. At six o'clock Ney sent an order to Kellerman to bring up one brigade. As Kellerman approached Ney galloped up and addressed him excitedly, " My dear general, a great effort is necessary; you must charge and break through the infantry in our front. Advance, and I will have you supported by Piré's cavalry." Kellerman, with Guiton's brigade of cuirassiers, trotted down the Charleroi-Brussels road and crossed the Gemioncourt brook. The following was then the position of the British troops. The single square into which the 42nd and 44th was now formed on the low ridge overlooking Gemioncourt, was suffering from the fire of the French artillery and skirmishers pressing across the valley from the Gemioncourt farm buildings. Halkett's three battalions were preparing for cavalry on the west side of the road. As the 69th, warned by Halkett's aide-de-camp, was in the act of forming square, the Prince of Orange rode up and loudly asked what the battalion was doing. The commanding officer explained that he had been ordered to form square; but the prince ordered him into line, saying, he did not believe that a cavalry charge was imminent—yet 800 sabres were at that moment crossing the brook within a few hundred yards. As Kellerman's horsemen crossed it the head of the column wheeled, and the regiments formed in succession as the rear cleared the bridge. In front of the 8th Cuirassiers rode Kellerman and Guiton. They passed round the flank of the 42nd and 44th square, and came opposite to the unfortunate 69th, which saw nothing in the tall corn until Kellerman perceiving that the regiment was unprepared, wheeled the cuirassiers by sections to their right and completely rolled up the British battalion. In a few minutes, 150 of the 580 men of the 69th were on the ground dead or dying, and the uninjured were dispersed. Some of the officers and men found shelter under the bayonets of the 42nd-44th square; Major Lindsay, Lieutenant Pigot, and Mr. Clarke, a volunteer, resisted with great desperation. Clarke killed three cuirassiers, and notwithstanding that he received twenty-two sabre-cuts he preserved the colour he was carrying.

Until now Kellerman had been successful; he had ridden over a battalion and had kept in square formation the rest of the British infantry; but his cuirassiers now suffered severely, as well from the fire of the battalions around them as from the British artillery on the Namur road. Several squadrons of cuirassiers and lancers attacked fiercely the square of the 28th. The men, however, encouraged by Picton's shout, "Twenty-eighth, remember Egypt!" remained firm and struck down their adversaries with deadly volleys. Kellerman collected his troopers and attempted to advance up the Brussels chaussée. Fired on from guns at case-shot range, the horsemen were also showered on by bullets from the wood and the houses of Quatre Bras, and presently Kellerman's horse fell dead on its rider. When Kellerman went down his cuirassiers turned and fled, regardless of the commands and entreaties of their officers. Galloping over all obstacles, they whirled Wathier's brigade off in a tumultuous *débâcle*. Kellerman was not seriously hurt, and clinging to the necks of two horses he ran out of action. Two miles from the field the fleeing mob of horsemen came on 2,500 dismounted cavalry, who were swept into the stampede, which ended only where stood the cavalry of the Guard. Foy's infantry began to give way, and but for Ney's resolution would have followed the fugitive cavalry. By nightfall the French were driven back to the positions they had held in the morning, the English holding Gemioncourt and the southern end of the wood of Bossu.

The losses at Quatre Bras sustained by the Anglo-allied army amounted to about 4,500 men; the French lost about 4,000. The 42nd suffered exceptionally heavily:

Lieutenant-Colonel Sir Robert Macara, K.C.B., Lieutenant George Gordon, Ensign George Gerrard, two sergeants, and forty-five rank and file were killed; Captain George Davidson died of his wounds; Brevet-Lieutenant-Colonel Robert Henry Dick, Captains Archibald Menzies, Donald McDonald, Daniel McIntosh, Robert Boyle and Mungo McPherson, Lieutenants Donald Chisholm, Duncan Stewart, Donald McKenzie, Hugh A. Fraser, John Malcolm, Alexander Dunbar, James Brander, George G. Munro, John Orr, and William Fraser, Ensign A. L. Fraser, Adjutant James Young, Quarter-Master Donald Macintosh, twelve sergeants, one drummer, and 215 rank and file were wounded. The total loss of the regiment was 298 officers and men.

The Duke of Wellington stated in his despatch: "I must particularly mention the Twenty-eighth, FORTY-SECOND, Seventy-eighth, and Ninety-second Regiments, and the battalion of Hanoverians."

The word "WATERLOO," borne on the colours of the regiment by royal authority, commemorates the gallantry it displayed at Quatre Bras; a medal was conferred on each officer and soldier; and the privilege of reckoning two years' service towards additional pay and pension on discharge was also granted to the men.

In the battle of Waterloo, in which the regiment was not heavily engaged, the 42nd had but five men killed; six officers and thirty-nine rank and file wounded. The six officers were: Captain Mungo Macpherson, Lieutenants John Orr, George Gunn Munro, Hugh Angus Fraser, James Brander, and Quarter-Master Donald Macintosh. It is interesting to remark that all those officers had been wounded at Quatre Bras, but that they nevertheless took part in the battle of Waterloo, where all were again wounded.

After spending several months in the vicinity of Paris the regiment came home in the end of 1815, and remained there until 1825 when it moved to Gibraltar. On 29th January, 1820, the colonelcy of the regiment was conferred on Lieutenant-General John, Earl of Hopetoun, G.C.B., from the 92nd Highlanders, in succession to General the Marquis of Huntly. Lord Hopetoun was a very distinguished officer. He was wounded before Alexandria, commanded a division of Sir John Moore's army in Portugal and Spain, fought at Coruña, and ultimately commanded the army which was victorious there. In 1813 he was appointed second in command in the Peninsula, and for his eminent services at the battles of Nivelle and Nive and the passage of the Adour, was made a G.C.B. He was later made a peer. Lord Hopetoun died in 1823. He was succeeded in the colonelcy of the 42nd, in September, 1823, by the Right Hon. Sir George Murray, G.C.B., G.C.H. After a distinguished early career in the army, Sir George served in the Peninsula as Wellington's quarter-master-general (gold cross and five clasps). After Waterloo, he served in France with the local rank of lieutenant-general until the return to England of the Army of Occupation in 1818. He was possessed of a great number of foreign orders. Sir George died in July, 1846.

# CHAPTER XXIV

### THE CRIMEAN WAR.

Movements of regiment from 1825 to 1841. Changes in its uniform. The kilt temporarily in disuse. Introduction of "spats" and the white shell-jacket. Guards of honour furnished by reserve battalion during Queen's visit to Scotland in 1842. Embarkation for East in 1854. Highland Brigade—42nd, 79th, and 93rd—commanded by Sir Colin Campbell. The Highland Brigade at the Alma. Lord Raglan's emotion. Sir Colin and the Highland bonnet. Regiment returned to England in July, 1856—reviewed by her Majesty. Its losses in action in the Crimea slight, but 227 men died there of wounds and disease.

In the end of 1825 the service companies of the 42nd were sent to Gibraltar, where the regiment remained for six years. In 1825 it was armed with the "Long Land Tower" musket, the only corps of the line to which it was issued; and in 1840 it was the first corps to receive the percussion musket, in both cases through the interest of Sir George Murray its colonel. On 25th November, 1828, Hon. Sir Charles Gordon, from half pay, became lieutenant-colonel of the regiment, *vice* Dick exchanged. After eleven years' service in Gibraltar, Malta, and the Ionian Islands, the 42nd returned home, and was quartered in Scotland and Ireland until 1841, when it was again sent to the Ionian Islands. While in Dublin, in 1839 the regiment received new colours. Sir Charles Gordon died in 1835, and Lieutenant-Colonel William Middleton succeeded to the command of the regiment on October 23rd of that year.

Many changes in the uniform of officers and men occurred between 1817 and 1840. In 1817 the kilt seems to have fallen into disuse, for the officers of the 42nd wore sky-blue trousers laced with gold, and these with the feather-bonnet! Blue-grey trousers, without the gold stripes, were taken into wear about 1823; and in 1829, trews of the regimental tartan fringed round the bottom and up the outer seams were introduced. At this period the officers' coatees were very richly laced, and officers of all ranks wore heavy bullion epaulettes. The epaulettes were later exchanged for "wings," which were worn until 1830, when epaulettes again became regulation and the lace on the breast of the coatee was done away with. The non-commissioned officers and men, however, wore "wings" until 1855, when epaulettes were abolished throughout the army. The white undress shell-jacket for the men was introduced in 1821, and has been worn by the Guards and Highlanders ever since. White gaiters, or "spats," came into use in 1826. The sergeants of the 42nd wore silver lace up to 1830, when it was ordered to be discontinued, to the great regret of the non-commissioned officers. On August 23rd, 1839, Lieutenant-Colonel George Johnstone obtained the lieutenant-colonelcy of the regiment, *vice* Middleton retired.

In April, 1842, the regiment was augmented from ten to twelve companies, in two battalions, viz. first and reserve, and from 800 to 1,200 rank and file. In September the reserve battalion, which was quartered at Stirling, furnished guards of honour at Perth, Dupplin Castle, Scone Palace, Drummond Castle, and Stirling, on the occasion of her Majesty's visit to Scotland. Major Macdougall received the brevet of lieutenant-colonel. Both battalions were serving in Malta in 1843.

On September 5th of that year Major D. A. Cameron became lieutenant-colonel in succession to Lieutenant-Colonel Johnstone, exchanged to half pay. On November 29th, 1843, Lieutenant-General Sir John Macdonald, K.C.B. was appointed to the colonelcy of the regiment, *vice* General Sir George Murray, removed to 1st Royal Regiment. Sir John Macdonald served in Egypt, at Copenhagen, and in the Walcheren Expedition. He served in Spain under Wellington, and was specially mentioned in despatches for his "unwearied exertions" at the battle of Barrosa. At the battle of the Nive and subsequent operations before Bayonne Sir John served as assistant adjutant-general. He received a medal for his services in Egypt, and the gold medal and clasp for Barrosa and the Nive. He was made a G.C.B. in 1847; he died 28th March, 1850. The regiment subsequently served at Malta, Bermuda, and Nova Scotia until 1852, when it returned home as a single battalion, the reserve battalion having been absorbed. On the death of Sir John Macdonald, Sir James Douglas, G.C.B. was appointed to the colonelcy of the regiment, 10th April, 1850. Sir James Douglas accompanied the expedition to South America under General Crauford on the staff of the quarter-master-general, and was engaged in the attack of Buenos Ayres. Subsequently he was under Sir Arthur Wellesley in Portugal, and was present at the battles of Roleia, Vimiero, and Coruña. He took part in the passage of the Douro, and in the battles of Busaco, Fuentes d'Onoro, Salamanca, and the Pyrenees, where he was wounded. He served in the battles of Nivelle, Nive, Orthez, and Toulouse, in which last action he was twice wounded and lost a leg. He received the gold cross with three clasps, and was nominated a K.C.B. Later he was appointed Governor of

Guernsey, and made a G.C.B. He died 7th March, 1862.

Early in 1854 the 42nd, under the command of Colonel A. D. Cameron, embarked for the East in consequence of hostilities with Russia. Landing at Scutari on June 9th, the regiment was brigaded with the 79th and 93rd, under the command of Major-General Sir Colin Campbell, afterwards Lord Clyde. On September 14th the allied armies of England and France landed in the Crimea; on the 19th they marched towards Sevastopol, and on the 20th they gained the battle of the Alma. The allied total amounted to about 63,000 men, with 128 guns. Lord Raglan commanded the British forces, Marshal St. Arnaud those of France. Of the first division, commanded by the Duke of Cambridge, the right brigade, commanded by Major-General Bentinck, consisted of three battalions of Guards; the left, commanded by Major-General Sir Colin Campbell, was the Highland brigade, consisting of the 42nd, the 79th, and the 93rd.

It fell to Sir Colin Campbell and his Highland brigade to protect the left flank of the British army, with three battalions to vanquish and put to flight eight Russian battalions, and to compel the retreat of four more. The arena of his exploit was the slopes and hollows of the Kourganè *terrain* to the Russian right of the great redoubt, from which the British light division had been forced to recoil with heavy loss. On the extreme Russian right flank and rear stood 3,000 horsemen, and to protect his own left Campbell had given the order to the 79th—the left regiment of his brigade—to go into column. But a little later, when he had ridden forward and so gained a wider scope of view, it became apparent to his experienced eye that he need fear nothing from the stolid array of Russian cavalry on his flank. He therefore recalled his order to the 79th, and allowed it to go forward in line. His brigade, after crossing the Alma, fell into direct *échelon* of regiments, the 42nd on the right being the leading regiment of the three, the 93rd in the centre, and the 79th on the left Just before the Guards began their advance on the redoubt which the right Vladimir column was still holding, Sir Colin was in his saddle in front of the left of the Coldstreams, talking occasionally with the Duke of Cambridge. When the Guards began their advance Sir Colin also proceeded to act. He discerned that by swiftly moving a battalion up to the crest in front of him he would be on the flank of the position about the great redoubt, where the right Vladimir column was confronting the Guards. This attitude of his would probably compel the retirement of the Vladimirs; if it did not, by wheeling to his right, he would strike the flank of the Russian column while the Guards were assailing its front. He had the weapon wherewith to effect this stroke ready to his hand in the 42nd, which having crossed the river, now stood ranged in line.

Before his brigade had moved from column into line, Campbell had spoken a few straightforward soldierly words to his men, the gist of which has been commemorated. "Now, men," said he, "you are going into action. Remember this: whoever is wounded — no matter what his rank—must lie where he falls till the bandsmen come to attend to him. No soldiers must go carrying off wounded comrades. If any man does such a thing his name shall be stuck up in his parish church. The army will be watching you; make me proud of the Highland brigade!" And now, when the time had come for action, and that rugged slope had to be surmounted, he rode to the head of the Black Watch, and gave to the regiment the command, "Forward, Forty-second!"

He himself with his staff rode rapidly in advance up to the crest. In his immediate front there lay a broad and rather deep depression, on the further side of which there faced him the right Kazan column of two battalions, on the left of which was re-forming the right Vladimir column, whose retreat from the vicinity of the redoubt had been compelled by the pressure of the Guards in front and flank. Both columns had suffered considerably; but assuming their previous losses to have been one-third of their original strength, they* still numbered 3,000 against the 830 of the 42nd. And when Sir Colin looked to his left, he saw on the neck bounding the left of the hollow another and a heavier column, consisting of two perfectly fresh battalions of the Sousdal Regiment. This last column, however, was stationary; and notwithstanding that the men were out of breath, Sir Colin sent the 42nd, firing as it advanced, straight across the hollow against the Kazan and Vladimir columns. The regiment had not gone many paces when it was seen that the left Sousdal column had left the neck and was marching direct on the left flank of the 42nd. Campbell immediately halted the regiment, and was about to throw back its left wing to deal with the Sousdal advance, when, glancing over his left shoulder, he saw that the 93rd—his centre regiment—had reached the crest. In its eagerness, the formation of that ardent regiment had become disturbed. Sir Colin rode to its front, halted it, re-formed it under fire, and then led it forward against

* Four battalions, *i.e.* the two forming the right Kazan column, and the two forming the right Vladimir column.

the flank of the Sousdal column. The 42nd meantime had resumed its advance against the Vladimir and Kazan columns.

Before the onslaught of the two Highland regiments the Russian columns were staggering, and their officers manifestly had extreme difficulty in compelling their men to retain their formation, when from the upper ground on the left was seen moving down yet another Russian column—the right Sousdal column—and heading straight for the flank of the 93rd. It was taken in the flagrant offence of daring to march across the front of a British battalion advancing in line. At that instant the 79th came bounding forward; after a moment's halt to dress their ranks the Cameron men sprang at the flank of the Sousdal column, and shattered it by the fierce fire poured into its huddled ranks. And now, the left Sousdal column almost simultaneously discomfited by the 93rd, and the Kazan and Vladimir columns which the Black Watch had assailed being in full retreat, the hill spurs and hollows became thronged by the disordered masses of the enemy. Kinglake, who was not present, thus brilliantly pictures the culmination of the triumph of the Highlanders: "Knowing their hearts, and deeming that the time was one when the voice of his people might fitly enough be heard, the Chief touched or half-lifted his hat in the way of a man assenting. Then along the Kourganè slopes, and thence westward almost to the causeway, the hillsides were made to resound with that joyous assuring cry which is the natural utterance of a northern people, so long as it is warlike and free." It is curious that nowhere in his vivid description of the part taken by the Highland brigade in the achievement of the victory of the Alma does Kinglake make any mention of the bagpipes. It is certain that they were in full blast during the advance of the regiments and throughout the fighting, and their shrill strains must have astonished the Russians, not less than did the waving tartans and nodding plumes of the Highlanders.

Sir Colin, ever careful in the midst of victory, halted his brigade on the ground it had already won, for his supports were yet distant; and mindful of his situation as the guardian of the left of the army, he showed a front to the south-east as well as to the east. The great Ouglitz column, 4,000 strong and still untouched, remained over against the halted British brigade. Chafing at the defeat of its comrades, it moved down from its height, striving to hinder their retreat and force them back into action. But the Ouglitz column itself had in its turn to withdraw from under the fire of the Highland brigade, and to accept the less adventurous task of covering the retreat of its vanquished fellow-columns.

Sir Colin wrote: "Lord Raglan came up presently and sent for me. When I approached him, I observed his eyes to fill and his lips and countenance to quiver. He gave me a cordial shake of the hand, but he could not speak. The men cheered very much. I told them I was going to ask the commander-in-chief a great favour—that he would permit me to have the honour of wearing the Highland bonnet during the rest of the campaign, which pleased them very much, and so ended my part in the fight of the 20th."

The brave and cool old soldier had had need to be on the alert, if ever man had; for he had to his hand but three battalions, and he had in his front no fewer than twelve Russian battalions, each one of which was numerically stronger than any one of his three. Nor were his opponents raw militia or reserve battalions such as confronted Prince Napoleon's division. The Russian regiments on the British side of the great post-road, the Vladimir, Sousdal, Kazan, and Ouglitz, constituted the famous Russian Sixteenth Division, the division d'élite of the Tzar's troops of the line; that same division which three and twenty years later won for the daring Skobeleff his electrical successes. It was twelve battalions of this historic division against whose massive columns Colin Campbell led his brigade of Highlanders in the old two-deep British line formation with the result he has told in his quiet sober manner. No wonder that Lord Raglan's "eyes filled, and his lips and countenance quivered" as, too much moved to speak, he shook the hand of the commander of the Highland brigade.

The request was at once granted, and the making up of the bonnet was secretly entrusted to Lieutenant and Adjutant Drysdale of the 42nd. There was a difficulty how to combine the heckle in the three regiments of the brigade. It was finally decided to have the upper third red for the 42nd, and the remaining two-thirds white at the bottom for the 79th and 93rd. Only about half-a-dozen men of the 42nd were concerned in the preparation of the bonnet. A brigade parade was ordered on the morning of 22nd September, on the battlefield of the Alma, "as the general was desirious of thanking the brigade for its conduct on the 20th." The square was formed in readiness for the chief's arrival, and he rode into it with the bonnet on. No formal signal was given, but he was greeted with such volumes of cheering that both the English and French armies were startled into wonderment as to what was going on. Such is the history of Sir Colin's feather bonnet.

The 93rd was the only regiment of the Highland brigade engaged in the memorable but chequered day of

Balaclava; but on the same afternoon, the other two battalions passed again under the command of the brigade commander. During the subsequent critical period, the 42nd and 79th held the ground between the 93rd camp and the foot of the Marine heights, and Vinoy's French brigade was sent to the high ground overlooking the Kadikoi gorge to strengthen Sir Colin in the command of his position. It so happened that the 42nd took no part in any of the important actions around Sevastopol. From the 19th October, the Highland brigade was commanded by Colonel Cameron of the 42nd, Sir Colin Campbell having been appointed to command all the forces in and about Balaclava. On the return from the Kertch expedition the regiment took up its position in front of Sevastopol. On June 18th it formed part of the reserve in the assault of the outworks of the fortress, and was subsequently engaged in siege operations. Sir Colin Campbell in conjunction with Colonel Cameron, the senior officer of the Highland brigade, had sketched out a plan for adoption, in case he should be called on to conduct the final assault. Colonel Cameron was to head the 42nd with a rush, while Sir Colin followed with the rest of the division in close support; and in this manner, pressed forward by the rest of the troops of the respective attacks, he believed that a lodgement would be effected and maintained by the weight of numbers in the rear. But Campbell's project was not destined to be accomplished. On the memorable 8th September, 1855, he was ordered to the front with the Highland brigade, to form the second reserve to the troops named for the assault of the Redan. That assault failed; and Sir Colin took the defence of the trenches with the Highland brigade on the withdrawal of the troops who had failed in the assault. While posting his troops in the trenches he was sent for by the commander-in-chief, to desire him to make preparations to assault the Great Redan on the following day with the Highland brigade, supported by the third division under General Eyre. But during the night the Russians evacuated Sevastopol. About 12.30 a.m. of the 9th, a sergeant of the 42nd on duty in the trenches, surprised at the silence in the Redan, ventured to enter it, and was followed by some volunteers of the same regiment. Nothing was heard but the heavy breathing and groans of the wounded and dying, who, with the dead, were the sole occupants of the massive work.

After the reduction of Sevastopol, the 42nd returned to Kamara, where it remained until the peace. Embarking at Kamiesch for England, the regiment landed at Portsmouth on July 24th, 1856, proceeded by rail to Aldershot, where it was reviewed by her Majesty, and thence was sent to Dover, in garrison with the 41st 44th, 79th, and 93rd Regiments. During the campaign only one officer and thirty-eight men of the 42nd were killed in action. But, apart from 140 officers and men sent to England on account of wounds and shattered health, there died of wounds and disease one officer and 226 men.

## CHAPTER XXV.

### THE INDIAN MUTINY.

The Indian Mutiny. Regiment landed at Calcutta in October and November, 1857. Sir Colin's gallop to the retrieval of Cawnpore. Windham's misfortunes. Forced march of part of regiment from Cheemee to Cawnpore—eighty miles in fifty-six hours—in time to take part in battle of Cawnpore on 6th December. Utter defeat of Gwalior Contingent. The 42nd the leading regiment in pursuit. Mansfield's inaction. Hope Grant's pursuit of Bithoor fugitives, in which 42nd shared. Capture of rebel guns. Regiment completed at Bithoor, December 22nd. Sir Colin's plan of campaign. Combat of Khoodagunge. The wild Irishmen of the 53rd. The havoc of rebels. Alison's vivid picture of return of victorious troops. Final reduction of Lucknow. Charge of Highlanders from the Dilkoosha on the Martinière. The Rohilcund campaign. Disaster of Rhooyah; death of Adrian Hope. Battle of Bareilly. Furious charge of Ghazis on 42nd. Dr. Russell's narrrow escape. Regiment, after ten years' service in India, came home in March, 1868. Unveiling of monument in Dunkeld Cathedral, April 2nd, 1872.

ON 9th October, 1855, Lieutenant-Colonel Alexander Cameron succeded Colonel D. A. Cameron in the command of the 42nd. On 11th December, 1856, the establishment was reduced to twelve companies. On 4th August, 1857, the regiment was reviewed by the Queen, who expressed herself highly satisfied with the appearance of the regiment. Between that date and the 14th it embarked for the East to take part in the suppression of the Indian Mutiny, and arrived at Calcutta in the following October and November. Sir Colin Campbell had withdrawn from Lucknow with great skill the garrison and its encumbrances. On the afternoon of November 24th, 1857, just as the life was quitting the worn frame of the noble Havelock, the relieving force with its unwieldy convoy of sick, women and children began its march for Cawnpore, its rear covered by Outram's division. For several days all communication had been cut off from General Windham, who had been left to hold Cawnpore with an inadequate force, and it was apprehended that the Gwalior Contingent had caught at the opportunity to assail the feeble garrison of that place. The thunder of the distant cannon waxed louder as the column advanced; and note after note from Windham, delivered by panting messengers, gave ominous intimation how greatly endangered had become the situation at Cawnpore.

Outspeeding his cavalry and horse-artillery, Sir Colin galloped on with his staff. Near the bridge over the Ganges, an officer reported that " Windham's garrison was at its last gasp." His soldierly nature chafed by the flaccid despondency which tone and expression alike disclosed, the hot old chief spurred his horse across the bridge, and rode straight for the entrenchment. As he galloped by, some of his old Crimean men recognised through the gloom the familiar face and figure; and cheer on cheer was raised as the word passed like lightning that the commander-in-chief had arrived. No more caitiff babble now of the garrison being " at its last gasp." With Sir Colin's coming disaster was no longer to be dreaded; and the situation was already retrieved in spirit.

Windham had not followed his chief's instructions to remain on the defensive. After four days of fighting, the hostile batteries had closed in around Windham's last defensive position near the bridge-head. A sally was made on the afternoon of the 28th, but it was ultimately repulsed with heavy loss and great discouragement. By nightfall the garrison had been obliged to take shelter in the entrenchment; and when Sir Colin rode into the work it had become the mark for the cannon-balls and even the musketry fire of the victorious rebels.

On the morning of the 29th the crossing of the troops began. The passage of the vast convoy lasted unceasingly for thirty-six hours. As the women and children, the sick and wounded crossed, the interminable *cortège* swept by the rampart of the fort, and encamped on the plain among the mouldering remains and riddled walls of the weak shelter wherein Wheeler's people had fought and died. Reprisals against the enemy had to be postponed until the convoy of families and wounded which had started down country for Allahabad on the night of December 3rd should have been far enough on the journey to be safe from danger at the hands of the rebels. Meanwhile, the communications having been restored, the current of reinforcements was resumed, and the eager soldiers needed only to recover from the fatigue of their upward march. On 3rd December the headquarters, and five companies of the 42nd under Lieutenant-Colonel Thorold marched with a column from Cheemee to Cawnpore—a distance of nearly eighty miles, which was covered in fifty-six hours, an extraordinary march in a tropical climate.

Sir Colin's hands were now free. The enemy, now increased to some 25,000 men, with forty guns, had their left strongly posted in the broken ground of the old cantonments between the city and the river. The hostile right was behind the canal on the southern plain, the Calpee road covered by the entrenched camp of the Gwalior Contingent. To fall on the enemy's right and prevent assistance being afforded it by their left, was the governing idea of Sir Colin's plan of attack. He determined to throw the whole weight of his force on the rebel right in the plain, strike at the camp of the Gwalior Contingent, establish himself on its line of retreat, and having thus separated it from the Bithoor force constituting the rebel left, to effect the discomfiture of both bodies in detail. The troops at his disposal amounted to 5,000 infantry, 600 cavalry, and thirty-five guns.

At 10 a.m. of the 6th Windham opened a heavy cannonade on the enemy's left between the city and the river, with the object of masking the main point of Sir Colin's attack. As this gradually slackened, Greathed, moving up to the line of the canal, engaged with a heavy musketry fire the enemy holding the edge of the city, for the purpose of detaining them in that position On Greathed's left, Walpole with his riflemen and the 38th crossed the canal, skirted the southern edge of the city, and then, bringing up his right shoulder, swept across the plain towards the enemy's camp. Simultaneously the columns of Hope and Inglis—the former consisting of the 4th Punjaubees, the 53rd, and the 93rd Highlanders, with the 42nd Highlanders in support in the centre; the latter consisting of the 32nd, 82nd, and 23rd Welsh Fusiliers—drove the enemy across the canal, followed them up closely, and pressed eagerly forward on the camp of the Contingent, hurling back the foe in utter confusion. So complete was the surprise, so sudden the onslaught, that the *chupatties* were found baking on the fires, the bullocks stood fastened to the carts, the sick and wounded were lying in the hospitals. By noon the enemy were in full flight by the road to Calpee. The 42nd, which had been near the rear when

T

the forward movement began, was now in the pursuit the leading regiment of all the infantry, having outstripped even the supple men of the Punjaubi Regiment. Such was the demoralisation of the Gwalior Contingent that the pursuit by Sir Colin, his staff and personal escort, along with Bourchier's battery, sufficed, without the cavalry, to keep the fugitives on the run. Gun after gun was captured in the chase. Sir Colin maintained the pursuit along the Calpee road for fifteen miles, capturing seventeen guns with their ammunition-waggons, and a great booty of material. The Gwalior Contingent, for the time being, was utterly discomfited. The defeat of the enemy would have been complete but for the escape of the Bithoor troops constituting the enemy's left in the ground between the city and the river. General Mansfield's stationary attitude permitted that section of the rebels to carry off their guns, and make good their retreat to Bithoor. His inaction would have more seriously detracted from the completeness of the British victory but for the success of the enterprise which Sir Colin committed to Hope Grant on the 8th. That gallant soldier hurried in pursuit of the Bithoor fugitives with some 2,500 men, of whom the 42nd soldiers were a part, and eleven guns. On the early morning of the 9th, he overtook them at Serai Ghaut, twenty-five miles above Cawnpore. Promptly opening fire, he drove them across the river and captured fifteen guns. Of the forty guns with which the rebels had advanced on Cawnpore, they had now lost all but one. Sir Colin had disposed of some 25,000 enemies, including the formidable Gwalior Contingent, at the cost of only ninety-nine casualties among the troops he had led to a success so signal.

Lieutenant-Colonel Cameron, commanding the regiment, and Major Priestley, who had remained behind at Calcutta, joined headquarters on December 12th. On the 22nd the five remaining companies of the regiment, under the command of Major Wilkinson, joined at Bithoor, and the strength was then complete. Sir Colin fully recognised the strong strategic temptation, before advancing up the Doab, to root out from Calpee the Gwalior Contingent, and so secure his flank and communications; but realising that it had been thoroughly cowed for the time, it was with no apprehensions on that score that he proceeded to carry out his project for the subjugation of the Doab by a concentric movement on Futtehghur. Three columns—from the north-west, from the south, and from the south-east—were simultaneously moving to converge on Futtehghur, but events forestalled this operation. On January 1st, 1858, Brigadier Hope with two infantry regiments reached the point, fifteen miles from Futtehghur, where the road crossed the Kala Nuddee stream by a fine suspension bridge, just in time to prevent its destruction. The enemy had occupied in great force the village of Khoodagunge on the further side, whence they opened a vigorous musketry fire covered by several heavy guns. Sir Colin ordered up his main body; meanwhile, he pushed the 53rd Regiment across the bridge with strict orders to remain on the defensive, to allow the cavalry to get behind the enemy and cut off their retreat to Futtehghur. When the main body began to cross, the 53rd, a regiment of stalwart Irishmen ever eager for fighting, conceived the idea that it was to be relieved, and this apprehension overwhelmed in the men their sense of discipline. All of a sudden they made a dash with loud cheers, and charged and captured several rebel guns. Sir Colin had intended to make a waiting

T 2

fight; when the hot-headed Patlanders interfered with this design he galloped up to the regiment in high wrath, and objurgated it in terms of extreme potency. But each volley of the chief's invective was drowned by repeated shouts of "Three cheers for the commander-in-chief, boys!" until, finding that the men were determined not to give him a hearing, the sternness of the commander gradually relaxed, and the veteran turned away with a laugh. He might have made his voice heard over the cheery clamour of the Irishmen, but that a few minutes earlier he had been hit in the stomach by a spent bullet, happily with merely the momentary inconvenience of loss of breath.

The rebels abandoned their guns and fled. But they had still to experience the stern mercies of Hope Grant and his horsemen. Making a détour and then suddenly wheeling to his right, he crashed in on the insurgent flank, moving on a narrow flank on the high road. Taken suddenly by surprise, the mutineers fled panic-stricken before this terrible onslaught. Hope Grant's cavalry, committing ruthless havoc with lance and sabre, maintained the pursuit for miles, and so demoralised was the foe that he never halted in his camp at Futteh-ghur, but rushed across the floating bridge into Rohilcund. The return of Grant's troopers to camp in the evening was described by Alison's vivid pen as a "stirring scene of war. The 9th Lancers came first, with three standards they had taken at their head; the wild Sikh cavalry rode in their rear. The Lancers waved their spears in the air and cheered; the Sikhs took up the cry, brandishing their bare tulwars over their heads; the men carrying the captured standards spread them to the wind. The 42nd, and the other regiments of the Highland brigade encamped close by, ran down and cheered the victorious cavalry, waving their feather-bonnets in the air. As Sir Colin rode back to camp through the tents of the Highland brigade, the cheering and enthusiasm of the men exceeded everything I had ever seen."

But political considerations intervened; Lord Canning was strongly in favour of immediately proceeding to the reduction of Lucknow. Sir Colin lost no time in giving loyal effect to the views of the Governor-General. Apart from the Nepaul contingent, on March 5th, 1858, Sir Colin Campbell stood before Lucknow at the head of nearly 25,000 men. Outram was sent across the Goomtee with an infantry division, a strong cavalry brigade, and five field batteries. At 2 p.m. of the 9th, the 42nd and 93rd swept abreast down the slope from the Dilkoosha, driving the enemy from their works in front of the Martinière; and then cleared of enemies the massive line of rebel defences till they reached the vicinity of Banks' House, where they remained for the night. Notwithstanding the severe fighting during the final reduction of Lucknow, the 42nd lost only five men killed; and Lieutenant Farquharson, who was awarded the Victoria Cross "for a distinguished act of bravery," and forty-one men wounded. The total loss in this herculean operation amounted to only 800 of all ranks. To have achieved a success so great at a cost so small was a result of which the most exacting commander might well have been proud. On 16th March, 1858, Colonel Green Wilkinson succeeded to the lieutenant-colonelcy of the regiment in succession to Lieutenant-Colonel Thorold; but on August 10th of the same year he was succeeded in the command by Lieutenant-Colonel Priestley, who died on the day after the headquarters of the regiment arrived at Stirling Castle on the return from India.

Lucknow captured and occupied, Sir Colin Campbell promptly set about the preparations for the Rohilcund campaign. His plan for the invasion of that province was based on the projected advance of two columns from opposite points; Walpole's force marching up from Lucknow, and a fine body of troops advancing from Roorkee under the command of Brigadier-General John Jones. Those columns, sweeping the country during their respective onward movements, were destined to converge on Bareilly, the capital of the province, which thus became the chief objective point of this strategical combination.

In the course of Walpole's march towards Rohilcund, there was reached on 15th April, some fifty miles from Lucknow, the jungle-fort of Rhooyah. The Rajah in possession refused to surrender. Walpole, without having previously reconnoitred the position, ordered an attack on the place by four companies of the 42nd. The attack was unfortunately delivered against the strongest face of the paltry place. The garrison took advantage of this folly to make an obstinate defence, with the result of heavy losses among the brave and persistent assailants, and of the failure to carry the fort. The enemy's well-directed fire obliged the troops to fall back after remaining in a most exposed position for six hours, during which time many casualties occurred. Brigadier Adrian Hope of the 93rd, Lieutenants Douglas and Bramley of the 42nd, and Willoughby of the Punjaubis here received their death-wounds. At length Walpole withdrew his force about sunset, and encamped about two miles off. During the night, the rebel chief retired quietly with all his men and material. Besides the officers above mentioned, the loss in the 42nd was one sergeant and six privates killed, and one officer

(Lieutenant Cockburn), three sergeants, and thirty-four privates wounded.

A daring deed of gallantry was performed by Quartermaster-Sergeant John Simpson of the 42nd. Having heard, when the troops had fallen back, that one of his officers had been left behind in the ditch, this brave man ran forward and rescued in the face of a withering fire, first Lieutenant Douglas and afterwards a private soldier, both of whom had been dangerously wounded. At the same time Private Davis of the 42nd brought in the body of Lieutenant Bramley, performing this duty of danger and affection under the very walls of the fort. Right worthily was the grant of the Victoria Cross made to the men who did those noble deeds: Quartermaster-Sergeant John Simpson, Lance-Corporal Alexander Thompson, and Private James Davis. But not even this display of gallantry could mitigate the gloom which fell on the column when Adrian Hope's death became known. The feeling against Walpole throughout the column was so strong as almost to endanger discipline, and until his death long after his name was execrated by the survivors of that time. In his despatch, Sir Colin Campbell singled out Adrian Hope for special mention. " The death of this most gallant and distinguished officer causes the deepest grief to the commander-in-chief. Still young in years, he had risen to high command; and by his undaunted courage, combined as it was with extreme kindness and charm of manner, he had secured the confidence of his brigade in no ordinary degree." The youngest son of General Sir John Hope, fourth Earl of Hopetoun, Adrian Hope, during his brief but brilliant career, had seen much service. He had campaigned against the Kaffirs in Africa, and had accompanied the late Sir William Eyre as major of brigade in the Crimea. Appointed to the 93rd Highlanders, he was borne on the strength of that regiment when he met his premature death.

The advance on Bareilly was begun on the morning of April 28th, and on the morning of May 5th the column marched on that place. About 11 a.m. a fierce onslaught, described by Sir Colin as " the most determined effort he had seen during the war," was delivered by a body of Ghazis, or Mussulman fanatics. Brandishing their tulwars, with heads carried low covered by their shields and uttering wild shouts of "*Deen! deen!*" they fell on with furious impetuosity and hurled the Punjaubis back on the 42nd. Giving ear to the injunctions of the veteran Campbell to keep cool and trust to the bayonet, the regiment never wavered; but some of the fanatics swept round its flanks and fell upon its rear. A brief but bloody hand-to-hand struggle ensued, and in a few moments every Ghazi was killed outright in the very ranks of the Highlanders. Colonel Cameron was dragged from his horse, and would certainly have been slain but for the timely and gallant interposition of Colour-Sergeant Gardiner, who bayoneted two of the fanatics and won for this brave act the Victoria Cross. General Walpole was wounded, and escaped with his life only by the promptitude with which the 42nd used the bayonet. When the Ghazis had been exterminated the Highlanders and Punjaubis advanced into the cantonments. In this fierce struggle, William Howard Russell, the famous correspondent of the *Times*, had a very narrow escape. A sowar had actually raised his tulwar to strike him down when Sergeant Forbes-Mitchell shot the rebel trooper. In the affair of Bareilly the 42nd had one private killed; and two officers, one sergeant, and twelve privates wounded.

In November, headquarters and left wing took up a position on the bank of the Sarda, to prevent the rebels crossing from Oude into Rohilcund. On the morning of 15th January, 1859, there was a sharp encounter with a superior rebel force which had crossed the Sarda, in which Captain Lawson was wounded and three sergeants were killed. With thirty-seven men Lawson kept 2,000 of the enemy at bay from sunrise to sunset, and two more Victoria Crosses were won by the Royal Highlanders. For their meritorious services during the Mutiny, the Royal Highlanders were authorised to add " LUCKNOW " to their roll of honours.

On 1st January, 1861, at the request of the regiment, Sir Hugh Rose, then commander-in-chief in India, came to Bareilly to present new colours to the regiment. After the old colours had been lodged, and the new presented to his Excellency and trooped with the usual ceremonies, Sir Hugh Rose addressed the regiment in a stirring speech. On September 12th of the same year the regiment was delighted by having its old and original name restored to it as a distinguished mark of honour. On July 8th her Majesty had been graciously pleased to authorise the Royal Highland Regiment to be distinguished, in addition to that title, by its earliest name—" THE BLACK WATCH." In March, 1862, Lieutenant-General the Marquis of Tweeddale was appointed colonel in place of the deceased Sir James Douglas. But in September of the same year the marquis became colonel of the 2nd Life Guards, and was succeeded by the regiment's former commander who had led it up the slopes of the Alma— Major-General Sir Duncan Cameron.

Sir Duncan Cameron served through the Eastern campaign of 1854-55 ; commanded the 42nd Highlanders at the Alma and the Highland brigade at Balaclava, on the Kertch expedition, siege and fall of Sevastopol, and the assault of the outworks on 18th June (medal with three clasps, C.B., Officer of the Legion of Honour, Sardinian and Turkish medals, and third class of the Medjidie). In the New Zealand war of 1863-65 he commanded the forces at Kolikara, Kohasoa, Tangariri, the Gate Pah, and other actions. For those services he was awarded the medal, received the thanks of the Legislative Council of the colony, and was made a K.C.B. From 1868 to 1875 he was governor of the Royal Military College; and in 1874 was promoted to be G.C.B. Sir Duncan died 8th June, 1888.

After ten years' service in India, the Black Watch came home in the beginning of March, 1868, and from Portsmouth immediately proceeded to Scotland where it was presently quartered in Edinburgh Castle. On Colonel Priestley's death, he was succeeded by Brevet-Lieutenant-Colonel J. C. McLeod, who had joined the regiment as ensign in 1846. The reception accorded to Scotland's favourite regiment on its arrival in Edinburgh was as enthusiastic as in the days of old when the military spirit was in its zenith. Its line of march was along Prince's Street, and the grand old corps was cheered vehemently at every step. Thirty-two years had elapsed since the regiment was last in Edinburgh, and there was little wonder at the hearty and genuine enthusiasm evoked by the return of the Black Watch. During their residence in Edinburgh, the Highlanders won the favourable opinions of all classes of the community, and kept up the ancient prestige and unbroken good name of the regiment.

On 2nd April, 1872, there occurred one of the most interesting events in the history of the Black Watch—

the unveiling in Dunkeld Cathedral of a fine monument, dedicated to the memory of the officers, non-commissioned officers, and men of the regiment who had fallen in war from its embodiment to the close of the Indian Mutiny. The monument was subscribed for by the officers of the regiment, and it was executed by Mr. John Steel, R.S.A., the celebrated Scottish sculptor. The sculpture, in white marble, represents an officer of the 42nd visiting the battle-field after an engagement in search of a missing comrade. The searcher has just discovered the body of his dead friend, and he stands with bared head, paying mute homage to departed valour. A marble slab below the sculpture bears the following inscription :—

IN MEMORY OF
THE OFFICERS, NON-COMMISSIONED OFFICERS,
AND PRIVATE SOLDIERS OF THE
42ND ROYAL HIGHLANDERS—THE BLACK WATCH—
WHO FELL IN WAR FROM
THE CREATION OF THE REGIMENT
TO THE CLOSE OF THE INDIAN MUTINY, 1859.

THE TEN INDEPENDENT COMPANIES OF THE FREACADAN DUBH, OR BLACK WATCH, WERE FORMED INTO A REGIMENT ON THE 25TH OCTOBER, 1739, AND THE FIRST MUSTER TOOK PLACE IN MAY, 1740, IN A FIELD BETWEEN TAYBRIDGE AND ABERFELDY.

ERECTED BY THE OFFICERS OF THE CORPS,
1872.

# CHAPTER XXVI.

## THE ASHANTI CAMPAIGN AND THE NILE EXPEDITION.

Ashanti campaign, 1874. The 42nd in battles of Amoaful and Ordah-su. Cyprus. Highland Brigade at Tel-el-Kebir. Combats of El-Teb and Tamai—severe loss in latter fight. Combat of Kirbekan. Death of General Earle. Return home of 42nd. Present Colonel commanding regiment.

IN 1873 a depôt centre for the Black Watch and its linked battalion, the 73rd, was established at Perth. At the close of the year, the regiment was ordered to the Gold Coast to join Sir Garnet Wolseley's expedition against Coffee Calcalli, the truculent king of Ashanti. For this service, kilts, doublets, and bonnets were given into store, and special clothing of drab cloth with pith helmets were issued to the men. The regiment arrived on the coast towards the end of January, 1874, and proceeded with the rest of the troops into the interior. When the column was delayed at Mansu, thirty miles inland, by the desertion of the native carriers, the Black Watch volunteered to act as porters, and actually performed this unwonted service for more than a day. On the 25th and 26th the Black Watch came up with Brigadier-General Sir Archibald Alison at its head; Colonel McLeod, commanding the regiment, had gone forward earlier in command of the advanced guard, and on the 26th he took Borobassi. On the 30th he was at

Quarman, within a short distance of the enemy's position.

The main body of the Ashantis were encamped on the hill rising towards the town of Amoaful. The British force consisted of four columns—a front column, a left column, a right column, and a rear column—all so disposed that when they closed up they would form a large square. The front column, under Sir Archibald Alison, consisted of the Black Watch commanded by Major Macpherson, and some detachments. The left column was commanded by Brigadier McLeod of the 42nd; the right, by Colonel Evelyn Wood. When, on the morning of the 31st, the front of the force was a few hundred yards beyond the village of Eginkassi, it was assailed by a heavy fire from a hidden enemy. Five companies of the Black Watch were already in skirmishing order, and the slugs were dropping thick and fast. There were few officers who did not receive some injury, and nearly 100 of the men were wounded. Captain Rait's shells soon forced the enemy to clear the road. The Black Watch took instant advantage of their gradual retirement. Sir Archibald Alison saw that the moment had come, and he bade the pipers play up. With a ringing cheer the Highlanders went straight at the concealed foe. The Ashantis gradually disappeared, and by 11 a.m. the village of Amoaful was in British occupation. Of the Black Watch, Major Baird was mortally wounded; Major Macpherson (Cluny), Captains Creagh and Whitehead, Lieutenants Berwick, Stevenson, Cumberland and Mowbray, and 104 men were wounded. After the long battle of Ordah-su on the morning of February 4th, in which Captain Moore and Lieutenants Grogan and Wauchope were wounded—the last severely, the troops entered Coomassie and gave three cheers for the Queen. The Black Watch was the first to enter, the pipers playing at its head; by half-past seven the whole force was in Coffee's capital, and the discomfiture of the Ashantis was complete, their king having fled.

The campaign thus at an end, Sir Garnet Wolseley brought his force back without delay to the coast. The last man was aboard ship by February 27th, and the Black Watch landed at Portsmouth on March 23rd, meeting with great enthusiasm. Among the officers of the Highland Regiment specially named for prominent services were Colonel McLeod, C.B., later made a K.C.B.; Majors Macpherson and Scott; Captains Farquharson, V.C., Furze, and Kidston; and Lieutenant Wauchope, who is now (in 1896) commanding a battalion of the regiment. The special thanks of both Houses were awarded to the troops, and honours were showered in profusion. Captains Bayley, Farquharson, V.C., and Furze were promoted to brevet-majors. The Victoria Cross was bestowed on Sergeant Samuel McGaw. The non-commissioned officers and men who were selected to receive medals "for distinguished conduct in the field," and had them presented by the Queen in presence of Colonel Sir John C. McLeod, K.C.B., commanding the regiment, were William Street, sergeant-instructor of musketry; Sergeant Henry Barton; Privates John White, George Ritchie, George Cameron, and William Bell; Piper James Wotherspoon; Privates Henry Jones, William Nichol, and Thomas Adams. Sergeant-Major Barclay was awarded the medal for "meritorious services" during the campaign. The word "ASHANTI" was added by royal authority to the "honours" on the colours already possessed by the regiment; and Ashanti War medals, by order of the Sovereign, were bestowed on all ranks.

The regiment remained at Portsmouth until November 15th, when it sailed for Malta under the command of Colonel Sir John McLeod, K.C.B., arriving there on the 27th, where it remained until ordered to Cyprus in the spring of 1878. From that disagreeable station it returned home in the following June, and after being quartered in the Isle of Wight and at Aldershot, was sent to Edinburgh in May, 1881. On 1st July, 1881, by Royal Warrant, infantry regiments of the line lost their numerical titles, and the old 42nd became known as the 1st Battalion the Black Watch (Royal Highlanders); while the 73rd or Perthshire Regiment became the 2nd Battalion. Thus the offspring of the old corps, after many decades of separation and independence, had come back to the bosom of the mother-regiment, and the two battalions were now linked in the closest bonds of consanguinity.

The first battalion of the Black Watch remained in Edinburgh until July, 1882, when it was ordered to Egypt on active service against Arabi Pasha. The battalion, under the command of Lieutenant-Colonel Macpherson, who had succeeded Sir John McLeod on 1st April, 1879, landed at Alexandria on 20th August, and joined at Ramleh the Highland brigade commanded by Sir Archibald Alison. On the 30th the brigade (1st Black Watch, 2nd Highland Light Infantry, Cameron Highlanders, and 1st Gordon Highlanders) embarked for Ismailia, where it arrived on 1st September. By the 10th Sir Garnet Wolseley was concentrated at Kassassin, and in the night of 12th–13th he advanced against Arabi Pasha's position at Tel-el-Kebir. The Highlanders attacked just before daybreak of the 13th, rushed the Egyptian entrenchments, and bore the brunt of the earlier portion of the assault. By 6.30 the fighting was over, and Arabi's entrenchments and camp were in British possession. The Black Watch lost Lieutenants Graham Stirling, J. McNeill, and Park (died of wounds); Sergeant-Major McNeil and five men killed; six officers and thirty-seven men wounded. After Arabi's defeat at Tel-el-Kebir the Black Watch accompanied the "Army of Occupation" to Cairo.

In February, 1884, the Black Watch under Lieutenant-Colonel Green, who on 1st July, 1881, had succeeded Colonel Macpherson in the command of the first battalion, proceeded to Suakim as part of Sir Gerald Graham's field-force which was to operate against the hostile tribes in the Eastern Soudan. On the 29th Graham's force marched to the relief of Tokar, and assailed the enemy's position at El-Teb. The Black Watch was in the thick of the fight, which for a time was very fierce, and it lost four men killed and two officers and nineteen men wounded. On 12th March the battalion took part in the battle of Tamai, where the fanatic Arabs broke into one of the squares, and were repulsed only by some very hard fighting. The Black Watch had Major Aitken and fifty-nine men killed; three officers and twenty-six men wounded. In April the battalion returned to Cairo, and took up its old quarters at Kasr-el-Nil.

On 23rd September, 1884, the Black Watch embarked for Assouan, and proceeded up the Nile in whale-boats to Dongola without serious mishap. Between Dongola and Corti a boat was swamped, and Major Brophy was drowned. The battalion arrived at Hamdab in January, 1885, and was attached to General Earle's force, which was intended to advance on Khartoum by way of Berber. On 10th February six companies of the Black Watch took part in the action of Kirbekan, and carried the

Arab position at the point of the bayonet. "The pipers struck up, and with a cheer the Black Watch moved forward with a steadiness and valour which the enemy was unable to resist, and which called forth the admiration of the general. . . . Without a check, the battalion advanced, scaled the rocks, and drove the enemy from their shelters." Meanwhile the cavalry had captured the enemy's camp, and the South Staffordshire (38th) having gallantly stormed the remaining portion of the position, the action of Kirbekan was won. The Black Watch lost Lieutenant-Colonel Coveney and five men killed; Lieutenant-Colonel Wauchope and twenty-one men were wounded. General Earle fell in the moment of victory. He was succeeded in the command by Major-General Brackenbury.

On 23rd February the River Column reached Huella, the furthest point the expedition was destined to penetrate; for when the tidings of the fall of Khartoum were received by Lord Wolseley, he sent a despatch ordering the column to commence its return journey.

Since then the Black Watch has not fired a shot in anger. On 27th June, 1884, the battalion arrived at Cairo "in splendid condition, and looking the picture of military efficiency." The bravery and good conduct of the Black Watch during the campaigns in Egypt, in Eastern Soudan, and on the Nile, cannot be too highly praised, and well did both officers and men deserve the rewards bestowed on them by their sovereign. Wherever the gallant old corps goes, it makes and leaves a good name; and so long as the Black Watch exists—in peace or in war, in camp or in quarters—it may be depended on to maintain the worthy and glorious reputation of the "Auld Forty Twa."

The venerable soldier who has been the colonel-in-chief of the Black Watch since 9th June, 1888—the Hon. Robert Rollo, C.B.—has served in the regiment from ensign to colonel. He embarked with the 42nd Highlanders for the East, served with the regiment in the campaign of 1854-55, and was brigade-major from the battle of Balaclava throughout the winter, until he took the command of his regiment. He commanded the 42nd on the Kertch expedition and surrender of Yenikali; at the siege of Sevastopol and assault on the outworks on June 18th (medal with clasps, brevet-lieutenant-colonel, Knight of Legion of Honour, fifth class of the Medjidie, and Turkish medal). He subsequently served in Canada as military secretary to Lieutenant-General Sir Fenwick Williams of Kars.

## CHAPTER XXVII.

### SOME PETS OF THE REGIMENT.

Of the many pets of the regiment, three were the most worthy of record—the dog "Pincher," "Donald" the deer, and the grenadiers' cat.

"Pincher" was a small, smooth-haired terrier which attached himself to the regiment during a march in Ireland, near Naas, its destination on returning home after the Peninsular War in 1814. Pincher was truly a regimental dog. If he had any partiality, it was slightly towards the light company. He remained with the regiment during the winter of 1814–15, and embarked with it for Flanders in the spring of the latter year; went into action with it at Quatre Bras, and was severely wounded in the neck and shoulder; but, like a good soldier, would not quit the field. He was again in action during the battle of Waterloo and accompanied the regiment to Paris, but did not learn the French language. Yet amidst the armies of the Continental nations Pincher never lost himself, came home, resumed his post, and went over to his native Ireland in 1817. His ultimate fate was sad. Late in that year or early in 1818, he went with some men going on furlough, who landed at Irvine in Ayrshire. Poor Pincher chased some rabbits in a warren, and was shot by a gamekeeper, to the deep and universal grief of the regiment when the melancholy intelligence reached it, which was not until one of the furlough men returned from Scotland to join. Meantime Pincher had not been seriously missed. Some remarks, indeed, were made at Armagh that Pincher was longer than usual on his rounds; but there was no anxiety felt regarding him, because it was well known that from the time of his joining the regiment in 1814, it mattered not how many detachments were out from headquarters, in turn he visited them all; and it was a standing wonderment how and by what instinct he found out each detachment in its turn. Poor Pincher was a good and faithful soldier's dog, and, like many a good soldier, died an inglorious death. His memory was sincerely respected while his generation existed in the regiment.

"Donald" the deer was with the depôt which awaited the regiment when it went into Edinburgh Castle, in September, 1836, after landing at Granton from Corfu. He was a callow youngster at this time, and not so formidable as that his antlers needed to be cut, but that had to be done later. He marched with the regiment during three days from Edinburgh to Glasgow, in June, 1837. He began to be somewhat mischievous that year, sometimes stopping the way when he chose to make his lair, or objecting actively to intruders on Glasgow Green when the regiment was exercising. But it was in Dublin, in the summer of 1838, that Donald discovered his true *métier*, and he promptly acted on the discovery. Without any previous training, he took his place at the head of the regiment alongside of the sergeant-major. Whether marching to and from the Phœnix Park for exercise, out-marching in winter, or at guard-mounting, on the days the 42nd furnished the band and staff Donald was never absent. He accompanied the regiment to all garrison field days, went to feed until the time came for going home—he did not care for manœuvres and evolutions—was often a mile away from the regiment, but was always at his post when the time came to march off. There was one exception. About the third field day, the 79th Regiment, also Highlanders, was on the ground for the first time, and Donald trotted up to them when the troops broke up. Donald somehow discovered his mistake, became uneasy and arrogant, and on reaching Island Bridge, where the 79th had to turn off to Richmond Barracks, calmly declined to accompany his new friends any farther. The colonel ordered half-a-dozen men to hand over their muskets to their comrades, and to drive Donald towards the Royal Barracks. He went willingly, and was evidently highly delighted to rejoin his own regiment at the park gate. He never again committed a similar mistake. When the regiment had the duty, he invariably went with the guard to the castle. The crowd on the way to and from the castle was always dense, since the Dublin population is constitutionally addicted to idling; but Donald made his way, and kept it clear too, and the roughs knew better than to attempt to annoy him. Indeed, he had been known to single out an obnoxious person who did so, and to give chase to him through the crowd. There never was any concern about Donald, as he could defend himself perfecly well. The Greys were in the Royal Barracks with the 42nd, and they permitted Donald to make his bed by tossing down their litter for him, and fed him daily with oats. But early in 1839 the Greys left, and were succeeded by the Bays. It was very soon understood that Donald and the new-comers did not understand each other. The Bays would not allow him to make his bed, nor did they give him

U *

oats; and Donald declared war against all Bays whenever and wherever they approached him, till at last a Bay trooper could scarcely venture to cross the Royal square without looking around to make sure that Donald was out of the way. His hostility gave rise to a clever sketch, drawn on the wall of the officers' room at the Bank guard, of the "Stag at Bay," wherein Donald was represented as having an officer of the Bays pinned up against a wall. In May, 1839, Donald made a nine-days' march to Limerick, although very foot-sore and out of temper, and woe to the ostlers in the stable-yard who interfered with him after a long and tiring day's march! Donald had another failing—one of which his countrymen are accused—a great liking for alcoholic liquids. His particular *wanities* were whisky and sherry. He suffered after a debauch, and it was forbidden to indulge Donald in these cravings. At Limerick, as soon as the officers' dinner-pipe went, he made his way to the mess-room windows, which were on the ground floor, in search of strong drink, until at length a severe fine had to be enforced on anyone giving it to him. By this time his temper had become so formidable, especially to strangers, that it was clear Donald could not be taken aboard ship to Corfu, even if the captain of the troop-ship would permit; and to the regret of all, it was decided that Donald must be transferred to strangers. Colonel Johnstone arranged with Lord Bandon, who promised that Donald should have the run of his lordship's park while the deer lived; and it was Donald's own fault that it was not so. It was really an affecting spectacle to see poor Donald overthrown, tied with ropes by those he loved so well, and put into a cart to be carried off. His cries were pitiful, and he actually shed tears—as indeed did some of his friends, for Donald was a universal favourite. Thus the regiment parted from dear old Donald, and nothing more was heard of him for many years.

In 1862, nearly twenty-two years later, Lieutenant-Colonel Wheatley, being appointed to the Cork district, took immediate steps to ascertain the subsequent history of Donald. The reply was, "That from the day he was set free in Bandon Park, he declined having any intercourse with either man or beast. That summer and winter he harboured in out-of-the-way places, to which no one could approach; and there had been so many complaints against him that about two years after the departure of the regiment Lord Bandon had reluctantly sanctioned his being shot." Poor Donald! the regiment and its ways furnished him the only home he ever knew, and his happiness had left him when separated from it.

The "Grenadiers' Cat" was picked up by a man of No. 1 Company in an encampment in Bulgaria, and embarked with the regiment at Varna for the Crimea. Having seen it in the bivouac at Lake Touzla, Lieutenant-Colonel Wheatley was induced, after the battle of the Alma had begun, to ask what had become of poor puss, when a man of the company replied, "It is here, sir," opening his haversack as he spoke. The animal looked out and surveyed the novel aspect of a battle with great contentment. It was shut up again in the haversack, and when inquiry was made next morning, it was found that "Bell" had escaped scatheless, and was among the men in the bivouac, well taken care of in so far as having its share of the rations. It appeared that the man who carried the cat and took care of it was exempted by the company from fatigue duties, his turn of carrying the company kettles, and other drudgery.

Like most pets, Bell did not come to a peaceful end. It finally became an inmate of the regimental hospital, that being the only quiet and safe refuge to be found for it, got worried, and died at Balaclava. Such was the end of Bulgarian Bell—the only instance, probably, of a cat going into action.

THE END.

# INDEX.

Abercromby, Lieut.-Colonel, 100
——, Major-General, 44, 49-53
——, Sir Ralph, 130, 132, 142, 146, 161, 166, 174-176, 197
Aboukir, Bay of, Battle of, 164
——, Engagement at, 167-170
——, ——, Losses at, 170-171
Alava, General, 237
Albemarle, George, 3rd Earl of, 74-85
Alexandria, Battle of, 179-195
——, ——, Disposition of British Force at, 177-178
——, ——, Disposition of French Force at, 178-179
——, ——, Losses at, 194-195
Alison, General Sir Archibald, 300-301, 303
Alma, Battle of the, 278-283
Almeida, 232
Alost, Action at, 130
Amherst, General, 67-70
Amoaful, Action of, 301
——, ——, Losses at, 301
Anderson, Colonel, 226
Arapiles, The, 237-238
Armiger, General, 92
Ashanti, Campaign of, 300-302
Ashford, Review before George III. at, 203
Astorga, 216

Badajos, 231
——, Siege of, 234-235
——, ——, Losses at, 235
Baird, Major-General Sir David, 197, 211-213, 221
Balaclava, Battle of, 284
Ball, Captain, 19
Bareilly, Affair at, 296
Barrington, General, 63-64
Basse-Terre, Attack on, 62
Belliard, General, 196
Bembibre, 217
Benevente, Action of, 215-216
——, Order issued at, 213-214
Bentinck, Lord William, 223-224
——, Major-General, 278
Beresford, Marshal, 249-253
Bernard, Duke of Saxe-Weimar, 264
Berthier, Marshal, 212
Bidassoa, Passage of the, 246

"Black Watch," Origin of the Name, 6
Blake, General, 211
Blakeney, General, 19
Blantyre, Lieut.-Colonel Lord, 230, 233
Bloomingdale, Action of, 104
——, ——, Losses at, 104
Blücher, Marshal, 262
Bonnet, General, 239
Bouquet, Colonel, 86-87
Brackenbury, Major-General, 305
Brandywine, Battle of, 110-111
——, ——, Losses at, 111
Brooklyn, Battle of, 102-103
——, ——, Losses at, 103
Brunswick, Duke of, 266-267
Buen Retiro, 240
Burgos, Retreat from, 242-244
——, Siege of, 240-242
——, ——, Losses at, 242
Busaco, Battle of, 232

Cambridge, Duke of, 278-279
Cameron, Lieut.-Colonel Alexander, 286, 290, 296
——, Major-General Sir Duncan, 277-278, 284, 297-298
Campbell, Alexander, Colonel, of Finab, 3, 20
——, Duncan, of Lochnell, 3
——, James, Ensign, of Glenfalloch, 29
——, John, of Carrick, 3, 29-30
——, ——, of Duneaves, 16-17
——, Lauchlan, Ensign, of Craignish, 29
——, Major-General John, 122
—— of Inveraw, 86
——, Richard, Captain, of Finab, 29
——, Ronald, Ensign, of Glenfalloch, 29
——, Sir Colin, 228, 244-245, 278-284, 286-296
——, Turkish General, 165
Carlisle, Castle of, 2
Castanos, General, 211
Cathcart, Lord, 139
Cawnpore, Battle of, 287-290
Charles Edward, Prince, 16, 34-35
Charlestown, Siege of, 119
Christie, Ensign, 269
Churchill, Brigadier-General, 144
Ciudad-Rodrigo, 231
——, Siege of, 234
Clausel, General, 238-240

Clayton, General, Commander-in-Chief in Scotland, 15
Clinton, General Sir Henry, 102, 112, 118
Cochrane, Captain Hon. Alexander, 168
Cocks, Major Somers, 240-241
Cole, General, 238
Colours, New, Presented, 1802, 203
Commanders, List of, Expedition to Egypt, 166
Coomassie, Capture of, 301-302
Coote, General, 196
Cope, Sir John, 34-35
Cornwallis, Earl, 101, 106-107
Corunna, Battle of, 219-227
——, ——, Losses at, 229
——, Retreat to, 211-218
Crauford, General, 215
Crawford, John Earl of, 7-8, 10, 12, 29
Croix des Bouquets, Fight at the, 246-247
Crump, Colonel, 64
Culloden, Battle of, 39
Cumberland, Duke of, 12, 17, 23-31, 74
"Cup," The Day of the, 202

Dalhousie, Lord, 179
Dalrymple, Major, 128
Debrissay, Colonel, 64
Demerara and Berbice, Descent on, 146
Dettingen, Battle of, 21
Deventer, Retreat to, 139
Dick, Lieut.-Colonel Robert Henry, 202
——, Major Henry Robert, 232, 269
Dickenson, Lieutenant, 244
Dickson, Lieut.-Colonel, 145, 199
"Donald," 308
Douglas, Admiral Sir James, 80
Dorth, General Baron, 23
Dowie, Private Andrew, Story of, 191-194
Ducharmey, Madame, 62-63
Duncan, Colonel, 187
Dundas, General Thomas, 128, 133

Earle, General, 304-305
Eglinton, Earl of, 198
Egypt, Losses in Campaign in, 197
Elliot, Lieut.-General, 75, 77
El Teb, Battle of, 304
——, ——, Losses at, 304
Elvina, 220-222
Erskine, Colonel, 173
——, Sir William, 101
Esla, Passage of the, 215
Expedition against Havannah, 74-85
—— ——, Losses on, 85
—— to St. Vincent, 153
—— —— Egypt, 164-197
—— —— ——, Commanders in, 166
—— —— ——, Regiments in, 166
—— —— French West Indies, 60
—— —— Louisburg, 47
—— —— L'Orient, 39
—— —— Quiberon, 39
—— —— the Acushnet River, 113
Eyre, General, 285

Fane, General, 251
Fergusson, Adam, Chaplain, 32, 41

Finchley Common, Regiment reviewed at, 17
Fletcher, Major, 167
Fontenoy, Battle of, 21-33
Forbes, Duncan, of Culloden, Lord President, 1-3, 13, 16, 34
Fort Duquesne, 43
—— Edward, 67
—— Louis, Attack on, 63
—— Pitt, Relief of, 86-87
—— St. André, 132
—— Washington, Capture of, 105
——, ——, Losses at, 105
—— William Henry, Siege of, 47
Fraser, General, J. J., 148
Fuentes d'Onoro, Battle of, 232-233
——, ——, Losses at, 233

Gamara Mayor, Combat at, 245
Gardiner, Colonel, 21
Gildermalsen, Action of, 133-134
——, ——, Losses at, 134
Glenfinnan, Standard hoisted at, 16, 35
Glenlyon, Old and Young, 37-38
Glenshiel, Action of, 2
Gordon, Hon Sir Charles, 275
——, Lord Adam, 124
Graham, Lieut.-Colonel Charles, 113, 120, 128, 145
——, Major-General Sir Thomas, 229, 236, 244, 246
——, Sir Gerald, 304
Grant, Colonel, 68, 72
——, Colonel of Ballindalloch, 3
——, Major-General, 102
——, Sir Hope, 290, 292
Green, Lieut.-Colonel, 304
Greenfield, General, 152
Greenock, Embarkation at, 1776, 99
"Grenadiers' Cat," The, 311-312
Grey, Major-General Sir Charles, 109, 111-113, 127, 148
Guadaloupe, Surrender of, 65-66

Halkett, General, 270
Hamerton, Colonel, 269
Hardinge, Captain Henry, 225-226, 265
Havannah, Conquest of the, 74-85
——, ——, Losses at, 85
Haviland, Colonel, 70, 72
Hawley, General, 35
Hill, Colonel, 173
——, General Lord, 250-253
Hope, Brigadier, 291, 294-296
——, General Hon. Sir John, 147-148, 204, 207-210, 229
Hopetoun, Earl of, 144
——, Lieut.-General John Earl of, 274
Hopson, Major-General, 60-62, 64
Howe, Brigadier-General, 144
——, General Sir William, 100, 102-103, 105
Hulst, Siege of, 39
Hunter, Major-General, 150, 153
Huntly, Marquis of, 124, 201, 203-204, 274
Hutchinson, Major-General, 161-195

# INDEX. 315

Ingoldsby, Brigadier, 26
Inverness, 2

Jenkins, Skipper, 6
Johnstone, Lieut.-Colonel George, 276

Keith, Earl Marischal, 2
——, Lord, 172
Kellerman, General, 270-272
Keppell, Brigadier-General, 144
——, Captain Hon. Augustus, 75, 77
——, General Hon. William, 77, 81-82
Kertch, Expedition to, 284
Khoodagunge, Action at, 291-293
Kirbekan, Action of, 304-305
——, ——, Losses at, 305
Knowles, Admiral, 74
Knyphausen, General, 105, 110, 118
Königseck, Count, 23-25

La Fausillé, Major-General, 75
Laborde, General, 213
Lake Champlain, 68-70
Lawson, Captain, 297
Lefebre-Desnouettes, General, 215-216
Leith, General, 238
——, Mutiny at, 115-118
Leslie, Lieutenant, 61
——, Lieut.-General, 124
Ligny, 262
Lincoln, General, 119
Loudoun, Earl of, 45, 47, 49
Lovat, Lord, 2-4
Lucknow, Capture of, 293
——, Relief of, 286
Ludlow, General, 187

McGregor, Gregor, "the beautiful," 16-17
Macara, Lieut.-Colonel, 246, 269
Macdonald, Lieut.-Colonel Donald, 144, 147
——, Lieut.-General Sir John, 277-278
——, Sir Archibald, 202
Macdougall, Major, 276
Macgregor, Sergeant, 108-109
Mackenzie, Major Kenneth, 161
Mackerras, Major, 167
Mackintosh, Laird of, 36
Maclean, Lieutenant, 63
Macleod, Sir John, 298, 300-303
Macmorran, Corporal, 244
Macpherson, Corporal, 19
——, Lieut.-Colonel, 303
Madrid, Entrance into, 240
Malcolm, Colonel, 148
——, Corporal, 19
——, Mr., Reminiscences of, 254-258
Malines, 130
Mandora, Battle of, 171-176
——, ——, Losses at, 175-176
Marmont, Marshal, 236, 239
Masséna, Marshal, 232
Mawhood, Colonel, 107
Maxwell, General, 107
Mayorga, Combat of, 214
Medows, General Sir William, 140
Melville, Lord, 1
——, Major, 62, 64

Menon, General, 172-184
Menzies, Sir Robert, 10
Middle Brook, 109
Middleton, Lieut.-Colonel William, 275
Minorca, Capture of, 160
Monckton, Major-General, 72
Montcalm, Marquis de, 45-47
Moore, Commodore, 60
——, General Sir John, 147, 150, 161-162, 170, 172, 209-227
Morne Chabot, Taking of, 147
—— Garnier, Attack on, 72
—— Tortueson, Skirmish of, 61
—— ——, Attack on, 72
Mornington, Lord, 131
Morshead, Major-General, 147, 151, 153
Munro, George, of Culcairn, 3
——, John, Lieut.-Colonel, 33, 40
——, Sir Hector, 207
——, Sir Robert, of Foulis, 11, 16, 22, 27, 30, 32
Murray, General, 69-70
——, General Lord John, 10, 25-26, 59, 92, 96-97, 122
——, Sir George, 275
——, Sir Patrick, 36
Musgrave, Lieut.-Colonel, 112
Mutiny, The Indian, 286-297

Napier, Major Charles, 221, 223-224
——, Sir William, 221
——, ——, Tribute to Sir John Moore, 227
Napoleon, Emperor, 216, 262
Nelson, Lord, 164
Ney, Marshal, 264-270
Nieuwport, Action at, 128
Nive, Battle of, 247-248
——, ——, Losses at, 248,
Nivelle, Battle of, 247
——, ——, Losses at, 247
Noailles, Marshal Duke of, 23
North America and West Indies, Losses in, 88
Nymeguen, Engagement at, 132-133

Oakes, Brigadier-General, 160, 182
Officers, List of, 1739, 8-9
——, ——, 1745, 36
——, ——, 1757, 46
——, ——, 1804, 205
Orange, Prince of, 265, 271
Ordahsu, Action at, 301
——, ——, Losses at, 301
Orthez, Battle of, 249, 251
——, ——, Losses at, 251
Oughton, General Sir Adolphus, 97
Outram, General, 287

Pack, General Sir Dennis, 238, 240, 264-270
Paget, Lord, 214-215
Percy, Lord, 105
Philadelphia, Entry into, 111
Pichegru, General, 139
Picton, General, 249-253, 263-266
"Pincher," 307-308
Pisquatua, Action at, 107-108

Pitt, Engineer, 240-241
Porto Rico, Attack on, 159
Prado, Don Juan de, 83
Prestonpans, Battle of, 35-37
Prideaux, General, 67
Priestley, Colonel, 298
Princetown, Combat of, 106 107
Promotions, Regimental, 44
Pulteney, Sir James, 162
Putnam, General, 102
Pyrenees, Battles of the, 246-247

Quatre Bras, Battle of, 265-273
——, ——, Losses at, 273

Raglan, Lord, 278, 282-283
Ramsay, Captain Norman, 232-233
Rebellion of 1745, 37
Redan, Assault of the, 285
"Red Feather," Story of the, 134 138
Regiments, List of, in Expedition to Egypt, 166
Regnier, General, 178, 179-187
Reille, General, 245, 249
Rhooyah, Fort of, Assault of, 294-295
Richelieu, Duc de, 27
Rodney, Admiral, 72
Rollo, Hon Robert, 306
——, Lord, 70, 72
Romana, General, 215
Rose, Sir Hugh, 297
Russell, Sir William, 296

St. Arnaud, Marshal, 278
St. Lucia, Landing on, 147
St. Sebastian, Capture of, 246
Salamanca, Battle of, 236-240
——, ——, Losses at, 239-240
Sarda, Action of, 297
Saxe, Marshal, 23-27
Sebastopol, Siege of, 284-285
——, ——, Losses at, 285
Second Battalion Raised, 59
Sempill, Lord, 12
Shaw, Farquhar, Private, 19-20, 22
Sheriffmuir, Battle of, 2
Simpson, Quartermaster-Sergeant John, 295
Sinclair, Sergeant, 200
——, Sir John, 200
Smith, Sir Sidney, 164, 167, 172, 188
Soult, Marshal, 212-221, 248-253
Spencer, Lieut.-Colonel Brent, 154, 195
Stephens, General, 107
Stewart, General Charles, 215
——, ——, of Garth, 4, 10, 17-18, 36
——, Lieut.-Colonel Alexander, 180-181
——, Major Sir Charles, 100
Stirling, Colonel Thomas, 99-101, 113-114, 120
——, Major, 181
——, Major-General James, Letter from, 222, 246
Stuart, Major-General Sir Charles, 160-161

Sullivan, General, 103, 110

Tamai, Battle of, 304
——, ——, Losses at, 304
Tartans chosen, 10-11
Tel-el-Kebir, Battle of, 303
——, ——, Losses at, 304
Ticonderoga, Siege of, 50-58
——, ——, Losses at, 53-54
——, Second Attack on, 68
Torres Vedras, 232
Toulouse, Battle of, 252-258
——, ——, Losses at, 253-254
——, Entry into, 259
Tournay, Siege of, 23
Trenton, Surprise of, 106
——, Action of, 107
Trinidad, Surrender of, 158
Tullibardine, Lord, Regiment of, 3
Tweeddale, Lieut.-General Marquis of, 297
——, Marquis of, 34

Uniform changed, 40

Vandamme, General, 130
Vaudreuil, Marquis de, 70
Velasco, Don Louis de, 82
Villa Franca, 217
Vimiera, Battle of, 209
*Virginia Gazette*, Article in, 88-89
Vittoria, Advance on, 244
——, Battle of, 245-246
Vizie, Capture of, 148-149
Vyse, Lieut.-General, 203

Waal, Passage of the, 133
Wade, Field-Marshal, 3, 17
Walcheren, Expedition to, 230
Waldeck, Prince of, 23, 25
Walmoden, General, 133
Walpole, General, 294, 296
——, Sir Robert, 1
Washington, General, 43-45, 103-105
Waterloo, Battle of, 273
——, ——, Losses at, 273
Wayne, General, 111
Weeley, Camp at, 204
Wellesley, Sir Arthur, 130-131, 209
Wellington, Duke of, 231-260, 261-274
Wheatley, Lieut.-Colonel, 202
Wheeler, General, 288
Whitelock, Brigadier-General, 144
White Plains, 104-105
Whyte, Major-General, 146
Wightman, General, 2
Wilford, Brigadier-General, 144
Winch, Colonel, 226
Windham, General, 287-289
Wolfe, General, 67
Wolseley, Sir Garnet, 300-302

York, Duke of, 127, 129, 130, 201

Ziethen, General, 261

---

PRINTED BY CASSELL & COMPANY, LIMITED, LA BELLE SAUVAGE, LONDON, E.C.

www.ingramcontent.com/pod-product-compliance
Lightning Source LLC
Chambersburg PA
CBHW070935230426
43666CB00011B/2449